Bayesian Argumentation

SYNTHESE LIBRARY

STUDIES IN EPISTEMOLOGY,

LOGIC, METHODOLOGY, AND PHILOSOPHY OF SCIENCE

VOLUME 362

For further volumes:
http://www.springer.com/series/6607

Frank Zenker

Editor

Bayesian Argumentation

The practical side of probability

 Springer

Editor
Frank Zenker
Philosophy
Lund University
Lund, Sweden

ISBN 978-94-007-5356-3   ISBN 978-94-007-5357-0 (eBook)
DOI 10.1007/978-94-007-5357-0
Springer Dordrecht Heidelberg New York London

Library of Congress Control Number: 2012953573

Printed on acid-free paper

Springer is part of Springer Science+Business Media (www.springer.com)

Foreword

This volume collects contributions to the international workshop on Bayesian Argumentation held on 22–23 October 2010 at the Philosophy Department of Lund University, Sweden.

I would like to express my gratitude to the Swedish Research Council (VR) and the Wenner-Gren Foundations for their generous financial support of this event, and to all speakers and participants for fruitful discussions.

Thanks are due to Stefan Schubert for useful comments on the introduction, to an anonymous reviewer and, last but not least, to Ties Nijssen, Ingrid van Laarhoven, and Christi Lue at Springer's Dordrecht office.

Lund, June 2012   Frank Zenker

Contents

Part IV Theoretical Issues

Bayesian Argumentation: The Practical Side of Probability

Frank Zenker

Abstract We give a brief introduction to the Bayesian approach to natural language argumentation, mainly oriented to readers more familiar with classical logic. Subsequently, we summarize the gist of each of the chapters so as to provide readers with an overview of the book's content.

1 Introduction

It is often found not too difficult to compare arguments with respect to their comparative strength or their rational persuasiveness. For present purposes, this may be understood as the capacity of reasons to reduce, sustain, or enhance the extent to which a rational agent endorses a conclusion. Perhaps, the easiest way of assessing argument strength consists in asking listeners for an opinion. But, clearly, what does persuade need not be coextensive with what *should* persuade.

A less simple way consists in deploying a normative standard—here the theory of probability, particularly its notion of evidential support—in order to answer two questions: First, what part of probability theory might be used toward arriving at a *normative* account that yields a motivated separation of natural language arguments into good and less good ones? Secondly, are the assessments of argument strength performed in laymen or institutional contexts (such as a court room) to some extent consistent with that theory?

Contributions to this volume converge upon the use of Bayes' theorem (which is introduced further below) as *the* norm in the light of which evidence—"arriving" in various forms, for example, as a third party report, a test result, or a direct observation—affects the endorsement of some hypothesis. A subset of these contributions also report data, some of which has been methodologically hardened

F. Zenker (✉)
Department of Philosophy & Cognitive Science, Lund University,
Kungshuset, Lundagård, 22 222 Lund, Sweden
e-mail: frank.zenker@fil.lu.se

F. Zenker (ed.), *Bayesian Argumentation: The practical side of probability*,
Synthese Library 362, DOI 10.1007/978-94-007-5357-0_1,
© Springer Science+Business Media Dordrecht 2013

in controlled experimental settings, on the extent to which arguers comply with this norm or not. Further contributions address challenges arising in (computationally) modeling rational agents and their argumentative interactions, while yet others offer novel solutions to long-standing "anomalies."

Below follows a brief introduction to the formal apparatus, particularly as it applies to the study of natural language argumentation, meant to "pave the way" for the novice reader. An overview of the book's content is provided in Sect. 3.

2   The Bayesian Approach to Argumentation

Bayes' theorem (Bayes and Price 1763) expresses the relations between a hypothesis, H, and evidence, E, in terms of probability, P. On a subjectivist interpretation, "probability" denotes *degrees of belief*. These degrees are mapped onto the unit interval $[0, 1]$ such that $P(H) = 1 - P(nonH)$. The relata are variously referred to as:

- $P(H)$ the *prior* or *unconditional probability* of a hypothesis (given no evidence)
- $P(E)$ the *marginal* or *a priori probability* of the evidence
- $P(H|E)$ the *direct* or *posterior* or *conditional probability* of a hypothesis given the evidence
- $P(E|H)$ the *inverse* or *conditional probability* of the evidence given the hypothesis (aka. the *likelihood of the evidence*)

To reach terms standardly used in the study of natural language argumentation (and episodes of reasoning thus suggested), "evidence" will be interpreted as reason, ground, or argument, and "hypothesis" as conclusion or proposal. Those used to representing argumentative structures as premise-conclusion complexes of the form $P_1, \ldots, P_n$; *ergo* C need to project premises into evidence and conclusion into hypothesis.

Bayes' theorem may count as noncontroversial and takes the following form,[1] where it is assumed—here and further below—that $0 < P(H) < 1$ and $0 < P(E) < 1$.

---

[1] To arrive at the theorem, one may start from a basic axiom of probability theory which states the probability of the conjunction of H and E, $P(H\&E)$, to be the probability of E multiplied by the probability of H given E, as expressed in (1):

$$P(H\&E) = P(E)P(H|E) \tag{1}$$

The same is stated in (2):

$$P(H\&E) = P(H)P(E|H). \tag{2}$$

This allows us to equate the right sides of (1) and (2) to reach

$$P(E)P(H|E) = P(H)P(E|H). \tag{3}$$

Upon which dividing both sides of (3) by $P(E)$ yields (BT)

$$\text{(BT)} \qquad P(H|E) = \frac{P(H)P(E|H)}{P(E)}$$

$$\text{(BT)} \qquad P(H|E) = \frac{P(H)P(E|H)}{P(E)}$$

The theorem may be said to relate the *direct* probability of a hypothesis conditional on evidence, $P(H|E)$, to the *inverse* probability of the evidence conditional on the hypothesis, $P(E|H)$. A more useful version—more useful because $P(E)$ can be expressed in extant terms[2]—is the following:

$$\text{(BT)} \qquad P(H|E) = \frac{P(H)P(E|H)}{P(H)P(E|H) + P(nonH)P(E|nonH)}$$

The basic idea underlying most uses of Bayes' theorem is that a hypothesis is supported by any evidence which is rendered (either sufficiently or simply) probable by the truth of that hypothesis. For the dynamic case, this entails that the probability of a hypothesis increases to the extent that evidence is more likely if the hypothesis were true than if it were false. (Novices may want to read the last sentence twice!)

The theorem allows calculating $P(H|E)$, which is the degree of belief in the hypothesis H to which (having received) evidence E does lead—or *should* lead, insofar as Bayes' theorem is treated as a normative update rule—provided assumptions on:

(i) The initial degree of belief in the hypothesis, $P(H)$. This is normally kept distinct from 1 or 0, for otherwise evidence will not affect $P(H)$. Hence, "good Bayesians" cannot (without "signing off" on evidence) entertain full belief, while dogmatists cannot (without inconsistency) fully endorse the Bayesian update rule.

(ii) Qualities of the evidence, $P(E)$. As explained in footnote 2, $P(E)$ can be calculated from the values of $P(H)$ and $P(E|H)$.

(iii) The relation between E and H, particularly how (much more) likely, or expectable, evidence would be if the hypothesis were true than if it were false. This comes down to comparing $P(E|H)$ with $P(E|nonH)$.

Bayes' theorem features two limiting cases. One captures a situation where a hypothesis *entails* the evidence—which, in logical terms, is expressed as H→E, or

---

[2] To express $P(E)$ in extant terms, note that the law of total probability states the probability of E to be the probability of H and E, plus the probability of *non*H and E (where "*non*H" designates the complement, or the negation, of H). In terms

$$P(E) = P(H\&E) + P(nonH\&E). \tag{1}$$

Expressed in conditional form (see the previous footnote), this yields

$$P(E) = P(H)P(E|H) + P(nonH)P(E|nonH). \tag{2}$$

as $P(E|H) = 1$ in probabilistic terms. The other captures the converse situation where evidence entails the hypothesis, expressed as $E \rightarrow H$ or $P(H|E) = 1$. Conveniently, among others, the following hold:

(1) $P(H|E) = 1$, iff $P(E|nonH) = 0$
(2) $P(H|E) < 1$, iff $P(E|nonH) > 0$
(3) $P(E|H)/P(E|nonH) > 1$, iff $P(H|E) - P(H) > 0$

In words, (1) we have full belief in the hypothesis given the evidence, *if and if, and only if (iff)* we have a zero degree of belief in the evidence given the negation of the hypothesis. (2) We have less than full belief in the hypothesis given the evidence, *iff* our degree of belief in the evidence given the falsity of the hypothesis is greater than zero. (3) The ratio of the evidence likelihoods—that is, the degree of belief in the evidence given the hypothesis over the degree of belief in the evidence given the negation of the hypothesis—is greater than one, *iff* the difference between the degree of belief in the hypothesis given the evidence (aka. the posterior probability) and the degree of belief in the hypothesis (aka. the prior probability) is greater than zero.

Put differently, (1) and (2) assert that *fully* endorsing H (as true *vis-à-vis* E) requires E to be *completely* unexpectable under the assumption that H is false. Conversely, as long as E is somewhat expectable under the assumption that H is false, H cannot be fully endorsed (as true *vis-à-vis* E). And (3) asserts that a difference between prior and posterior probability—thus, any support lent to the hypothesis by the evidence—is mirrored by a likelihood ratio greater than 1.

Perhaps instructively for those more familiar with classical logic, when the relation between evidence and hypothesis is neat enough for the truth of one to ensure the truth of the other, Bayes' theorem "degrades" to the biconditional of deductive logic, $H \leftrightarrow E$.[3] Therefore, some hold that much of what can be done in classical logic may be done with (limiting case instances of) Bayes' theorem. Where such neat relations are not at hand, the theorem traces the effect that (receiving) evidence makes (or should make) on the degree to which a hypothesis is supported *vis-à-vis* endorsing the negation of the same hypothesis, provided a

---

[3] Floridi (2009) provides an instructive example, here slightly adapted. Unrealistically(!), it assumes *perfect* antivirus software: "Maggie thought that, *if* 'the email was infected' [abbreviated as the hypothesis H], *then* 'the antivirus blocked it' [abbreviated as evidence E], and since the quarantine folder contains only emails blocked by the antivirus, then all the emails in it must be infected. More formally, she reasoned that: '$H \rightarrow E$, E *therefore* H'. Jill explains to Maggie that the previous inference is a typical fallacy (called: *affirming the consequent*), but that she should not feel silly at all. For, consider Bayes's theorem once again. Look at the formula $P(E|nonH)$ [...] which indicates the probability that the antivirus blocks the email (E) when the email is not infected (*nonH*). *Suppose we have perfect, infallible antivirus software*. This will generate no false positives (no mistakes). But if there are no false positives, that is, if $P(E|nonH) = 0$, then $P(H|E) = 1$ and Bayes's theorem is degraded to a double implication: '$H \leftrightarrow E$, E *therefore* H', which is what Maggie perhaps had in mind. On the other hand, if there are some false positives, that is, if $P(E|nonH) > 0$, then $P(H|E) < 1$ and the formula bears a strong family resemblance to the fallacy of *affirming the consequent*: '$H \rightarrow E$, E *therefore* H', which is what Maggie might also have had in mind" (Floridi 2009: 399).

prior degree of belief in the hypothesis and an estimate of the likelihood of the evidence.

Since, formally, this is very much as it should be, challenges arise "only" in interpreting the Bayesian terms and in reasonably choosing the numerical values by which these terms express the kinds of evidential considerations featured in natural language arguments. Take, for instance, the contention that hypotheses should be submitted to *severe* tests, and that arguments which report severe tests are stronger (or more persuasive) than those reporting less severe tests. In Bayesian terms, this means the probability of obtaining evidence (in case the hypothesis is true) should be comparatively low. So, assuming two tests to choose from, the *more severe* should sport a lower value for $P(E|H)$.

As pointed out above, evidence supports ("strengthens") or undermines ("weakens") a hypothesis or else is irrelevant to it. The degree of confirmation (or support) that evidence lends to a hypothesis may be expressed as the difference between the posterior and the prior probability of a hypothesis: $P(H|E) - P(H)$. A second and equally defensible measure of support is the likelihood ratio: $P(E|H)/P(E|nonH)$.[4] These measures have been proposed as estimates of the *force of an argument*, since they express the magnitude of a change of conviction which receiving evidence brings about *vis-à-vis* a prior conviction. Relatedly, the absolute degree of conviction to which receiving an argument leads—that is, the posterior probability—may then be used to estimate the *strength of an argument*.

This coinage goes back to Oaksford and Hahn who observe that, consequently, the *relative* degree of conviction which evidence brings about may be the same, even if two agents differ with respect to the prior probabilities they endorse. This holds as long as discussants do not disagree about properties of the evidence such as being obtained from a trustworthy source or by a reliable method. Conversely, arguers would have to differ in ways that point beyond the priors for their disagreement to remain rationally reconstructable. In this limited but important sense, Bayes' theorem promises to provide a normative theory of argument strength, given assumptions on the quality of reasons.

With a view to natural language argumentation, the Bayesian approach recommends itself for its precise expressions, and—other than by successfully explaining the quality of arguments/fallacies *vis-à-vis* various contexts and audiences—also receives support from recent results in the study of human reasoning. According to authors such as Evans (2002), humans may generally not count as "deduction machines." Rather, much of man-made reasoning appears to be consistent with some of the assumptions made in probabilistic modeling. Nevertheless, for reasons of computational complexity alone (Korb 2004), it is clear that humans are not "Bayesian machines" either.

The Bayesian approach to natural language argumentation is a quasi-natural choice, firstly, for the study of any argument which seeks to support, or undermine, a claim on the basis of statistical data. After all, on the Bayesian approach,

---

[4] For other support measures, see Fitelson (2001) and Pfeifer (Chap. 10, this volume).

the standards appealed to—that is, those of inductive logic—will, in one way or another, be part of the reconstructive apparatus and thus be available in argument evaluation.

Secondly, empirical research on message persuasiveness should find the Bayesian approach natural when explaining the differential persuasiveness of messages *vis-à-vis* various sources, contexts, and audiences. For instance, when receiving identical messages from a reliable *versus* an unreliable source, in the first case, $P(E|H)$ may reasonably be taken to exceed $P(E|nonH)$, providing one way of modeling the impact of trust on the degree to which a message is believed or not.

Finally, the Bayesian approach challenges the view that the reconstruction and evaluation of natural language argumentation must either rely on informal means or else be unrealistically confined to a comparatively small class of arguments which instantiate deductively valid structures. Surely, branding the Bayesian approach as *the* solution appears equally unrealistic. Nevertheless, as the contributions to this volume demonstrate, formal tools such as Bayes' theorem have a rightful place both in argument reconstruction and argument evaluation.

3   Chapter Overview

Comprising theoretical backgrounds and disciplines as diverse as cognitive science, jurisprudence, and philosophy, contributions remain unified with respect to the normative standard to which they relate. While chapters are self-contained, readers may appreciate the division into the Bayesian approach to argumentation, the legal domain, modeling rational agents, and theoretical issues.

3.1   The Bayesian Approach to Argumentation

Ulrike Hahn, Mike Oaksford, and *Adam J.L. Harris*, in Chap. 2, lay out a Bayesian perspective on testimony and argument. Normally treated as independent variables or alternative routes to audience persuasion, the authors build on empirical studies which validate a rather precise connection between source and content considerations of argument. This yields an alternative to standard default and plausibility treatments and crucially differs from the latter with respect to the principle employed for evaluating linked argumentation structures. Rather than the so-called MAXMIN principle, their contribution deploys Bayes' theorem, and extends the investigation to cases of witnesses who differ not only with respect to the reliability of testimony, but also with respect to the argumentative strength of its content. After contrasting possible ways of modeling source reliability either exogenously or endogenously, the authors proceed to a "rehousing" of argumentation schemes within a Bayesian framework, resulting in a network representation of Walton's well-known critical questions for the appeal to expert opinion. As they content, "reasoning appropriately about source reliability in any given context involves Bayesian inference within a suitable model. How complex that model needs to be depends on the context, such as the relevant dimensions of variation within that context."

Mike Oaksford and *Ulrike Hahn*, in Chap. 3, report on an empirical study that investigates why *ad hominem* argumentation is found convincing, and contrast their findings with recent empirical results obtained from the perspective of the normative pragma-dialectical model. In the latter, the reasonableness of an *ad hominem* argument is construed as a function of the discussion stage in which it occurs. The argument form is deemed an illegitimate move (aka. a fallacy) only in the opening stage of a critical discussion, where it violates the "Freedom Rule" (according to which discussants may not prevent each other from forwarding a standpoint). In contrast, Oaksford and Hahn deploy a Bayesian model which, among others, respects considerations of source reliability. Moreover, they also vary further conditions such as the initial degree of belief in a conclusion, and whether the *ad hominem* appears as a pro or a con argument. Although further empirical investigation into this and other argument forms is deemed necessary, their study partly fails to corroborate—and thus challenges—the explanation offered on the pragma-dialectical model, insofar as they find "no differences between different types of argumentum ad hominem, where the freedom rule was violated, and a control, which introduced no violation of the freedom rule."

3.2 The Legal Domain

Matthias Grabmair and *Kevin D. Ashley*, in Chap. 4, distinguish four kinds of interdependent uncertainties that lawyers must plan for in litigation cases, then illustrate these vis-à-vis the claim of trade-secret-misappropriation recently brought against Facebook founder Mark Zuckerberg. Typically, in deciding what legal claim to assert, lawyers will profit from a structured assessment of what is normally called the "strength of a case." It is for this purpose, then, that factual, normative, moral, and empirical uncertainties become relevant, insofar as winning or losing a case may be understood as a function of having estimated these correctly, or not. Employing an extension of the Carneades argumentation model, the authors use probability values to model that audiences (here, judges and juries) may accept or reject some statement or principle to some degree, or else be undecided about it. This inference is a function of probability values representing the audiences' belief in certain assumptions and assessments of an argument's persuasiveness. The resulting Bayesian model, which uses argument weights, can represent pro and con arguments for or against some claim. Moreover, it allows for dynamic weights. The authors further suggest and illustrate that weights can be subject to argumentation as well. Thus, a formal model of legal argument mandates among other things "the moral assessment of a case (e.g., by a judge) to influence the probability with which certain legal arguments will prevail over others."

Amit Pundik, in Chap. 5, presents a case study on the use of statistical evidence in criminal courts and defends the standpoint that, under certain assumptions, courts can have good reasons to refrain from the use of statistics, and experts delivering them. His case involves the correct diagnosis of sudden infant death syndrome (SIDS) and addresses the question whether public and scholarly attention has been wrongly directed to the statistics—which, as it happened, were seriously flawed. Pundik reviews and rejects extant explanations that purport to show why the SIDS statistics have led to a wrongful charge against an innocent mother, then draws on the theory of contrastive explanation to provide an alternative account. According to this theory, the statistics on spontaneous child death would have made sense in the context of this trial only if they had been compared with statistics on the preferred contrast class (here, particular acts of murder). Pundik argues that, regardless of whether a comparison of probabilities between contrasting explanations is in fact possible, it should not be conducted as part of criminal proceedings. He concludes that his case study "should serve as a warning against any attempt to prove the fact of causation using statistical evidence about the rate of potential exonerating causes."

3.3   Modeling Rational Agents

Erik Olsson, in Chap. 6, presents a computer-based simulation environment, called *Laputa*. This provides a Bayesian model of group interaction which may be interpreted as exchanges of arguments for or against some proposition p among agents/inquirers. Provided certain constraints are met—among others, that message sources are independent, that inquirers cooperate in the sense of providing arguments that are novel to their interlocutors, that arguing pro (con) p entails personally endorsing (not) p to a reasonable degree, and that proponents deem their own arguments sound—agents can be modeled to update both their degree of belief in p and their degree of trust in the message source. From this basis, Olsson proceeds to show that, over time, agents in the group will polarize in the sense of endorsing ever greater degrees of belief in p, while assigning ever less trust to those agents endorsing not p (or vice versa). Consequently, he can suggest that "polarization on the belief level is accompanied, in a sense, with polarization on the trust level." Moreover, he can demonstrate that, on this model, seemingly minute differences between degrees of belief and degrees of trust will, over time, lead to polarization. Consequently, these simulations support the claim "that even ideally rational inquirers will predictably polarize or diverge under realistic conditions."

Gregor Betz, in Chap. 7, provides an outline of his recent theory of dialectical structures and investigates the relation between such structures and truth-likeness (*verisimilitude*). Among others, his theory serves to reconstruct attack and support relations between premises and conclusion at the level of complex debates (aka. "controversies"). In turn, this provides the basis for a structured evaluation of the positions endorsed by proponents and opponents. In particular, the pre-theoretic idea of a "(comparative) strength of justification" can be rendered formally precise by means of the notion "degree of justification"—which obeys Bayes' rule—and that of "degree of partial implication." Given assumptions on background knowledge, Betz's account yields ways of measuring the inferential density of a given state of a debate. Consequently, hypothetical debate progressions may be subjected to computer simulation, in order to investigate the relation between the degree of justification, the inferential density, and the proportion of true sentences. As he demonstrates, "[a]dopting positions with a high degree of justification fosters the achievement of a basic epistemic aim [i.e., to acquire true beliefs], and that's why degrees of justification should guide the belief-forming process of rational beings."

Robert van Rooij and *Kris de Jaegher*, in Chap. 8, address argumentation from the perspective of game theory. Their starting point is the observation that "[w]e communicate more than standard game theory predicts." Moreover, standard game theory is seemingly unable to explain deception and the strategic manipulation of messages. This suggests that standard game theory suffers from one or the other idealized assumption which reduces its explanatory power in application to natural language argumentation. Of these assumptions they identify, and then significantly relax, the following three: what game is being played is common knowledge, agents are completely rational, and the assessment of probabilities and subsequent decision making is independent of the way alternatives and decision problems are stated (framing effects). In each case, they demonstrate in a formally precise way that explanatory scope increases when assumptions are deemed false. For instance, that suboptimal outcomes are chosen, or dominated strategies nevertheless played, may be explained by participants' lack of insight into the full breadth of options. In line with recent criticisms of the ideal rational agent assumption, their general conclusion is that "we talk and argue so much because we believe others are bounded rational agents."

3.4 Theoretical Issues

Tomoji Shogenji, in Chap. 9, addresses the long-standing contention that circular argumentation or reasoning is defective or fallacious. For instance, it is widely considered bad reasoning to invoke perceptual evidence to support the reliability of our sense apparatus since the reasoning already assumes the reliability of our sense apparatus when it invokes perceptual evidence. To rebuke what he calls the "myth of epistemic circularity," Shogenji distinguishes two senses of the term "assume"— namely, to presuppose the truth of the hypothesis and to envision the truth of the hypothesis. According to Shogenji, assuming the truth of the hypothesis in the second sense is no more problematic than assuming the negation of the hypothesis in the reasoning of *reductio ad absurdum*. In *reductio ad absurdum*, we establish the truth of the conclusion by envisioning the falsity of the hypothesis and deriving a contradiction from it. In a similar way, Shogenji proposes a procedure of envisioning the truth of the hypothesis and then the negation of the hypothesis, to compare their respective degrees of coherence with the evidence. He demonstrates in the Bayesian framework that the evidence raises the probability of the hypothesis if the evidence is more coherent with the truth of the hypothesis than it is with the negation of the hypothesis. Applying this procedure to the perceptual support of the reliability of our sense apparatus, Shogenji contends that when the perceptual evidence is more coherent with the hypothesis of reliability than it is with the negation of the hypothesis, the evidence raises the probability of the reliability hypothesis without epistemic circularity.

Niki Pfeifer, in Chap. 10, contrasts probabilistic with deductive logical treatments of natural language arguments that contain conditionals and argues for a combination of both. He stresses the importance of conditionals which are uncertain and which allow for exceptions such as the classic "birds can fly" from default logic. Working within the framework of coherence based probability logic—a combination of subjective probability theory and propositional logic—probability values are attached directly to the conditional event, and probabilities are conceived as degrees of belief. Pfeifer's account traces "how to propagate the uncertainty of the premises to the conclusion" in a deductive framework and yields a formal measure of argument strength that depends on two factors: the "location of the coherent probability interval" on the unit interval and the "precision" of the probabilistic assessment, that is, the distance between the tightest coherent lower and the upper probability bounds of the conclusion. Thus, on Pfeifer's account, standard problems incurred when working with traditional measures of confirmation (e.g., How to connect premises containing conditionals? How to conditionalize on conditionals?) are avoided, while the intuition that strong arguments should be those that imply precise assessments of the conclusions with high probability is recovered.

Jonny Blamey, in Chap. 11, presents a novel solution to the preface-paradox by invoking considerations of stake size. The paradox pivots on the tension that arises when the degree of belief that is assigned to the conjunction of a set of propositions compares with the degree of belief assigned to each conjunct in a manner that lets the *whole* (the conjunction) come out as different from the sum of its *parts* (the conjuncts). This is normally accounted for by our intuitive tendency to be certain of each conjunct in a set of statements forming a conjunction, but to be less than certain of the conjunction seen as a whole. Working within the framework of evidential probability, Blamey builds on the idea that "the same evidence can fully justify a belief at low stakes but not fully justify the same belief at high stakes." More precisely, he lends himself of a betting model of belief, equates the value of knowledge with the value of the stake, and pairs this with the idea that a conjunction has greater informational content than the conjuncts such that "conjoining the propositions escalates the informational content exponentially by 1 over the conditional probability between the conjuncts." Consequently, Dutch books (i.e., bets resulting in sure losses) can be avoided provided, among others, that Blamey's *minimum constraint* is assumed to hold, according to which one "cannot prefer a bet at smaller stakes to a bet at larger stakes for the same price." Thus, it is shown not to be incoherent to remain less than evidentially certain at high stakes, while one may very well be evidentially certain at low stakes.

References

Bayes, T., & Price, R. (1763). An essay towards solving a problem in the doctrine of chance (By the late Rev. Mr. Bayes, communicated by Mr. Price, in a letter to John Canton, M. A. and F. R. S). *Philosophical Transactions of the Royal Society of London, 53*, 370–418.

Evans, J. S. T. B. (2002). Logic and human reasoning: An assessment of the deduction paradigm. *Psychological Bulletin, 128*(6), 978–996.

Fitelson, B. (2001). *Studies in Bayesian confirmation theory*. Dissertation, University of Wisconsin at Madison. http://fitelson.org/thesis.pdf. Accessed 22 June 2012.

Floridi, L. (2009). Logical fallacies as informational shortcuts. *Synthese, 167*, 317–325.

Korb, K. (2004). Bayesian informal logic and fallacy. *Informal Logic, 23*(2), 41–70.

Part I
The Bayesian Approach to Argumentation

Testimony and Argument: A Bayesian Perspective

Ulrike Hahn, Mike Oaksford, and Adam J.L. Harris

Abstract Philosophers have become increasingly interested in testimony (e.g. Coady, Testimony: A philosophical study. Oxford University Press, Oxford, 1992; Kusch & Lipton, Stud Hist Philos Sci 33:209–217). In the context of argumentation and persuasion, the distinction between the content of a message and its source is a natural and important one. The distinction has consequently attracted considerable attention within psychological research. There has also been a range of normative attempts to deal with the question of how source and message characteristics should combine to give rise to an overall evaluation of evidential strength (e.g. Walton, Witness testimony evidence: Argumentation, artificial intelligence, and law. Cambridge University Press, Cambridge, 2008). This chapter treats this issue from the perspective of the Bayesian approach to argument (Hahn & Oaksford, Psychol Rev 114:704–732, 2007a; Hahn et al., Informal Log 29:337–367, 2009) and summarises empirical evidence on key intuitions.

> there is no species of reasoning more common, more useful, and even necessary to human life, than that which is derived from the testimony of men, and the reports of eyewitnesses and spectators. (Hume 1977, p. 74)

U. Hahn (✉)
School of Psychology, Cardiff University, Cardiff, UK

Department of Psychological Science, Birkbeck College, University of London, London, UK
e-mail: u.hahn@bbk.ac.uk

M. Oaksford
Department of Psychological Science, Birkbeck College, University of London, London, UK

A.J.L. Harris
Department of Cognitive, Perceptual and Brain Sciences,
University College London, London, UK

F. Zenker (ed.), *Bayesian Argumentation: The practical side of probability,*
Synthese Library 362, DOI 10.1007/978-94-007-5357-0_2,
© Springer Science+Business Media Dordrecht 2013

1   Introduction

Within philosophy, appreciation of the fact that much of what we believe is derived from the assertions of others has meant that testimony, after many decades of neglect, has become a topic of considerable interest (e.g. Coady 1992; Kusch and Lipton 2002; Adler 2006). The focus here has largely been on the extent to which testimony may be said to give rise to 'knowledge', and how it relates to other sources of knowledge, in particular, perception.

In keeping with this emphasis, there has been a long tradition of psychological research that has focused on the reliability of testimony. Motivated particularly by the issue of evaluating witnesses in legal contexts, there has been much research both into how reliable people are as witnesses, even where they are well intentioned, and into how people evaluate the reliability of witness evidence. Limitations on reliability arise not just from simple 'forgetting' but from the reconstructive nature of memory which makes memory sensitive to the way information is elicited (e.g. Loftus 1975); consequently, research has identified factors relating to the characteristics of the event, the witness and the procedures by which testimony is gained (see, e.g. Wells and Olsen 2003, for a review). Studies concerned with the evaluation of witnesses have examined factors affecting how people weigh and interpret evidence (e.g. Carlson and Russo 2001; Schuller et al. 2001; Weinstock and Flaton 2004); they have also examined people's responses to different types of testimony such as testimony by experts or by children and so on (e.g. Eaton and O'Callaghan 2001; ForsterLee et al. 2000; Krauss and Sales 2001), and they have tried to examine how testimony is seen relative to other types of evidence (e.g. Skolnick and Shaw 2001).

Motivated by the epistemological importance of testimony, the reception of testimony has also been a recent concern within developmental psychology. Not only is much of what we think we know derived from the testimony of others, but it is, to a considerable extent, acquired early in life. Developmental research has established that, contrary to long-held beliefs, even young children are not uniformly credulous. Rather, they display considerable selectivity in who they choose to learn from. Specifically they will select informants with whom they have had previous interactions and prefer those for whom past interactions have indicated reliability and expertise (for a review, see Harris and Corriveau 2011).

However, testimony need not be viewed as just a particular kind of evidence. It is also a very general feature of argumentative discourse. In any argument, reasons are necessarily advanced by a specific agent; they are not simply abstract propositions floating about. The presentation of an argument can itself be viewed as a type of testimony (see also Adler 2006), and the inherent combination of argument content with an argument source raises the question of how the source should be taken into account. Here, a common view seems to have been that arguments should 'speak for themselves' and that the source should play no role. This is manifest in the fact that arguments involving characteristics of the source itself have traditionally been viewed as fallacious. The ad hominem argument, which seeks to undermine the credibility of the source (e.g. Walton 1998; see also Oaksford and Hahn, this volume), is a staple of the traditional catalogue of fallacies (e.g. Woods et al. 2004) and is routinely featured in textbooks on critical thinking (e.g. Bowell and Kemp 2002; Hughes et al. 2010; Rainbolt and Dwyer 2012). The reasoning behind this is that properties of the speaker are insufficient to undermine an argument. Likewise, the appeal to authority (or argumentum ad verecundium, Walton 1998), which seeks support for a position from the credentials of the speaker, is viewed as fallacious because the fact that the speaker is of high standing is irrelevant to the argument itself and does nothing to improve it.

In keeping with this, there is also a long social-psychological tradition of research on persuasion that has treated message content and message source as two more or less independent variables that are associated with psychologically distinct routes through which we are persuaded. Specifically, persuasion research has distinguished between analytical and heuristic routes to persuasion (e.g. Chaiken 1980; Petty et al. 1981; Petty and Cacioppo 1984; Eagly and Chaiken 1993). The analytic route is characterised by careful scrutiny of the message content in order to determine the merits of the argument, whereas the heuristic route is characterised by more low-effort, shallow processing which focuses on putatively superficial and readily available characteristics of the message such as the perceived credibility of the source, the attractiveness or likeability of the source, or the quality of presentation. Although it has been acknowledged that there may be circumstances in which characteristics of the source may themselves be considered as cues that are relevant in analytic processing (e.g. Petty and Wegener 1999; see also Kruglanski and Stroebe 2005), source characteristics, by and large, have been associated with qualitatively inferior evaluation.

One may ask, though, whether such a separation between source and content is really normatively desirable. Clearly, there are cases where one is in a position to evaluate everything about the content of an argument. In this case, it is not clear what source considerations could add. However, at least as prevalent seem cases where there may be some uncertainty about the content – concerning, for example, its veracity or completeness. Here, source characteristics could provide additional information, at least in principle, and it would seem questionable to ignore information that could be inductively useful. Moreover, a strict separation between content and source presupposes a fundamental distinction between 'argument' and 'evidence', given that reliability considerations seem essential to testimonial evidence. There may be some types of reasons which should be viewed as only one or the other. However, there would seem to be many more where no real distinction exists, and this can be seen nowhere more clearly than in the overlap between the supposedly fallacious appeal to authority and the testimony of experts. Hence, it should also come as no surprise that more recent treatments of the fallacies have moved away from treating either ad hominem arguments or appeals to authority as always fallacious (see, e.g. Tindale 2007, and examples therein).

This then raises the questions of how source considerations should be taken into account, how fallacious and non-fallacious ad hominem arguments should be distinguished (see also Oaksford and Hahn, this volume) and, more generally, how source and content characteristics should be combined in the overall evaluation of an argument or piece of evidence.

In this chapter, we examine these questions both from a Bayesian perspective and from the perspective of plausible reasoning, drawing out and contrasting theoretical positions and comparing them with experimental data concerning people's intuitions.

2   Testimony, Argumentation and the 'Third Way'

Argumentation typically involves uncertainty. In arguing, we seek to convince those who are not yet fully convinced of a position. There is no point seeking to convince further someone who is already fully convinced of a position, nor is there, practically, much point in trying to convince someone of a position that they are certain is actually wrong. This severely limits the role of classical logic in everyday argument, and most everyday arguments are not logically valid (see, e.g. Toulmin 1958; Perelman and Olbrechts-Tyteca 1969). Appropriate norms for rational argument must consequently deal naturally with uncertainty. The probability calculus provides the standard formal tool for dealing with uncertainty. However, many authors have held the view that probabilities are inappropriate or insufficient for dealing with argumentation (for references and discussion of some of these critiques, see, e.g. Hahn and Oaksford 2006b) and have advanced the view that there is some third form of reasoning, in addition to deduction and induction, that requires formal development. Specifically, 'plausible reasoning' may constitute such a third option (see, e.g. Pollock 2001; Walton 2004). However, despite many differences in detail, one may consider as proponents of a potential 'third way' any of the many default logics, non-monotonic logics and logics of practical reasoning that have been proposed (see, e.g. Prakken and Vreeswijk 2002, for an overview). Furthermore, not only may these 'third way' approaches be considered as candidates for formalising argumentation, they are frequently advanced as tools for dealing with uncertainty per se.

A central concept within this third way tradition is the notion of 'presumption' or 'default' (see Rescher 1976). A presumption is a position that is adopted, 'as a rule', in the absence of specific counter-indication. A dialectic borrowing from law, the notion of presumption is closely related to another legal import, the concept of burden of proof (for an overview and critical evaluation of the burden of proof in the context of argumentation, see Hahn and Oaksford 2007b). The basis for presumption is plausibility. Rescher (1977), for example, states this as follows:

> Presumption favors the most *plausible* of rival alternatives-when indeed there is one. This alternative will always stand until set aside (by the entry of another, yet more plausible, presumption). (p. 38)

Plausibility, for Rescher, is not a matter of probability but rather of how well something 'fits' within our overall framework of cognitive commitments.

Interestingly, testimony plays an important role in this for Rescher:

> The standing of sources in point of authoritativeness affords one major entry point to plausibility. In this approach, a thesis is more or less plausible depending on the reliability

of the sources that vouch for it- their entitlement to qualify as well-informed or otherwise in a position to make good claims to credibility. It is on this basis that 'expert testimony' and 'general agreement' (the consensus of men) come to count as conditions for plausibility. (p. 39)

This thread is developed further by Walton (2008) who explicitly adopts the 'third way' approach based on defaults and defeasible claims as a framework for 'modeling rational thinking about witness testimony as a kind of evidence' (p. 3). Walton shares Rescher's ready dismissal of probability as a tool (see, e.g. Walton 2008, pp. 92–102, 2001; Rescher 1976, in particular, pp. 28–39; for counterarguments, see, e.g. Hahn and Oaksford 2006b; note also, however, that despite some discussion of Bayesianism, Walton typically seems to think of probabilities as 'objective', 'statistical' quantities, see, e.g. Walton 2008, pp. 206–209). Walton rejects the view that witness testimony may be seen as inductively strong (2008, p. 99). He seeks instead to provide rational, normative guidance on testimony by characterising 'the appeal to witness testimony' as a particular kind of argument with its own structure, that is, its own premises and conclusions, and requirements or queries that must be satisfied in order for the argument to be cogent. Specifically, Walton tries to establish a so-called argumentation scheme for witness testimony. An argumentation scheme is a stereotypical pattern of inference that is characterised by its specific type of premises and conclusion, along with the nature of the inferential link between the two (see also, e.g. Walton 1996, 2008; Verheij 2003). This scheme-based approach seeks to broaden the range of circumstances in which a conclusion can be viewed as rationally derived from a set of premises which are assumed to be true in order to capture the many informal arguments that are beyond the reach of classical logic. In general, the conclusion is defeasible (held tentatively subject to further information), and the rationality of a particular scheme rests on the fact that the defeasible inference or presumption is typically plausible, given what we know about the world.

For testimony, Walton provides a number of related schemes, the most basic of which is the 'argument from a position to know' and of which the 'argument from expert opinion' (discussed more extensively below) is a subtype. Walton's paradigmatic example concerns a dialogue in which someone lost in a foreign city asks a stranger for directions to the central station. Here, the person seeking directions presumes that the stranger is familiar with the city, and the underlying scheme in such a dialogue, the 'argument from a position to know' (Walton 1996, p. 61), has the following structure:

Major premise: Source *a* is in a position to know about things in a certain subject domain containing a proposition *A*.
Minor premise: *a* asserts that *A* (in domain *S*) is true (false).
Conclusion: *A* is true.

This scheme shifts 'a probative weight' from the premises to the conclusion (see also Walton et al. 2008) which is rendered defeasibly plausible or acceptable.

However, matching the argument from a position to know are three critical questions:

CQ1. Is *a* in a position to know whether *A* is true (false)?
CQ2. Is *a* an honest (trustworthy, reliable) source?
CQ3. Did *a* assert *A* is true (false)?

In a given case, the argumentation scheme is evaluated in light of these critical questions. When such a question is asked the probative weight 'shifts'; and it shifts back again only if the question is answered satisfactorily.

Identifying the structure of particular types of arguments is an important and interesting issue for argumentation research. However, at the end of the day, the practically most pressing question in evaluating any particular argument or line of reasoning is *how strong* it should be considered to be. Normative frameworks must also have something to say about this issue. Such summary evaluation needs to reflect the fact that evidence can be more or less compelling, and that, often, multiple sources of evidence must be combined. The majority of 'third way' approaches arguably bypass this evaluation question altogether, not just in the context of testimony. Walton (2008) also suggests that finding satisfactory answers to the question of evaluating strength in the case of testimony is more difficult than just drawing out its structural characteristics. However, Walton (2008) does draw together various evaluation rules that have been proposed in the literature and expands on these to provide a framework for the evaluation of plausible arguments.

Integral to this are two different evaluation contexts that according to Walton (2008, see also Walton 1992) need to be distinguished: these are what are known in the argumentation literature as *linked* and *convergent* arguments (or 'coordinative' and 'subordinative' argumentation, see also van Eemeren and Grootendorst 2004, and Johnson 2000, for discussion and further references). In a convergent argument, a number of arguments each independently support a claim. By contrast, in linked arguments, arguments depend on each other and provide support for the claim only in combination. Although this distinction is not captured by classical logic, Walton maintains that it is fundamental in dialectic contexts because these two types of arguments can be attacked (or need to be defended) in very different ways. In the case of a linked argument, the proponent will seek out the weakest of the premises because once this fails, the whole argument fails. However, this strategy is not sufficient in the case of a convergent argument because 'taking out' one premise still leaves the other intact as a separate line of support.

For linked arguments, Walton proposes that the overall strength of the argument is determined by the weakest link. This so-called MIN rule (see also Walton 1992) follows on from proposals by Rescher (1976) and Pollock (2001).

Rescher put forward Theophrastus' rule as a *consequence condition* for plausible reasoning:

> when a set of mutually consistent propositions in a given set of propositions with plausibility values entails some other proposition in that set, the resulting proposition cannot be less plausible than the least plausible among them. (Rescher 1976, p. 15)

Pollock (1995, pp. 95–101) generalised Theophrastus' rule to chains of arguments through 'the weakest link principle' (p. 99):

> the degree of support of the conclusion of a deductive argument is the minimum of the degrees of support for its premises.

Walton, however, is explicit in extending this weakest link principle to arguments that are not deductively valid (e.g. Walton 2008, p. 96).

For convergent arguments, by contrast, a different rule is required, and for these, Walton (1992, 2008) recommends the MAX rule, whereby the overall plausibility of the conclusion corresponds to the plausibility of the strongest of the independent lines of support (or is at least as strong).

The result then is the so-called MAXMIN rule (Walton 1992, p. 43, 2008), whereby a reasoner is instructed to,

> At each local argument in the sequence of connected argumentation, use the least plausible premise rule if the argument is linked, and use the most plausible premise rule if the argument is convergent

Testimony and source reliability, for Walton (2008), involve linked arguments. The content and the source of a testimonial statement are not independent lines of support that stand one without the other but rather are inextricably linked. In the remainder of this chapter, it will be argued that the MAXMIN rule does not provide an appropriate approach to testimony and that it conflicts with fundamental intuitions. Before dealing with the case of testimony specifically, however, some general concerns regarding the MAXMIN rule will be discussed.

3   Some Problems for MAXMIN

A fundamental problem for the consequence condition, and with it the MIN rule, involves conjunction. From A and B, it follows deductively that A & B. Hence, it should be the case by these rules that[1]

$$\text{Plausibility}(A\&B) \geq \text{MIN Plausibility}(A),\ \text{Plausibility}(B) \qquad (1)$$

However, intuitive examples can readily be found where this does not seem to be the case. Walton (1992) discusses two; the first is as follows:

A = Jones is less than 5 ft tall.
B = Jones is an all-star forward on the NBA for the Los Angeles Lakers.
Conclusion (A&B) = Jones is a less than 5-ft-tall all-American forward on the NBA Los Angeles Lakers.

---

[1] In fact, because it is the case both that $A,B \vdash A\&B$ and that $A\&B \vdash A$ as well as $A\&B \vdash B$, the MIN rule (Eq. 1) can only be satisfied consistently in the case of the conjunction by assuming that Plausibility($A\&B$) = MIN Plausibility(A), Plausibility(B) (see also Walton 1992, pp. 36, 37; Rescher 1976, p. 16, Theorem 3).

Here, even if there is evidence to support the plausibility of both A and B individually, the plausibility of an extremely successful less than 5-ft-tall basketball player seems rather limited.

The problem here may be that the two statements seem to point in opposite directions and may thus possibly be addressed by an additional condition Rescher (1976) specified on plausible inference, namely, that the propositions in the set must be 'logically compatible and materially consonant with one another' (p. 15). This condition would seem to raise more problems than it solves in that it remains entirely unclear how this is to be assessed (see also Walton 1992), and it indicates, furthermore, the limitations of the rule, which now leaves such simple cases without evaluation procedure.

However, the compatibility condition is also insufficient in that neither logical nor probabilistic conflict is required to generate problematic examples as is clear from Walton's second example:

A = The first flip of this coin will be heads.
B = The second flip of this coin will be heads
Conclusion $(A\&B)$ = Both the first and the second flip of this coin will be heads.

A and B are entirely compatible, but their conjunction nevertheless seems less plausible than each of them individually, and, as Walton (1992) concedes, 'plausibility seems to parallel probability in this case' (p. 38). It is the contention of this chapter that this is true in other cases also.

This particular case (which links also to Kyburg's 1961, 'lottery paradox' and Makinson's 1965, 'preface paradox,' see Wheeler 2007, for a review, and on the preface paradox see also Blamey, this volume[2]), however, is particularly transparent, in that there are clear probabilities we are willing to attribute to coin tosses. The example illustrates that conjunction is not 'probability functional' (Adams 1998). Whereas conjunctions such as E and L and E *or* L are *truth-functional* in the sense that their truth values are functions of the truth values of E and L, they are not *probability functional* because their probabilities are not functions (solely) of the probabilities of E and L. By the same token, probabilities are not simply 'degrees of truth' as in many-valued logics, and the combination of probability and logic must respect the unique inference and combination rules of each if it is to be successful.

---

[2] The lottery paradox concerns the tension between the fact that it seems rational to believe that each individual ticket of a lottery is likely to lose, yet the conjunction of all of these individual beliefs is false. The preface paradox involves imagining the statements of a book each of which engenders great confidence but which are likely to include an error. Much has been said about these 'paradoxes' of rational acceptance. On the present view, what they illustrate is the simple point made here, namely, that one would not want to evaluate conjuncts without consideration of the relationships between statements. The 'paradoxes' are consequences of the way seemingly 'objective' probabilities concerning lottery tickets or coin flips combine. Hence, any theory of rational belief that wishes to reflect basic mathematical facts about processes of sampling with (coin tosses) or without replacement (lotteries) must respect these combination properties also.

For probabilities, in fact, the conjunction of two events can be *no more probable* than the less probable of the two events, that is,

$$P(A\&B) \leq \text{MIN } P(A), P(B) \tag{2}$$

and violations of this in judgement are known as the 'conjunction fallacy' (e.g. Tversky and Kahneman 1983). That is, in the case of probabilities and their conjunction, the 'weakest link' does not provide a *lower bound* on strength as stipulated by the consequence condition and the MIN rule but rather an *upper bound*.

Probabilistically, the value assigned to a conjunction is governed by the relationship

$$P(A\&B) = P(A) \times P(A|B) = P(B) \times P(B|A) \tag{3}$$

that is, the relationship between A and B, as captured by the conditional probabilities also matters.

Hence, in the specific example of the coin toss, with $P(A)$ and $P(B)$ each reflecting an unbiased coin at .5, $P(A\&B)$, by Eq. 3, equals .25. In other words, the probability of the conjunct can be lower than the minimum of either $P(A)$ or $P(B)$ and can be as low as zero. Specifically, the lower bound on the value of the conjunct is 0 if $P(A) + P(B) \leq 1$ and $P(A) + P(B)-1$ otherwise.[3] The coin example is troubling for the consequence condition because it would seem to otherwise fall squarely within its remit. The example may, however, be relegated into the role of an 'exception' if everyday arguments can be mapped on to probabilities only in exceptional circumstances or if it can be shown that our intuitions about everyday arguments clearly follow consequence condition and MIN rule instead. It will be the goal of the remainder of this chapter to show that neither is, in fact, the case.

4   A Bayesian Perspective

At the heart of the Bayesian perspective on testimony is Bayes' theorem – a normative rule for updating beliefs based on new evidence[4]:

---

[3] If $P(A) + P(B)$ is greater than 1, then $P(A \& B)$ will be at a minimum when $P(A \& \neg B) = 1-P(B)$. Therefore, $P(A \& B)$ will be at a minimum when it equals $P(A)-(1-P(B))$, that is, $P(A) + P(B)-1$. Note also that this means it is the sum of the two probabilities that determines the lower bound on the probability of the conjunct, not the minimum of these two probabilities.

[4] The term 'evidence' is used here and in the following to refer to anything that might be considered in support of a hypothesis (i.e., a 'reason'). Hence, the term is used more broadly here than in many discussions of testimony; specifically, something can be evidence for a hypothesis even if that hypothesis turns out to be false, that is, what is often referred to as 'potential evidence' (Achinstein 1987); likewise, the term 'evidence' as used here includes information which, objectively, turns out not to be diagnostic (cf. Graham 1997); information which is subjectively non-diagnostic is likewise referred to as evidence in this chapter and simply constitutes evidence that is maximally weak.

$$P(h|e) = \frac{P(h)P(e|h)}{P(h)P(e|h) + P(\neg h)P(e|\neg h)} \qquad (4)$$

according to which one's posterior degree of belief in a hypothesis, h, in light of the evidence, $P(h|e)$, is a function of one's initial, prior degree of belief, $P(h)$, and how likely it is that the evidence one observed would have occurred if one's initial hypothesis was true, $P(e|h)$, as opposed to if it was false, $P(e|\neg h)$. These latter two quantities $P(e|h)$ and $P(e|\neg h)$ may be thought of as the 'hit rate' and 'false positive rate' of a diagnostic test. Their ratio, the so-called likelihood ratio, provides a natural measure of the diagnosticity of the evidence – that is, its informativeness regarding the hypothesis in question.

Crucially, if $P(e|h) > P(e|\neg h)$, then receipt of the evidence will result in an increase in belief in h, whereas if $P(e|h) < P(e|\neg h)$, then receipt of the evidence will result in a decrease, and if the two are equal, our beliefs remain unchanged. Moreover, the magnitude of the difference between $P(e|h)$ and $P(e|\neg h)$ will influence directly how much change in belief is brought about –more reliable evidence will lead to higher posterior degrees of belief. Finally, where there is more than one piece of evidence their combined impact is readily derived through sequential application of Bayes' theorem, taking the posterior at each step as the new prior that is combined with the next piece of evidence in order to calculate its impact.

This captures naturally the simple case in which multiple independent witnesses all provide the same testimony. This may be illustrated with a further example of Walton's (1992, p. 42):

> Virgil said sincerely that there is a fire.
> Vanessa said sincerely that there is a fire.
> Therefore, there is a fire at the university.

where Virgil is a highly reliable source and Vanessa somewhat less reliable. From the Bayesian perspective, this means that the ratio $P('Virgil\ says\ fire'|fire)/P('Virgil\ says\ fire'|no\ fire)$ is greater than that of $P('Vanessa\ says\ fire'|fire)/P('Vanessa\ says\ fire'|no\ fire)$. Consequently, Virgil's testimony on its own will lead to greater degrees of belief in the presence of a fire than Vanessa's. However, receiving Vanessa's independent evidence will further increase our belief in the presence of a fire, as will every further witness even if they are yet less reliable (as long as we assume the relevant likelihood ratio is greater than 1). In other words, each witness has their own impact on our conviction, with that impact scaled by their reliability.[5]

From the perspective of plausible reasoning, it constitutes a convergent argument because each premise provides a separate, independent line of evidence, consequently the MAX rule is applied (Walton 1992, p. 42). In the best case, this leaves the exact plausibility of the conclusion under-defined because the rule stipulates simply that "in a convergent argument the conclusion is *at least as*

---

[5] This simple case is also familiar from, for example, Bayesian treatments of the Humean position on miracles; see, e.g. Tucker (2005) and references therein.

plausible as the most plausible premise" (p. 42, italics added), or, at worst, this ignores entirely Vanessa's testimony (and an army of potential further witnesses like her) if for convergent arguments we "take the maximum of the value of the premises" (p. 44). Either way, this seems a less satisfactory treatment.

This case, however, is really only the most simple case of testimony. More subtle, and considerably less well-examined, issues arise when witnesses differ not just in the reliability of their testimony but also in its content. These issues will be the focus of the remainder of this chapter.

5 Message Content and Message Source: Exploring Norms and Intuitions

Where witnesses differ not just in reliability but also in the content of their testimony, the impact of both of these factors on the believability (or plausibility) of the conclusion needs to be taken into account.

There are two ways in which source reliability might be factored into a Bayesian model of a given task. The first is to consider source reliability as an exogenous variable; that is, inherent characteristics of the evidence – or message content – and the characteristics of the source providing that evidence are (implicitly) combined into a single, overall likelihood ratio (as in, e.g. Birnbaum and Mellers 1983; Birnbaum and Stegner 1979; Corner and Hahn 2009). In other words, evaluation is based on the subjective probability of the composite evidence E 'that specific message from that specific source' conditional on truth or falsity of the hypothesis, that is, $P(E|H)$ and $P(E|\neg H)$.

The second possibility is to model source reliability endogenously, capturing it through an explicit variable(*s*) in the model (as in, e.g. Bovens and Hartmann 2003; Friedman 1987, see also Goldman 1999; Hahn et al. 2009; Hahn and Oaksford 2007a, b; Pearl 1988; Schum 1981, 1994). This involves a cascaded inference in a hierarchical model. Figure 1 shows a simple hierarchical model in which to capture an evidence report from a partially reliable source. This model captures explicitly the fact that what is received is a *report* of some evidence through a partially reliable source, not the evidence directly. In other words, it naturally captures cases of testimony where evidence of an event is based on witness description, not on first-hand experience.

The likelihood ratio associated with such an evidence report, E_{rep}, is described by Eq. 5 is:

$$\frac{P(E|H)[P(E_{rep}|E,H) - P(E_{rep}|\neg E,H)] + P(E_{rep}|\neg E,H)}{P(E|\neg H)[P(E_{rep}|E,\neg H) - P(E_{rep}|\neg E,\neg H)] + P(E_{rep}|\neg E,\neg H)} \tag{5}$$

Here, $P(E_{rep}|E,H)$ represents the probability of an evidence report, E_{rep}, to the effect that the evidence E obtains, given that both E *and* H (the hypothesis) are true,

Fig. 1 A hierarchical model in which the reliability of the reporting source is captured explicitly. Three levels are distinguished: the underlying hypothesis H, the evidence E and the source's actual report of that evidence E_{rep}

and so on (see also Schum 1981). If the witness is completely reliable and reports only the true state of the evidence, then Eq. 5 reduces simply to the standard direct relationship between evidence and hypothesis. An immediate, general characteristic of testimony arises from this formalisation. Specifically, the evidential characteristics of the report vis à vis the hypothesis are a *multiplicative combination* of the diagnosticity of the evidence itself and the characteristics of the reporting source, that is, the source's own hit and false alarm rate regarding the true state of that evidence.

If we contrast sources high and low in reliability and contrast arguments from these sources that are either weak or strong, then this multiplicative combination means that we should see not only independent contributions on posterior degree of belief of source reliability and argument strength, but these factors should interact (see Fig. 2 below). This is indeed what is observed in recent experimental studies of argumentation.[6] Specifically, participants in Hahn et al.'s (2009) studies saw arguments such as the following:

> Dave: This drug is safe.
> Jimmy: How do you know?
> Dave: Because I read that there have been fifty experiments conducted, and they didn't find any side effects.
> Jimmy: Where did you read that?
> Dave: I read it in the journal Science just yesterday.
>   (strong content/reliable source)

---

[6] While there have been very detailed examinations of the impact of source credibility within social psychology (e.g. Birnbaum et al. 1976; Birnbaum and Stegner 1979; Birnbaum and Mellers 1983), these studies have not simultaneously manipulated the diagnosticity of the message content. Finally, both message content and source characteristics have been manipulated simultaneously in a large number of social psychological studies of persuasion (e.g. Chaiken 1980; Petty et al. 1981; Petty and Cacioppo 1984, of many). However, differences in theoretical focus have meant that the data from these studies have typically not been analysed in such a way as to address the question of how these two factors combine because as indicated in the 'Introduction', persuasion researchers have typically considered source and content as alternatives that are indicative of two separate cognitive routes to persuasion and have consequently used these factors almost exclusively as a means by which to isolate these different routes. Hence, a comprehensive review by Pornpitakpan (2004) lists fewer than a handful of studies examining the combined effects of message source and content on persuasion.

or,

> Dave: This drug is safe.
> Jimmy: How do you know?
> Dave: Because I read that there has been one experiment conducted, and it didn't find any
> side effects.
> Jimmy: Where did you read that?
> Dave: I got sent a circular email from excitingnews@wowee.com
> (weak content/unreliable source)

as well as the combinations 'strong content/weak source' and 'weak content/strong source'. Figure 2 shows the resultant ratings of convincingness given by participants. The convincingness of the arguments were affected both by the nature of the source and the content of the argument, with a statistical interaction between the two, in line with the Bayesian norm. This interaction can be seen in the Figure in the ratings for the strong content/reliable source, which sees an extra 'boost' relative to the difference between reliable and unreliable source in the weak argument condition. This may be contrasted, once again, with the evaluation suggested by a plausible reasoning perspective. As noted above, Walton (2008) states that such cases should be considered as *linked arguments*. On receiving an argument from a source of given reliability, one can attack either the argument itself or the reliability of the source. Undermining the reliability of the source will also undermine the argument (unless of course that argument has some independent basis). Hence, the two components form a linked argument, in which, according to the MIN rule, the overall strength depends on the weakest link. If the plausibility of the conclusion is set to the weaker of the two components, however, then evaluation will necessarily be blind to one of the dimensions of variation considered in the matrix of Fig. 2 panel (a) and the data of panel (b). Specifically, if the degree of plausibility assigned to the claim that the source is reliable is less than the plausibility value assigned to the content of either the weak or strong argument, then the variation in strength of content is immaterial. Conversely, if the plausibility value attached to the source is higher than that attached to the argument content, then the variation in reliability is without consequence. Thus, the MIN rule would seem to violate fundamental intuitions about argument strength across such simple sets of arguments.

This limitation stems from the fact that the weakest link idea is implemented in what is in effect a 'loser takes all' fashion. At fault here is not the intuition that the impact of testimony should somehow be limited by the reliability of the source, but rather the specific way in which this fundamental intuition is implemented. Notably, there is a way in which source reliability caps the influence of evidence within a Bayesian framework as well (see also Oaksford and Hahn this volume). Returning to Eq. 5 above and its multiplicative nature, we had noted that if the witness is completely reliable and reports only the true state of the evidence, then Eq. 5 reduces simply to the standard direct relationship between evidence and hypothesis. By the same token, where the evidence is entirely deterministic and arises if and only if the hypothesis is true (i.e., $P(E|H) = 1$, $P(E|\neg H) = 0$), the hit and false positive rates of the witness completely determine the characteristics of

a

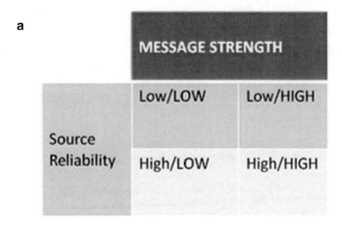

b

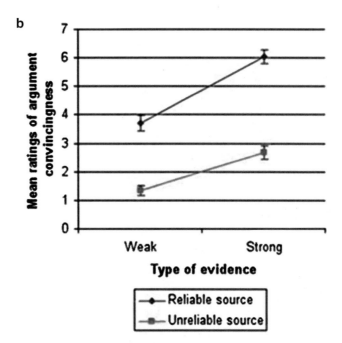

Fig. 2 Varying both source reliability and argument strength. *Panel (a)* highlights the factorial combinations arising from contrasts of weak and strong evidence combined with low and high source reliability; *Panel (b)* shows data from a corresponding experimental manipulation in Exp. 1 from Hahn et al. (2009).

the report. From this latter case, it can be seen that less than perfect reliability of the witness necessarily reduces the overall diagnosticity of the evidence received. How diagnostic the report can be and hence what posterior degree of belief it can bring about is capped by the reliability of the witness (see Hahn et al. 2009).

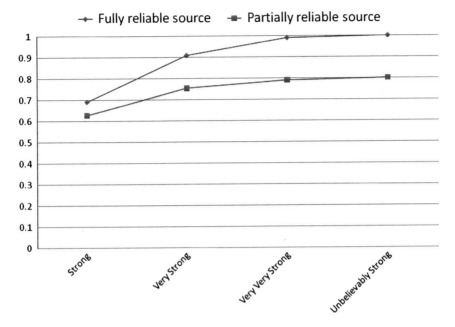

Fig. 3 The figure contrasts the relative impact of receiving the same message (varying in evidential strength as measured by the likelihood ratio) given variation in the reliability of the reporting source. The *x*-axis captures message strength, and the *y*-axis indicates resultant degree of conviction measured as posterior degree of belief (with the prior always set to .5)

The effects of this are demonstrated in Fig. 3 which contrasts the resultant posterior degree of belief arising from message content that ranges in strength from weak to extremely strong (as measured by the likelihood ratio associated with the content itself) when that evidence is received from a partially as opposed to fully reliable source. In other words, the Bayesian perspective captures naturally the sense that limits on the reliability of the source must limit the ultimate conviction in the conclusion that their argument brings about, but it does so without the counter-intuitive consequences of the MIN rule or weakest link principle.

Finally, there has been interest recently in considering another way in which message content and source reliability interact, namely, not just as distinct factors that determine how convincing an argument is, but rather as sources of evidence that may be seen to possess inferential value *about each other*. This intuition is captured in a further hierarchical model of evidence from partially reliable sources by Bovens and Hartmann (2003).

Again, the hypothesis (or conclusion) at stake, the source and the evidence presented by the source all have an explicit representation within a simple Bayesian belief network. This simple network is shown in Fig. 4. The network captures the intuition that what a source actually reports, E_{rep}, is determined both by the 'actual' evidence and the reliability of the source, in that a less than fully reliable source

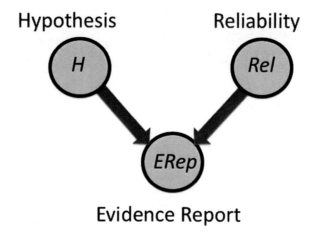

Fig. 4 A simple explicit model of hypothesis, evidence and source. The model shown consists of three binary variables representing the hypothesis or claim in question, H, the evidence report provided by the source and a variable governing the reliability of the source, Rel. As indicated by the arrows, the evidence report is influenced by both the truth/falsity of the hypothesis and whether or not the source is reliable; however, the reliability of the source and the truth/falsity of the hypothesis itself are assumed (in this model) to be independent

may misreport the evidence in question. But it differs from the hierarchical model of Fig. 1 above in exactly which relationships and factors are represented explicitly and hence which can be explicitly reasoned about. The above model of Fig. 1 distinguishes as explicit variables the 'actual' evidence E and the source's report, E_{rep}. By contrast, the present model in Fig. 4 wraps this distinction into a direct relationship between hypothesis H and report. But it represents as an explicit variable the reliability of the source, Rel, whereas the former model captures the reliability of the source in the relationship (i.e., likelihood ratio) between E and E_{rep}. The two models share all the general characteristics discussed so far, namely, the multiplicative relationship between message content and message source in their effect on posterior degree of belief, and, the fact that the degree of reliability of the source 'caps' the impact of the source's evidence (see also Hahn et al. 2009). However, by representing the reliability of the source as a separate variable, the model of Fig. 4 captures the intuition that the content of the message potentially has an impact not just on our degree of belief in the conclusion (hypothesis) but also on how reliable we consider the source to be, even in those circumstances where we are by no means certain in our beliefs. Receiving an evidence report that conflicts with our beliefs about the hypothesis can influence not just our belief in that hypothesis but also, simultaneously, lower our belief in the source's credibility.

Bovens and Hartmann (2003) demonstrate a number of interesting consequences of this model for central questions in epistemology, and the underlying intuition is embodied also by the agents in Olsson and Angerer's simulations of knowledge in networks of interacting agents (see, e.g. Olsson, this volume). Empirical support for this intuition, finally, stems from a recent study (Jarvstad and Hahn 2011, Exp. 2) demonstrating that participants readily drew conclusions about the degree of reliability of a source based on the content of a source's very simple communications, even though participants had no way of being sure about that content (see also Reimer et al. 2004).

6 Rehousing Argumentation Schemes Within a Bayesian Framework

We have sought to demonstrate thus far that the evaluation rules for plausible reasoning conflict both with the Bayesian framework and with common intuition. This does not, however, mean that the argumentation schemes and the critical questions that accompany them within Walton's defeasible reasoning framework are without merit. Rather, they genuinely capture criteria that are typically relevant. The critical questions introduced in the context of the example of the visitor asking for directions above are ones that are clearly relevant, and it is where, in the normal course of affairs, we have reason to believe that the criteria they describe are met that the inference from testimony to the actual location of the central station seems justified.

At the same time, it is the contention of the Bayesian approach that notions such as 'relevance', 'typically' and 'in the normal course of affairs' can be handled naturally within the probability calculus (see, e.g. Pearl 1988; and in the argumentation context specifically, also Hahn and Oaksford 2006a, b). Moreover, the calculus captures naturally dynamic changes in relevance through the notion of *conditional independence* (see Pearl 1988): the probability of outcome A in light of variable B may be different in the presence of C, than it is without it, and such dependence relationships are captured naturally in the graph structures of Bayesian belief networks that we have drawn on already.

So for example, in the network of Fig. 1 above, the testimonial report E_{rep} will *cease* to be relevant if – for whatever reason – we gain access to the evidence, E, itself, once the state of F is *known*, receiving a report on its state no longer leads us to increase our belief in H (relatedly, experimental evidence from the persuasion literature finds that the impact of source reliability is moderated by the recipient's own 'expertise'; see, e.g. Ratneshwar and Chaiken 1991). Bayesian belief networks represent relevant variables (as nodes) and capture directions of influence between them as weighted links and do so in such a way that supports probabilistic inference (i.e., the propagation of beliefs). In the remainder, we thus seek to provide a simple example of how an argumentation scheme can be represented within this formalism. For this example, we use Walton's argumentation scheme for the argument from expert opinion, which is a subtype of the argument from position to know outlined above.

Appeals to expert opinion arise in any situation in which we lack specialised knowledge in a domain and, in some cases, might be the only option we have

Table 1 The six critical questions for the appeal to expert opinion (Adapted from Walton 2008, p. 218)

Expertise question	How credible is the source, S, as an expert source?
Field question	Is S an expert in the field that H is in?
Opinion question	What did S assert that implies H?
Trustworthiness question	Is S personally reliable as a source?
Consistency question	Is H consistent with what other expert sources assert?
Backup evidence question	Is S's assertion based on evidence?

available to us (e.g. consulting our G.P. to diagnose a set of symptoms). Such appeals can take the form of the fallacy of *ad verecundiam,* if the appeal is made to 'parties having no legitimate claim to authority in the matter at hand' (Copi and Cohen 1994, p. 119). The task of evaluating the strength of an appeal to expert opinion is essentially, therefore, one of evaluating the expertise of the party to whom the appeal is made. Walton (1997, 2008, p. 218) outlined six critical questions for evaluating the strength of an appeal to expert opinion (Table 1). As we shall see, these six questions are well captured within a Bayesian network.

Figure 5 shows a simple Bayesian network within which it is possible to evaluate the answers to all six of the questions outlined by Walton (Table 1), and here, we outline how each question is addressed within the network. Walton (2008, p. 218) defines the credibility of S as an expert source as being the question of whether S has mastery of a domain of knowledge or skill. We will conflate the expertise question and the field question as the expertise will only be of relevance if it is in the particular domain under consideration. These questions are therefore captured by the prior probability assigned to 'expertise'. Of course, the network could be extended to the top right to allow for parents of this node, enabling evidence to be presented in support of S's credentials. Such nodes could be direct representations of Walton's five subquestions critical to determining whether S might be called an expert, pertaining to qualifications, references, record of experience, record of successful predictions and record of previous projects reviewed by other experts.

'What did S assert that implies H?' In Fig. 5, S is directly asserting that H is true. S might, however, choose to assert only an intermediate fact (e.g. 'Evidence' in Fig. 5). In this instance, the degree to which this assertion implies H results from the likelihood ratio at 4 $\frac{P(Evidence|H)}{P(Evidence|\neg H)}$.

'Is S personally reliable as a source' is captured by the prior degree of belief assigned to the 'trustworthiness' node. As with the 'expertise' node, the network could be extended to provide evidence for S's trustworthiness.

'Is H consistent with what other experts assert?' Nodes 'H_{rep} (from S2)' and 'H_{rep} (from S3)' represent the reports of different experts on the notion of whether or not H is true.

'Is S's assertion based on evidence?' This question is captured by the opinion question already covered. Note, though, that the network can be extended for cases in which S's statement is based on more than a single item of evidence.

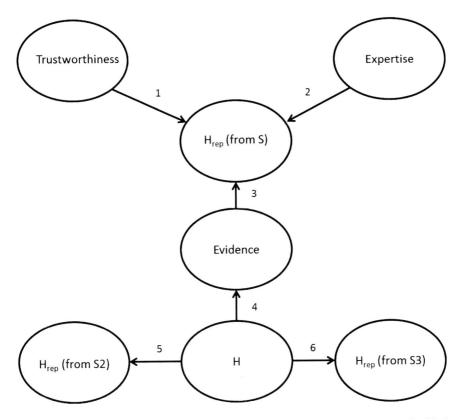

Fig. 5 A Bayesian network representation of the appeal to expert opinion, within which all critical questions raised by Walton (2008) can be addressed

Figure 5 therefore illustrates how central features of appeals to expert opinion can be captured within a Bayesian network. According to the known evidence and the assignment of conditional probability values, the network prescribes not only how likely H is to be true, but information also propagates through the network, updating degrees of belief in the expertise and trustworthiness of the expert source (as in Jarvstad and Hahn 2011, Exp. 2).

Hence, it is the contention of this chapter that significant progress can be achieved by marrying the insights of scheme-based approaches with the formal framework of probability and that this will supply the satisfactory framework for evaluation that is presently missing (on such combination, see also Grabmair and Ashley, this volume).

From this perspective, reasoning appropriately about source reliability in any given context involves Bayesian inference within a suitable model (see also Lagnado et al. 2012). How complex that model needs to be depends on the context, such as the relevant dimensions of variation within that context. Where multiple sources all report the same content, it is not necessary to separate out content and source. Where the specific factors determining reliability are irrelevant or simply unknown, summary representation through a single variable 'reliability' will suffice. In other contexts, it will be useful to separate out personal trustworthiness and expertise, such as in the model of Fig. 5., or possibly sincerity, observational sensitivity, and objectivity (lack of bias), as in Schum (1994); or as Goldman (1999) puts it, competence, opportunity, and honesty. Sometimes it may also be useful to distinguish different cognitive processes affecting the reliability of the report (e.g. Friedman 1987). Though specific contexts may require either more detail or less, the criteria that scheme-based approaches have sought to identify are ones that are often likely to be a concern and hence are good candidates for our models. This chapter has tried to describe the basic building blocks from which such models are assembled and the key conceptual implications that the nature of these building blocks has for thinking about testimony.

7   Concluding Remarks

Testimony, as many have argued recently, is central to the way we acquire information about the world and form our beliefs and opinions. Hence, testimony is central also to argumentation. This was long overlooked, and thinking about argument was dominated by the view that arguments should somehow 'stand for themselves', independently of the person advancing them. Consequently, considerations of the source were branded fallacious. Walton's work on the ad hominem (Walton 1998) and ad verecundiam fallacies (Walton 1997) has done much to challenge that view, and the present upsurge on philosophical interest in testimony lends support to this challenge.

Nevertheless, there may be areas of argumentation where source considerations are unnecessary or inappropriate. One important limit for the relevance of source reliability considerations has already been mentioned: where the recipient of an argument possesses independent means by which to verify its content, consideration of the source becomes unnecessary.

At the same time, the examples considered in this chapter have been limited to statements that involve facts. They have not concerned statements that are purely about values ('democracy is good'), and there may be limits to the role of testimony in contexts of practical reasoning because value statements possess different criteria of evaluation. Certainly, the Bayesian framework as discussed so far applies only to conclusions that are true or false. However, many arguments involving values concern the choice of actions under conditions of uncertainty, and such choice falls under the normative scope of decision theory. Here, recent work on consequentialist arguments ('we should not raise taxes, because it will ruin the economy'), including the purportedly fallacious 'slippery slope argument' ('if we allow medical screening of embryos, it will be designer babies next'), shows how such arguments can be captured in a Bayesian, decision-theoretic framework (Hahn and Oaksford 2006a, 2007a; Corner et al. 2011; Thompson et al. 2005). Examining in detail the way testimony might operate in such contexts that involve both fact and values seems an important issue for future research.

Finally, it is worth mentioning other research on the fallacies of argumentation that draws on the probability calculus because the range of argument forms and examples discussed in these works (see, e.g. on the 'argument from ignorance', Oaksford and Hahn 2004; on circular arguments Shogenji 2000; Hahn and Oaksford 2006a, 2007b; Hahn 2011; Shogenji, this volume) add to the examples discussed in this chapter in making clear that the application of Bayesian probability as a formal framework is not, as some have assumed, limited to arguments that are overtly numerical or statistical.

References

Achinstein, P. (1987). Concepts of evidence. *Mind, 87*, 22–45.

Adams, E. W. (1998). *A primer of probability logic*. Stanford: CSLI.

Adler, J. (2006). Epistemological problems of testimony. In *Stanford Encyclopedia of Philosophy*. Stanford: Stanford University.

Birnbaum, M. H., & Mellers, B. (1983). Bayesian inference: Combining base rates with opinions of sources who vary in credibility. *Journal of Personality and Social Psychology, 45*, 792–804.

Birnbaum, M. H., & Stegner, S. E. (1979). Source credibility in social judgment: Bias, expertise and the judge's point of view. *Journal of Personality and Social Psychology, 37*, 48–74.

Birnbaum, M. H., Wong, R., & Wong, L. K. (1976). Combining information from sources that vary in credibility. *Memory & Cognition, 4*, 330–336.

Blamey, J. (this volume). Upping the stakes and the preface paradox. In F. Zenker (Ed.), Bayesian argumentation: The practical side of probability (pp. xx–xx). Dordrecht: Springer

Bovens, L., & Hartmann, S. (2003). *Bayesian epistemology*. Oxford: Oxford University Press.

Bowell, T., & Kemp, G. (2002). *Critical thinking: A concise guide*. London: Routledge.

Carlson, K., & Russo, J. (2001). Biased interpretation of evidence by mock jurors. *Journal of Experimental Psychology: Applied, 7*, 91–103.

Chaiken, S. (1980). Heuristic versus systematic information processing and the use of source versus message cues in persuasion. *Journal of Personality and Social Psychology, 39*, 752–766.

Coady, C. A. J. (1992). *Testimony: A philosophical study*. Oxford: Oxford University Press.

Cohen, L. J. (1982). What is necessary for testimonial corroboration? *British Journal for the Philosophy of Science, 33*, 161–164.

Copi, I. M., & Cohen, C. (1994). *Introduction to logic* (9th ed.). New York: Macmillan.

Corner, A., & Hahn, U. (2009). Evaluating science arguments: Evidence, uncertainty & argument strength. *Journal of Experimental Psychology: Applied, 15*, 199–212.

Corner, A. J., Hahn, U., & Oaksford, M. (2011). The psychological mechanism of the slippery slope argument. *Journal of Memory and Language, 64*, 153–170.

Eagly, A. H., & Chaiken, S. (1993). *The psychology of attitudes*. Belmont: Thompson/Wadsworth.

Eaton, T. E., & O'Callaghan, M. G. (2001). Child-witness and defendant credibility: child evidence presentation mode and judicial instructions. *Journal of Applied Social Psychology, 31*, 1845–1858.

ForsterLee, L., Horowitz, I. A., Athaide-Victor, E., & Brown, N. (2000). The bottom line: the effect of written expert witness statements on juror verdicts and information processing. *Law and Human Behavior, 24*, 259–270.

Friedman, R. (1987). Route analysis of credibility and hearsay. *Yale Law Journal, 96*, 667–742.

Goldman, A. I. (1999). *Knowledge in a social world*. Oxford: Oxford University Press.

Grabmair, M., & Ashley, K. D. (this volume). A survey of uncertainties and their consequences in probabilistic legal argumentation. In F. Zenker (Ed.), *Bayesian argumentation: The practical side of probability* (pp. xx–xx). Dordrecht: Springer.

Graham, P. J. (1997). What is testimony? *Philosophical Quarterly, 47*, 227–232.

Hahn, U., & Oaksford, M. (2006a). A Bayesian approach to informal argument fallacies. *Synthese, 152*, 207–236.

Hahn, U., & Oaksford, M. (2006b). Why a normative theory of argument strength and why might one want it to be Bayesian? *Informal Logic, 26*, 1–24.

Hahn, U., & Oaksford, M. (2007a). The rationality of informal argumentation: A Bayesian approach to reasoning fallacies. *Psychological Review, 114*, 704–732.

Hahn, U., & Oaksford, M. (2007b). The burden of proof and its role in argumentation. *Argumentation, 21*, 39–61.

Hahn, U., Harris, A. J. L., & Corner, A. J. (2009). Argument content and argument source: An exploration. *Informal Logic, 29*, 337–367.

Hahn, U. (2011). The problem of circularity in evidence, argument and explanation. *Perspectives on Psychological Science, 6*, 172–182.

Harris, P. L., & Corriveau, K. H. (2011). Young children's selective trust in informants. *Philosophical Transactions of the Royal Society B, 366*, 1179–1190.

Hughes, W., Lavery, J., & Doran, K. (2010). *Critical thinking: An introduction to the basic skills* (6th ed.). Peterborough: Broadview Press.

Hume, D. (1977) *An enquiry concerning human understanding* (E. Steinberg, Ed.). Indianapolis: Hackett Publishing Company.

Jarvstad, A., & Hahn, U. (2011). Source reliability and the conjunction fallacy. *Cognitive Science, 35*, 682–711.

Johnson, R. H. (2000). *Manifest rationality: A pragmatic theory of argument*. Mahwah, NJ: Lawrence Erlbaum.

Krauss, D. A., & Sales, B. D. (2001). The effects of clinical and scientific expert testimony on juror decision making in capital sentencing. *Psychology, Public Policy, and Law, 7*, 267–310.

Kruglanski, A. W., & Stroebe, W. (2005). The influence of beliefs and goals on attitudes: Issues of structure, function, and dynamics. In D. Albarracín, B. T. Johnson, & M. P. Zanna (Eds.), *The handbook of attitudes* (pp. 323–369). Mahwah, NJ: Erlbaum.

Kusch, M., & Lipton, P. (2002). Testimony: A primer. *Studies in the History and Philosophy of Science, 33*, 209–217.

Kyburg, H. E., Jr. (1961). *Probability and the logic of rational belief*. Middletown: Wesleyan University Press.

Lagnado, D. A., Fenton, N., & Neil, M. (2012). Legal idioms: A framework for evidential reasoning. *Argument and Computation, 4*, 1–18. Online first.

Loftus, E. F. (1975). Leading questions and the eyewitness report. *Cognitive Psychology, 7*, 560–572.

Makinson, D. C. (1965). The paradox of the preface. *Analysis, 25*, 205–207.

Oaksford, M., & Hahn, U. (2004). A Bayesian approach to the argument from ignorance. *Canadian Journal of Experimental Psychology, 58*, 75–85.

Oaksford, M., & Hahn, U. (this volume). Why are we convinced by the Ad Hominem argument?: Bayesian source reliability or pragma-dialectical discussion rules. In F. Zenker (Ed.), *Bayesian argumentation: The practical side of probability* (pp. xx–xx). Dordrecht: Springer.

Olsson, E. J. (this volume). A Bayesian simulation model of group deliberation. In F. Zenker (Ed.), *Bayesian argumentation: The practical side of probability* (pp. xx–xx). Dordrecht: Springer.

Pearl, J. (1988). *Probabilistic reasoning in intelligent systems*. San Mateo: Morgan Kaufman.

Perelman, C., & Olbrechts-Tyteca, L. (1969). *The new rhetoric: A treatise on argumentation*. Notre Dame: University of Notre Dame Press.

Petty, R. E., & Cacioppo, J. T. (1984). Source factors and the elaboration likelihood model of persuasion. *Advances in Consumer Research, 11*, 668–672.

Petty, R. E., & Wegener, D. T. (1999). The elaboration likelihood model: Current status and controversies. In S. Chaiken & Y. Trope (Eds.), *Dual process theories in social psychology* (pp. 41–72). New York: Guilford Press.

Petty, R. E., Cacioppo, J. T., & Goldman, R. (1981). Personal involvement as a determinant of argument-based persuasion. *Journal of Personality and Social Psychology, 41,* 847–855.

Pollock, J. L. (2001). Defeasible reasoning with variable degrees of justification. *Artificial Intelligence, 133,* 233–282.

Pollock, J. L. (1995). *Cognitive carpentry*. Cambridge, MA: Bradford/MIT Press.

Pornpitakpan, C. (2004). The persuasiveness of source credibility: A critical review of five decades' evidence. *Journal of Applied Social Psychology, 34,* 243–281.

Prakken, H., & Vreeswijk, G. A. W. (2002). Logics for defeasible argumentation. In D. M. Gabbay & F. Guenthner (Eds.), *Handbook of philosophical logic* (2nd ed., Vol. 4, pp. 219–318). Dordrecht/Boston/London: Kluwer Academic.

Rainbolt, G. W., & Dwyer, S. L. (2012). *Critical thinking: The art of argument*. Boston: Wadsworth.

Ratneshwar, R., & Chaiken, S. (1991). Comprehension's role in persuasion: The case of its moderating effect on the persuasive impact of source cues. *Journal of Consumer Research, 18,* 52–63.

Reimer, T., Mata, R., & Stoecklin, M. (2004). The use of heuristics in persuasion: Deriving cues on source expertise from argument quality. *Current Research in Social Psychology, 10,* 69.

Rescher, N. (1976). *Plausible reasoning*. Assen: Van Gorcum.

Rescher, N. (1977). *Dialectics: A controversy-oriented approach to the theory of knowledge*. Albany: State University of New York Press.

Schuller, R. A., Terry, D., & McKimmie, B. (2001). The impact of an expert's gender on jurors' decisions. *Law and Psychology Review, 25,* 59–79.

Schum, D. A. (1981). Sorting out the effects of witness sensitivity and response-criterion placement upon the inferential value of testimonial evidence. *Organizational Behavior and Human Performance, 27,* 153–196.

Schum, D. A. (1994). *The evidential foundations of probabilistic reasoning*. Evanston: Northwestern University Press.

Shogenji, T. (2000). Self-dependent justification without circularity. *British Journal for the Philosophy of Science, 51,* 287–298.

Shogenji, T. (this volume). Reductio, coherence, and the myth of epistemic circularity. In F. Zenker (Ed.), *Bayesian argumentation: The practical side of probability* (pp. xx–xx). Dordrecht: Springer.

Skolnick, P., & Shaw, J. I. (2001). A comparison of eyewitness and physical evidence on Mock-Juror decision making. *Criminal Justice and Behavior, 28,* 614–630. doi:10.1177/009385480102800504.

Thompson, V. A., Evans, J. S., & Handley, S. J. (2005). Persuading and dissuading by conditional argument. *Journal of Memory and Language, 53,* 238 257.

Tindale, C. W. (2007). *Fallacies and argument appraisal*. New York: Cambridge University Press.

Toulmin, S. (1958). *The uses of argument*. Cambridge: Cambridge University Press.

Tucker, A. (2005). Miracles, historical testimonies, and probabilities. *History and Theory, 44,* 373–390.

Tversky, A., & Kahneman, D. (1983). Extensional versus intuitive reasoning: The conjunction fallacy in probability judgment. *Psychological Review, 90,* 293–315.

van Eemeren, F. H., & Grootendorst, R. (2004). *A systematic theory of argumentation. The pragma-dialectical approach*. Cambridge: Cambridge University Press.

Verheij, B. (2003). Dialectical argumentation with argumentation schemes: An approach to legal logic. *Artificial intelligence and Law, 11,* 167–195.

Walton, D. N. (1992). Rules for plausible reasoning. *Informal Logic, XIV,* 33–51.

Walton, D. N. (1996). *Argument schemes for presumptive reasoning*. Hillsdale: Lawrence Erlbaum.

Walton, D. (1997). *Appeal to expert opinion*. University Park: Pennsylvania State Press.

Walton, D. N. (1998). *Ad Hominem arguments*. Tuscaloosa: The University of Alabama Press.

Walton, D. M. (2001). Abductive, presumptive, and plausible arguments. *Informal Logic, 21*, 141–169.

Walton, D. N. (2004). *Relevance in argumentation*. Mahwah: Erlbaum.

Walton, D. N. (2008). *Witness testimony evidence: argumentation, artificial intelligence, and law*. Cambridge: Cambridge University Press.

Walton, D., Reed, C., & Macagno, F. (2008). *Argumentation schemes*. Cambridge: Cambridge University Press.

Weinstock, M., & Flaton, R. (2004). Evidence coverage and argument skills: cognitive factors in a juror's verdict choice. *Journal of Behavioral Decision Making, 17*, 191–212.

Wells, G. L., & Olsen, E. A. (2003). Eyewitness testimony. *Annual Review of Psychology, 54*, 277–295.

Wheeler, G. (2007). A review of the lottery paradox. In W. Harper & G. Wheeler (Eds.), *Probability and inference: Essays in honour of Henry E. Kyburg, Jr* (pp. 1–31). London: King's College Publications.

Woods, J., Irvine, A., & Walton, D. (2004). *Critical Thinking: Logic & The Fallacies*. Toronto: Prentice Hall.

Why Are We Convinced by the Ad Hominem Argument?: Bayesian Source Reliability and Pragma-Dialectical Discussion Rules

Mike Oaksford and Ulrike Hahn

Abstract There has been little empirical research on the ad hominem argument. What there is has been carried in the tradition of the pragma-dialectic approach by investigating the reasonableness of the ad hominem argument which is determined by the discussion stage in which it is deployed (van Eemeren et al., Fallacies and judgements of reasonableness. Springer, Dordrecht, 2009). The experiment reported in this chapter investigates how convincing people find the ad hominem argument from the emerging Bayesian epistemic perspective on argumentation (Hahn and Oaksford, Psychol Rev 114:704–732, 2007), in which people are argued to be sensitive to the reliability of the source of an argument. The experiment varied source reliability, initial degree of belief in the conclusion, and whether the ad hominem was a pro or a con argument. A Bayesian account of the effect of reliability on posterior degree of beliefs after hearing the argument provided excellent fits to the data. Moreover, the results were not consistent with the pragma-dialectic approach, as no differences were observed between conditions where a discussion rule was violated and a control condition where it was not violated. However, further experimentation is required to fully establish this conclusion.

Much of what we know of the world comes to us second-hand (e.g. Coady 1992). We actually pick up few of our beliefs via direct experience. Rather most of our beliefs derive from being told in the classroom, on the TV, in the newspapers, in books, by our parents, by our bosses, or by our friends. Whether or to what degree

M. Oaksford (✉)
Department of Psychological Science, Birkbeck College, University of London,
Malet Street, London WC1E 7HX, UK
e-mail: mike.oaksford@bbk.ac.uk

U. Hahn
Department of Psychological Science, Birkbeck College, University of London,
Malet Street, London WC1E 7HX, UK

School of Psychology, Cardiff University, Cardiff, Wales, UK

F. Zenker (ed.), *Bayesian Argumentation: The practical side of probability*,
Synthese Library 362, DOI 10.1007/978-94-007-5357-0_3,
© Springer Science+Business Media Dordrecht 2013

39

we believe what we are told depends on many factors. For example, it depends on the coherence of what we are told with other beliefs and information (see, e.g. Olsson 2005; Shogenji 1999; Bovens and Hartmann 2003; Harris and Hahn 2009). However, it also depends critically on the source of the information. We are less likely to believe a proposition on being told that our informant was a sociopath, and we are more likely to believe experts than novices. It is perhaps not surprising therefore that our standards of argumentation embody some assessment of the credibility of an informant. For example, (1) seems a reasonable argument:

(1) Person A suggests that person B should invest in A's company.
    Person C argues against A's suggestion by pointing out that A is a sociopath.

One might argue that whether A is a sociopath or not is irrelevant to whether investing in A's company will yield B a profit. However, human beings are in what has been called the "finitary predicament" (Cherniak 1986); they most often simply do not have the time or access to information to make more informed decisions. In financial terms, the man in the street is most often an "outsider" rather than an "insider". Without insider knowledge, C's interjection that A is a sociopath, and hence likely to act solely in her own interests rather than B's is highly relevant to B's decision whether or not to invest in A's company. Had more people identified Bernie Madoff as a sociopath, fewer may have lost their shirts investing with him in financial deals they never looked into further.

A problem for argument (1), which is seemingly against the person rather than the proposition they are advancing, is that it has traditionally been viewed as fallacious: it is an instance of the classical reasoning fallacy, the *argumentum ad hominem*. For example, what distinguishes (1) from (2):

(2) Person A (B's doctor) suggests that person B should give up smoking.
    Person C argues against A's suggestion by pointing out that B smokes herself.

(2) seems clearly fallacious as whether B's doctor smokes or not cannot influence the beneficial health effects that B will experience by giving up smoking. Here, the reliability of the source of this advice is not only irrelevant but known to be irrelevant. That is, in this case, we do have insider information. It is now common knowledge that smoking is bad for your health in a way that it was not common knowledge that investing in Bernie Madoff's company would lead you to lose money. This epistemic difference seems to be important for how convinced people are by an ad hominem argument. That is, the extent to which B now believes that she should give up smoking or invest in A's company, given C's ad hominem argument, depends in part on what they already believe about these propositions.

An epistemic approach to reasoning fallacies, that may be able to capture these intuitions, has recently been adopted by a variety of researchers. For example, Ikuenobe (2004) argued that "a fallacy is fundamentally an epistemic error, involving the failure to provide in the form of a premise, adequate proof for a belief, or proposition in the form of a conclusion" (p. 193). However, he avoided articulating any explicit epistemic principles about what constitutes adequate proof or evidence. Hahn and Oaksford (2006, 2007) adopt a related approach arguing that when the relevant arguments are reformulated with the conclusion as the hypothesis and the premise as the evidence, then Bayes' theorem provides a useful account of the epistemic adequacy of proof or what they call *argument strength*. There has been very little empirical research on argumentative fallacies. This is particularly true of the argumentum ad hominem, where other than the work summarised by van Eemeren et al. (2009), no other empirical studies appear to have been carried out on this fallacy. In this chapter, we report the results of an experiment investigating the effects on people's degree of belief in the conclusion of an ad hominem argument. We will conclude that a Bayesian source reliability model (Hahn et al. 2009) provides a good account of people's judgements of how persuaded they are by these arguments, which do not seem to be particularly sensitive to violations of *pragma-dialectical* discussion rules (see, *The Pragma-Dialectical Approach*, and van Eemeren et al. 1996, 2009).

We begin this chapter with a review of the types of the argument ad hominem that have been identified in the literature. We then introduce the pragma-dialectical approach to the argument ad hominem and the experimental research that has been done on how *reasonable* these arguments are perceived to be (van Eemeren, et al. 2009). We then introduce the Bayesian approach to argumentative fallacies and derive some predictions for an experiment. We then describe the experiment and the results. In the discussion, we outline the conclusion that we draw from this research.

1   Types of the Argumentum Ad Hominem

Three types of the argumentum ad hominem have been identified in the literature. These are the *abusive*, the *circumstantial*, and the *tu quoque* ("you, too") forms. According to Walton (2000, 2009), all forms of the argument ad hominem attempt to undermine a person's argument for a proposition by suggesting that the person is of "bad character". As Walton observes, this means that these arguments can have non-fallacious uses, "the real function of an *ad hominem* argument (when properly used) is to attack an arguer's credibility in order to criticise the argument she advocates", Walton (2000, p. 102).

The form of the abusive argument ad hominem is as follows (from Walton 2000):

(3) Person A is of bad character.
    Therefore, A's argument X should not be accepted.

An example of this type of argument is given in (3′):

(3′) Person A knows nothing about cars.
    Therefore, A's argument that you should buy a Ford should not be accepted.

This is the same form as (1) above. Accusing someone of lack of knowledge or of being a sociopath without further substantiation is potentially abusive. This is also known as the *direct* form of the argument. As we will see, according to many theorists (van Eemeren, et al. 2009; Walton 2000, 2009), whether this use of the argument ad hominem is fallacious depends on the stage of argumentation and the type of argumentation in which our interlocutors are engaged.

The form of the circumstantial, or *indirect*, argument ad hominem is as follows (from Walton 2000):

(4) A advocates argument X.
   A has carried out an action, or set of actions, that imply that A is personally committed to the opposite of X.
   Therefore A is a bad person.
   Therefore A's argument X should not be accepted.

An example of this type of argument is given in (4′):

(4′) A advocates using company C because it is the best.
   A has married the daughter of the CEO of C and so may not be personally committed to C being the best.
   Therefore, A is a bad person.
   Therefore, A's argument for employing C should not be accepted.

In this type of argument ad hominen, a circumstantial inconsistency is pointed out, that is, there is circumstantial evidence that A would advocate this argument even if he didn't personally believe it.

The *tu quoque* type of the argument ad hominem is a special case of the circumstantial argument type in which the circumstantial inconsistency involves A (not) carrying out exactly the actions that she is advocating people should (not) carry out. This is identical to argument (2) above:

(5) A advocates not smoking.
   A smokes herself and so cannot be personally committed to not smoking.
   Therefore A is a bad person.
   Therefore A's argument for not smoking should not be accepted.

We now look at how these fallacies have been dealt with in the pragma-dialectical approach to argumentation.

2   The Pragma-Dialectical Approach

In their *pragma-dialectical* approach, van Eemeren and Grootendorst (2004) developed a normative theory of discourse rules that define the illegitimate moves that the participants in an argument can make at different stages and in different types of arguments. Some moves may be fallacious in the context of one type of argument but not in another. For example, in a *quarrel*, "where each participant tries to hit out verbally at the other ... [and which is] characterised by an almost total absence of logical reasoning and by heightened emotions" (Walton 1990, p. 414), arguing ad hominem may be appropriate. However, in a *critical discussion*, in which the goal is to "resolve a difference of opinion by means of methodical exchange of discussion moves" (van Eemeren and Grootendorst 2004, p. 22), arguing ad hominem might not be appropriate. Following the pragma-dialectical approach in this regard, we concentrate here solely on the critical discussion in which some kind of rational standard seems to be required.

In the pragma-dialectical approach, fallacies arise because the participants in an argument make wrong moves, that is, moves not licensed by the rules of discourse. Whether the ad hominem argument is fallaciously used in a critical discussion depends on the stage to which the argument has progressed. This argument may be used perfectly legitimately at the *argumentative* stage of a critical discussion if one party has made an appeal to authority in order to support a standpoint that they have introduced earlier at the *confrontation* stage. So, for example, A may propose that smoking is bad for you, and B may enquire why A believes this. At this point, A may argue that his doctor informed him that smoking is bad for you, that is, A makes an appeal to authority to backup his claim introduced at the confrontation stage. A and B have now entered the argumentative stage of the critical discussion, at which point it is legitimate for B to question A's appeal to authority by pointing out that A's doctor himself smokes which seems to belie his ability to act as an authoritative source. However, in (5), where A is the doctor introducing this argument himself at the confrontation stage, it would not be legitimate to disallow his introduction of this claim by deploying the *tu quoque* ad hominem argument. For van Eemeren et al. (2009, p. 21), deploying the ad hominem argument at the confrontation stage constitutes a violation of the *freedom rule* that "discussants may not prevent each other from advancing standpoints or from calling standpoints into question". This is because the goal of a critical discussion is, as we stated above, to "resolve a difference of opinion by means of methodical exchange of discussion moves". If the doctor's introduction of the claim that smoking is bad for you is dismissed at the confrontation stage simply because he himself smokes then there is no possibility of moving forward in resolving any difference of opinion between the doctor and his interlocutor.

Van Eemeren et al. (2009) have also investigated people's attitudes to the argument ad hominem in a series of experiments. These experiments used all three types of the argument ad hominem which were always introduced in the confrontation stage of a critical discussion. Consequently, the arguments were always deployed such that their use was fallacious and constituted a violation of the freedom rule. A control condition was also used that did not violate the freedom rule. General conversational pragmatics also suggests that within the different types of argument ad hominem there will be differences in how reasonable each is viewed. Van Eemeren et al. (2009) hypothesise that general issues of politeness indicate that the abusive form will be less reasonable than the circumstantial and the circumstantial less reasonable than the tu quoque. In order to rule out any general politeness explanation of the results, van Eemeren et al. (2009) also used three different discussion contexts, a domestic discussion, a political debate, and scientific discussion. The important distinction is between the scientific context and the remaining two. One would expect people to be particularly sensitive to violations of discussion moves in scientific discussion as this is one of the paradigmatic examples of a critical discussion where the goal is to get things right. Thus, if people are sensitive to the reasonableness or soundness of an argument then one would expect them to consider fallacies in a scientific discussion to be less reasonable than fallacies in the other two discussion contexts.

As the discussion in the last paragraph indicates, the dependent variable used in van Eemeren et al.'s (2009) experiments was a rating of *reasonableness*. The idea behind this variable was to—as far as possible—address people's understanding of the discourse rules governing argumentation in a critical discussion. That is, by analogy with logic, van Eemeren et al. were attempting to assess the soundness of the discussion rules regardless of specific content used. They suggest that differences in reasonableness between discussion contexts do not mean that different norms apply in each context but rather that the criteria for the application of the same norms may vary from context to context.

Briefly summarising their results, they found that all the arguments ad hominem implying a violation of the freedom rule were judged less reasonable than the control condition where there was no violation of this rule. They also found that the individual arguments differed in reasonableness in the order predicted, that is, the abusive form was judged less reasonable than the circumstantial and the circumstantial was judged less reasonable than the *tu quoque*. Moreover, overall, the use of any of these argument forms was judged less reasonable in the scientific discussion context than the other two contexts, and their use was judged equally reasonable in the domestic and political contexts. In sum, van Eemeren et al. (2009) argue that people are sensitive to violations of the freedom rule and to the pragmatics of politeness but that the observed differences between discussion contexts rule out a general politeness explanation of their results.

3   The Bayesian Approach

In this section, we briefly introduce the Bayesian approach to argumentation and where it contrasts with the pragma-dialectical approach. In the latter approach, fallacies arise because the participants in an argument make wrong moves, that is, moves not licensed by the rules of discourse. For example, here are two arguments ad hominem cited in van Eemeren et al. (2009, p. 56) but deriving from Brinton (1995):

(6) Candidate Jones has no right to moralise about the family; he was once seen arguing with his wife.
(7) Candidate Jones has no right to moralise about the family; since he cheats on his wife.

(6) seems much less acceptable than (7). This difference cannot reside in the discourse context which is the same in both cases, a political discussion, nor in the type of ad hominem argument as they are both the direct or *abusive* form of this

argument. Consequently, for the pragma-dialectical approach, the difference between these arguments seems to have to reside in the type of the argumentative discourse in which people are engaged and in the stage of the argument (van Eemeren and Grootendorst 2004). So, in (7) a rule must have been violated, but in (6) no rule has been violated.

Our Bayesian account begins from the observation that pairs of arguments like (6) and (7) would seem to be differentially acceptable even in the same argumentative context. So assuming a critical discussion, they could both be used fallaciously in the confrontation stage violating the freedom rule, but nonetheless it could be argued that (7) is more convincing than (6). Moreover, both would be acceptable as refutations of Candidate Jones' authority to moralise about the family in the argumentative stage. But again, (7) would be more convincing than (6). Thus, it seems perfectly feasible for both (6) and (7) to occur in the same argumentative context, for example, a critical discussion, and at the same stage but (7) would still be more convincing than would (6). According to the Bayesian theory, the difference must be due to the difference in the content of the argument, which is analysed using Bayesian probability theory to provide an account of *argument strength*. Thus, the approach attempts to capture the uncertain nature of argumentation, emphasised by previous researchers (e.g. Perelman and Olbrechts-Tyteca 1969), while also providing a normative standard, as emphasised in the pragma-dialectical approach.

Before discussing the technicalities of the Bayesian approach, it is worth contrasting it with van Eemeren et al. (2009) by quoting them in detail here. They are commenting on the contrast between their approach and the large body of empirical work on *persuasion* in social psychology (for a recent review, see, e.g. Johnson et al. 2005; for a detailed treatment, see, e.g. Eagly and Chaiken 1993):

> Although it may by and large be expected that there will be some connection between the persuasiveness of argumentation and the reasonableness of argumentation (who would let themselves be convinced by unreasonable argumentation?), it should nevertheless be clear that the contents of the two terms, *persuasiveness* and *reasonableness*, do not coincide. Sound, or in other words reasonable, argumentation does not have to be perceived as convincing *per se*. Other more psychologically tinted factors such as someone's original attitude regarding the defended standpoint, the credibility of the source, the involvement of whoever must be convinced of the defended standpoint, and so on, play a part in convincing that is not to be underestimated. (Van Eemeren et al. 2009, pp. 32–33)

Our Bayesian approach attempts to make sense of how persuaded or convinced somebody is by an argument by providing a *rational analysis* of argumentation in Anderson's (1990) sense.

According to Anderson (1990), rational analysis requires six steps:

Step 1. Specify precisely the goals of the cognitive system.
Step 2. Develop a formal model of the environment to which the system is adapted.
Step 3. Make minimal assumptions about computational limitations.
Step 4. Derive the optimal behaviour function given 1–3 above. (This requires formal analysis using rational norms, such as probability theory and decision theory.)
Step 5. Examine the empirical evidence to see whether the predictions of the behaviour function are confirmed.
Step 6. Repeat, iteratively refining the theory.

Paraphrasing van Eemeren et al. (1996, p. 5), the goal of argumentation is to increase (or decrease) "the acceptability of a controversial standpoint for a listener or reader, by putting forward a constellation of propositions intended to justify (or refute) the standpoint before a 'rational judge'" (step 1). The environment is given in part by the audience, its prior beliefs about a subject and the *rational judge* constraint (step 2). For the moment, we leave step 3 to one side (perhaps to be incorporated on iterating the process at stage 6). To provide step 4, we employ Bayesian probability theory to capture how far someone's prior degree of belief in a controversial standpoint should be modified by propositions advanced for or against it. The experiment we report later in this chapter initiates step 5.

Our approach can be seen as pursuing complimentary goals to both the empirical research on persuasion and the pragma-dialectical approach. On the one hand, we provide a much needed evaluative account of argument persuasiveness in social psychology (Voss and Van Dyke 2001); on the other hand, we supplement a normative account of the reasonableness of argument with a normative account of how convincing people should find these arguments.

The Bayesian approach uses Bayes' theorem and the subjective or epistemic interpretation of probability (Gillies 2000) to capture, "someone's original attitude regarding the defended standpoint" and "the credibility of the source". Bayes' theorem is as follows:

$$(8) \qquad P(C|a) = \frac{P(a|C)P(C)}{P(a|C)P(C) + P(a|\neg C)P(\neg C)}$$

Bayes' theorem states that one's posterior degree of belief in a conclusion, C, in light of an argument, a, $P(C|a)$, is a function of one's initial, prior degree of belief, $P(C)$ (i.e. "someone's...original attitude"), and how likely it is that the argument one is presented with is true if one's initial conclusion was true, $P(a|C)$, as opposed to if it was false, $P(a|\neg C)$. The ratio of these latter two quantities, the likelihood ratio, provides a natural measure of the diagnosticity of the argument—that is, its informativeness regarding the conclusion in question. The most basic aspect of diagnosticity is that if $P(a|C) > P(a|\neg C)$, then the argument will result in an increase in belief in C, whereas if $P(a|C) < P(a|\neg C)$, then the argument will result in a decrease. This has immediate implications for arguments from different sources. We can imagine an encounter with someone who we believe to be truthful as opposed to someone who we believe to be a liar: information from the truthful source will increase our belief in the conclusion, whereas we will consider the opposite of what the liar says to be more likely to be true.

We adopt the same approach to source reliability as Hahn et al. (2009; see also Bovens and Hartmann 2003). The argument, a, above is always a report by one of the interlocuters of the evidence that they take to support or refute C. Factoring in the reliability, R, of the source can be achieved by decomposing the likelihoods to incorporate R in the marginals, for example,

$$(9) \qquad P(a|C) = P(a|C, R)P(R) + P(a|C, \neg R)P(\neg R)$$

(and similarly for $P(a|\neg C)$). An unreliable informant is assumed to be as likely to emit argument a as $\neg a$ whether the conclusion is true or false, that is. $P(a|C,\neg R) = P(a|\neg C,\neg R) = .5$. This decomposition allows the contributions of the argument to altering degrees of belief to be separated out from source reliability. Hahn et al. (2009) showed that because of the multiplicative relation between the probability that the source is reliable, $P(R)$, and the likelihoods, source reliability places limits on the posterior degree of belief. They did this by varying the likelihood ratio due solely to the argument, that is, $P(a|C,R)/P(a|\neg C,R)$, and the probability that the source is reliable, $P(R)$. For example, for a completely reliable source, $P(R) = 1$, assuming an uninformative prior, $P(C) = .5$, as the argument likelihood ratio increases the posterior, $P(C|a)$, approaches 1. However, with $P(R) = .6$, the posterior asymptotes at $P(C|a) = .8$ as the argument likelihood ratio increases.[1]

This analysis captures our initial intuition that the reliability of an informant and prior knowledge interact such that the less knowledge you have the greater effect the ad hominem argument should have. The argument ad hominem is a counter argument which should dissuade someone from believing a conclusion given a prior argument. Prior to the ad hominem attack, a general *principle of charity* constrains an audience to view an interlocutor's utterances as making true statements (Davidson 1974; Wilson 1959). The ad hominem argument is an attack on this assumption to undermine the conclusion. In (1), for example, before hearing C's ad hominem argument, B *assumes* A is reliable, that is, $P(R) \approx 1$, and even though he is initially uncertain, $P(C) = .5$, he should now be highly confident that he should invest in A's company, $P_1(C|a) = .995$. However, C then informs him that the reliability assumption is wrong and that A is unreliable, for example, $P(R) = .5$, and so, re-computing, this reduces B's confidence so that $P_2(C|a) = .75$ a reduction of .245. Of course, if the source is assumed to be completely unreliable, $P(R) = 0$, there will be no change in degree of belief, that is, $P(C) = P_1(C|a)$. However, if B has some prior knowledge that inclines him to believe the conclusion already, as in (2), for example, $P(C) = .8$, the assumption that his doctor is reliable, that is, $P(R) \approx 1$, should lead to the conclusion that she should give up smoking with even higher confidence, $P_1(C|a) = .999$. Moreover, learning that her doctor smokes and so may be unreliable will not reduce B's degree of belief by much, so with $P(R) = .5$, $P_2(C|a) = .92$, that is, a reduction of only .076. Thus, by incorporating prior beliefs a Bayesian model seems to explain the epistemic differences between examples (1) and (2). Figure 1 illustrates this behaviour and also shows what happens if the argument likelihoods are not deterministic, that is, $P(a|C,R) = 1$ and $P(a|\neg C,R) = 0$. Figure 1 shows the models behaviour when $P(a|C,R) = .8$ and $P(a|\neg C,R) = .2$, that is, the argument likelihood ratio is 4.

---

[1] In this example and the next, a deterministic relationship is assumed between the conclusion and the argument, such that the conclusion guarantees the argument with probability 1 if true and probability zero if false.

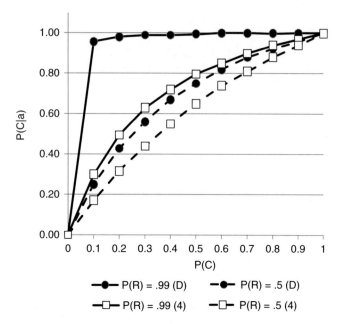

Fig. 1 The behaviour of the model showing changes in the posterior, $P(C|a)$, varying the prior, $P(C)$, with two different argument likelihoods (D = deterministic, 4), and two reliabilities, $P(R)$ (.99, .50)

4 An Experiment on the Argument Ad Hominem

We conducted an experiment using the argument ad hominem, but in contrast to van Eemeren et al. (2009), we asked participants to rate how convinced one of the interlocutors should be by these arguments in a critical discussion. The materials we used were derived from van Eemeren et al.'s (2009) study. However, we also derived *pro* and *con* versions of these arguments. The con version is the standard usage of the ad hominen argument which we illustrate using the *abusive* form used in the experiment:

(10) A: After listening to him, I think it might be possible that Ford cars simply drive better.
  B: Actually, you should be certain that they don't drive better.
  A: Why do you think that?
  B: Because how would he know? He doesn't know the first thing about cars.

Initial degree of belief ($P_1(C|a)$), that is, "after listening to him", was partially manipulated by replacing the phrase "I think it might be possible" (weak) with "I strongly believe" (strong) in the opening comment. Person A always expresses an initial opinion based on hearing an argument from a third party in support of the claim that, "Ford cars simply drive better". Creating a pro argument involved a simple change in the opening comment:

(11) A: Even after listening to him, I think it might be possible that Ford cars don't
drive any better.
B: Well, you can be certain that they don't drive better.
A: Why do you think that?
B: Because how would he know? He doesn't know the first thing about cars.

Here, B's ad hominem argument against the third party is in the same direction as
A's opening claim because A still doesn't believe it despite the argument. We took
two measures in this experiment. After B's final ad hominem attack, participants
were asked how convinced A should now be in the claim that "Ford cars *simply*
(don't) drive (any) better" on a 0–100 scale. That is, we measured $P_2(C|a)$ for A after
B argues that $P(R) < 1$. In a second phase of the experiment, we also measured
participants' assessment of A's degree of belief in their opening comment ($P_1(C|a)$).
This comment is of course conditioned on having heard an argument by a third
party supporting the claim that "Ford cars simply drive better". That is, we measured
$P_1(C|a)$, that is, before A had any reason to believe that $P(R) < 1$, that is, when A, by
the principle of charity, should assume that $P(R) \approx 1$. The measurement was taken
on the same 0–100 scale.

In these dialogues, the argument put forward by the third party remains fixed.
Moreover, it is assumed that that reliability remains fixed across types of ad hominem
argument at least when the principle of charity holds. That is, when participants judge
A's opening claim for $P_1(C|a)$ *before* B argues that $P(R) < 1$. With all elements of
the likelihood ratio fixed the only way the posterior, $P_1(C|a)$, can vary is if the prior,
$P(C)$, varies. Let us consider Fig. 1 for the $P(R) = .99$, argument likelihood ratio
(LR) $= 4$ case. When $P_1(C|a) = .8$, which might be the case when the conclusion is
strongly believed based on the con argument materials, $P(C) = .5$. If, when presented
with the con argument where the conclusion might only be possible, $P_1(C|a)$ falls to
.63, then, assuming everything else remains the same, $P(C)$ must fall to .3. So, because
in the materials everything else remains fixed, differences in $P_1(C|a)$, that is, *before* B
argues that $P(R) < 1$, must equate to changes in A's prior degree of belief, $P(C)$.
In fitting the model to our data, we will use the prior ratings of $P(C|a)$, when $P(R) \approx 1$,
to calculate $P(C)$, which we will assume is updated, on learning that $P(R) < 1$.

This analysis is also consistent with intuition. Compare the following intra-
individual case:

(12) A After listening to him, I think it might be possible that Ford cars simply
drive better.
A After listening to him, I strongly believe that BMW cars simply drive better.

Assuming A has heard exactly the same argument in both cases for why Fords/
BMW drive better than, say Saabs, and assuming a principle of charity, it seems
intuitively clear that A must have believed that BMWs drive better than Fords
before hearing the argument put forward by this third party. Moreover, the following
interindividual case seems intuitively to prompt the same explanation:

(13) A After listening to him, I think it might be possible that Ford cars simply
drive better.
A' After listening to him, I strongly believe that Ford cars simply drive better.

If A and A′ have heard exactly the same argument in both cases and assuming a principle of charity, it is intuitively clear that A′ must have believed that Fords drive better more than A before they heard the argument put forward by this third party. Example (12) is more convincing than (13) because A and A′ might differ in terms of gullibility, which is better modelled by differences in the argument likelihoods they assign to the same argument.

The principle quantitative prediction for this experiment is that the results can be shown to conform to the pattern in Fig. 1, making reasonable assignments of values to the parameters of the model. This hypothesis creates further predictions. So, in all cases, the judgement of convincingness taken in the second phase of the experiment, corresponding to $P_1(C|a)$ when $P(R) \approx 1$ (which we refer to as the 1st posterior), should be higher than when taken in the first phase, corresponding to $P_2(C|a)$ when $P(R) < 1$ (which we refer to as the 2nd posterior). Con arguments, where the initial claim is affirmative (e.g. "Ford cars drive better"), should have higher convincingness than pro arguments where the initial claim is negative (e.g. "Ford cars don't drive better"). Furthermore, when A's initial claim is strong ("I strongly believe"), convincingness should be higher than when this claim is weak ("I think it might be possible"). However, differences for weak or strong initial claims are only likely to come out in interactions. For example, a weak pro argument should come out just below .5, a weak con argument just above .5; but a strong pro argument should come out well below .5 and strong con well above. But this means that the mean of the weak and strong arguments would be predicted to be about the same, that is, .5 approximately. So while an interaction with pro vs. con arguments is predicted, there should be no main effect of weak vs. strong initial claims. There are other hypotheses about which we are neutral that can be tested. For example, if judgements of how convinced people are by an argument show some role for soundness, as investigated by van Eemeren et al. (2009) using the reasonableness measure, then differences between the types of the argument ad hominem would be predicted. That is, the *tu quoque* would be judged more convincing than the *circumstantial*, and the *circumstantial* would be judged more convincing than the *abusive*. Moreover, if people are sensitive to violations of the freedom rule in judgements of how convincing they find an argument, then convincingness should be lower for all the ad hominem argument types than for the control condition.

5   Method

Participants. Thirty two participants were recruited from undergraduate psychology students at Birkbeck College, University of London. Twenty one of the participants had English as their first language. The remainder were also English speakers and readers. The participants were unpaid and not familiar with the materials used in the study.

Design. The experiment was a 2 × 4 × 2 × 2 completely within subjects design with posterior judgement (1st vs. 2nd posterior), Ad hominen fallacy type (abusive, circumstantial, tu quoque, and a non-fallacious control), initial claim strength (weak vs. strong), and argument direction (pro vs. con) as independent variables and convincingness ratings (0–100) as the dependent variable.

Materials. The materials were contained in a two-part booklet. Part 1 established estimates of people's 2nd Posterior degrees of belief in the conclusion. Part 2 established estimates of people's 1st posterior degrees of belief in the conclusion. Part 1 had 17 pages with instructions and two practice dialogues on the first page. The 16 experimental dialogues were arranged in random orders and displayed one per page on the subsequent 16 pages. The 16 dialogues comprised a set of 4 dialogues for each of the 4 fallacy levels. Each dialogue was composed of a four-line fictional exchange between two interlocutors, A and B. Within each fallacy dialogue set, interlocutor B presents an identical argument for each of the four dialogues, for example, "Because how would he know? He doesn't know the first thing about cars". However, the position of interlocutor A changes across the four dialogues as the argument direction, pro vs. con., and the strength of A's initial were manipulated, for example, "After listening to him, I *think it's possible* (strongly believe) that Ford cars *simply* (don't) drive better". See the Appendix for the materials for all four dialogues including the control.

The reason for placing the directional manipulations in A's opening statement rather than in B's arguments is that *ad hominem* arguments by definition always "damn the source". It was therefore simpler and required less manipulation of the remaining dialogue content to hold B's *ad hominem* argument as unidirectional. After each dialogue, participants were instructed to rate how convinced they felt that A should now be in their opening statement having listened to the argument present by B. The rating was on a scale of 0% (not convinced at all) to 100% (completely convinced).

Part 2 contained a prior belief questionnaire. Two practice examples were followed by the 16 opening statements made by interlocutor A in each of the part 1 dialogues. Participants were asked to provide ratings on the same scale as above of how strong they thought A's belief was in each of their opening statements. The remainder of part 2 contained questions about the participants followed by a short-written debrief explaining the purpose of the experiment.

Procedure. Participants were tested individually under laboratory conditions and were not timed. They were initially given a consent form to be signed and an information sheet containing details of the purpose of the project. Participants were then given the two-part booklet and instructed to work through the dialogues in part 1 in order, providing an argument strength estimate for each dialogue before moving onto the next one. Once the dialogues in part 1 were completed, the participants were instructed to complete the initial questionnaire and the final questions in part 2 before being debriefed.

6   Results and Discussion

The results of the experiment are shown in Table 1. The raw data using the 0–100 ratings were first transformed into the 0–1 probability scale by dividing by 100. For the pro arguments, this gave an estimate of $P(\neg C|a)$ and so these were further transformed by subtracting from one to give an estimate of $P(C|a)$ which acted as the dependent variable. Before assessing the overall fit of the Bayesian model to these data, we first statistically assessed the other hypotheses outlined in the introduction to this experiment. We conducted a $2 \times 4 \times 2 \times 2$ ANOVA with posterior judgement (1st vs. 2nd posterior), ad hominem fallacy (abusive, circumstantial, tu quoque, and a non-fallacious control), initial claim strength (weak vs. strong), and argument direction (pro vs. con) as within subjects factors and with $P(C|a)$ as the dependent variable.

As predicted, there was a main effect of posterior judgement such that 2nd posterior, $P_2(C|a)$ (mean $= .37$, SE $= .016$), corresponding to $P(C|a)$ when $P(R) < 1$, was significantly lower than the 1st posterior, $P_1(C|a)$ (mean $= .50$, SE $= .009$), corresponding to $P(C|a)$ when $P(R) \approx 1$, $F(1, 31) = 81.88, MSe = .06$, $\eta^2 = .73, p < .0001$). Again as predicted, con arguments (mean $= .53$, SE $= .025$), where the initial claim is affirmative (e.g. "Ford cars drive better"), had higher $P(C|a)$ values than pro arguments (mean $= .34$, SE $= .013$), where the initial claim is negative (e.g. "Ford cars don't drive better"), $F(1, 31) = 33.62$, $MSe = .30$, $\eta^2 = .52, p < .0001$). There was no significant main effect of initial claim strength, $F(1, 31) = 1.40$, $MSe = .03$, $\eta^2 = .04$, $p = .25$). However, this variable, as predicted, interacted strongly with other factors. As discussed in the introduction to this experiment, it interacted strongly with pro vs. con arguments. The difference between pro and con arguments was far greater when the initial claim was strong (pro: mean $= .27$, SE $= .003$; con: mean $= .61$, SE $= .017$) than when it was weak (pro: mean $= .41$, SE $= .025$; con: mean $= .45$, SE $= .015$), $F(1, 31) = 95.61, MSe = .06$, $\eta^2 = .76, p < .0001$). It interacted much more weakly with posterior judgement. The difference between 1st and 2nd posterior was greater when the initial claim was weak (1st posterior: mean $= .50$, SE $= .009$; 2nd posterior: mean $= .35$, SE $= .016$) than when it was strong (1st posterior: mean $= .50$, SE $= .011$; 2nd posterior: mean $= .38$, SE $= .019$), $F(1, 31) = 4.54$, $MSe = .01$, $\eta^2 = .13$, $p < .05$. There were a variety of other weak three-way interactions, which mainly involved the type of ad hominem argument.

There was no main effect of ad hominem argument type, $F(3, 93) = 1.10$, neither were any of the Helmert contrasts significant, that is, control vs. tu quoque, the control vs. tu quoque and circumstantial collapsed, and the control vs. tu quoque, circumstantial and the abusive collapsed . In particular, the comparison between the control and the fallacies collapsed was not significant, $F(1, 31) < 1$. Ad hominem argument type did show a weak two way interaction with strength of initial claim, but it was further modified by a three-way interaction with pro vs. con arguments, $F(3, 93) = 5.42$, $MSe = .01$, $\eta^2 = .15$, $p < .005$. To explore these possible effects further, we reasoned that it is the comparative effects of the

Table 1 Results of the experiment showing the mean $P(C|a)$ values (SDs) for initial claim strength (weak or strong), pro vs. con argument, 1st vs. 2nd posterior (post) judgement, for each fallacy type and the control

	Weak claim				Strong claim			
	Pro argument		Con argument		Pro argument		Con argument	
Fallacy	1st post	2nd post	1st post	2nd post	1st post	2nd post	1st post	2nd post
Abusive	.48(.28)	.38(.22)	.52(.14)	.39(.21)	.34(.22)	.32(.26)	.66(.17)	.51(.21)
Circumstantial	.47(.21)	.30(.24)	.54(.19)	.35(.16)	.32(.20)	.22(.22)	.68(.20)	.51(.18)
Tu quoque	.51(.15)	.35(.17)	.51(.15)	.40(.20)	.23(.19)	.21(.21)	.74(.19)	.51(.16)
Control	.44(.20)	.31(.23)	.56(.17)	.35(.19)	.26(.23)	.23(.29)	.77(.16)	.54(.23)
Totals (SE)	.48(.03)	.34(.03)	.53(.02)	.37(.02)	.29(.03)	.25(.04)	.71(.03)	.52(.02)

different argument forms on changing degree of belief that are important to determining whether differences in the soundness of these forms affects how convincing they are as well as how reasonable. Interactions with pro vs. con arguments or the strength of the initial claim, while important for testing the Bayesian model, are tangential to whether these different argument forms have differential effects. We therefore investigated the difference between argument types by looking at 2nd posterior ratings alone summed across these other variables and the 1st posterior–2nd posterior difference scores aggregated in the same way.

Looking solely at the 2nd posterior ratings, there was a significant effect of ad hominem argument type, $F(3, 93) = 2.54$, $MSe = .01$, $\eta^2 = .08$, $p < .05$ (one-tailed). Reverse Helmerts contrasts showed that the abusive argument form had higher mean $P(C|a)$ than the other argument types collapsed, $F(1, 31) = 5.74$, $MSe = .01$, $\eta^2 = .16$, $p < .025$, and that there were no significant difference between circumstantial and tu quoque collapsed with the control, nor between tu quoque and the control. Thus, the abusive form does not lead to as low values of $P(C|a)$ as the other ad hominem argument types, and there are no differences between these other types and the control. We also analysed the 1st posterior–2nd posterior difference scores. There was a significant effect of ad hominem argument type, $F(3, 93) = 2.37$, $MSe = .01$, $\eta^2 = .07$, $p < .05$ (one-tailed). Replicating the analysis for the 2nd posterior rating alone, reverse Helmerts contrasts showed that the abusive argument form lead to a lower difference in $P(C|a)$ than the other argument types collapsed, $F(1, 31) = 6.34$, $MSe = .01$, $\eta^2 = .17$, $p < .01$, and that there were no significant differences between circumstantial and tu quoque collapsed with the control, nor between tu quoque and the control. We also looked at all pairwise comparisons using paired t-tests. Only the comparisons with the abusive form approached significance but even these were not significant once an appropriate Bonferroni correction for multiple tests was applied.

These results would appear to indicate that, in contradistinction to van Eemeren et al's. (2009) predictions, how convincing we find the argument ad hominem is not affected by the soundness of these arguments. People appear as convinced by the argument ad hominem when the freedom rule is violated (*circumstantial*, *tu quoque*) than when it is not (*control*). It could be argued that this result arises because of the way we have set up these arguments means that the participants interpret the two interlocuters as in the argumentative stage and not in the confrontational stage. In the argumentative stage, the freedom rule is not violated. One might argue that both A and B have heard C produce her argument for or against the conclusion and so for both of them the argument has been admitted as a legitimate topic of debate. However, presumably an argument only begins when two interlocuters disagree on a matter. Even for the pro argument, A and B differ in the degree to which the conclusion should be believed. Despite C's argument, A may still strongly believe the conclusion, but B's ad hominem argument is designed to take A to being totally convinced. The first two lines of each dialogue set up, this disagreement and hence must be interpreted as at the confrontational and not at the argumentative stage. Moreover, if all these arguments are at the argumentative stage, why is the abusive type less convincing as no pragma-dialectical rule has been violated (although post hoc t-tests did not support this difference). So there is good reason to argue that these dialogues are indeed in the confrontational stage and that despite the consequent violation of the freedom rule, two versions of the argument ad hominem were as convincing as a control even though they violated the freedom rule.

A possible explanation for the lack of difference between ad hominem argument types is that we have used too few exemplars and that those we have used, as it happens, are all similar in reasonableness because they cross cut discourse context. We used van Eemeren et al's (2009, Table 3.3, p. 68) domestic context abusive type (mean reasonableness: 3.29), their political context circumstantial type (mean reasonableness: 4.19), and their scientific context *tu quoque* type (mean reason-ableness: 3.66). The *tu quoque* is only rated low in reasonableness in this context, which might explain the lack of differences. We would need to introduce more exemplars to truly rule out any difference in convincingness between the circum-stantial and the *tu quoque*. However, the differences in reasonableness between the arguments we used predicts a linear trend such that *circumstantial* > *tu quoque* > *abusive* if soundness also affects how persuasive people find these arguments. And ignoring the control, this linear trend was significant in our data, $F(1, 31) = 5.82$, $MSe = .01$, $\eta^2 = .16$, $p < .025$, providing some evidence that how persuaded people are by these arguments is sensitive to their perceived reasonableness in different contexts. Nonetheless, the principle result of no differences with the control remains, which indicates that these judgements may not be sensitive to violations of the freedom rule.

We now turn to modelling the overall pattern of results using the Bayesian source reliability model. Given the very minimal differences between the types of ad hominem argument and the lack of differences between these argument types and the control, we modelled the aggregate data shown in the final row of Table 1. There are quite a number of parameters that could vary to model this data but to guard against over fitting we chose to fix most of these to the values used to illustrate the model in Fig. 1. The argument likelihood was set to 4 ($P(a|C, R) = .8$; $P(a|\neg C,R) = .2$); $P(a|C,\neg R)$ and $P(a|\neg C,\neg R)$ were set to .5; and $P(R)$

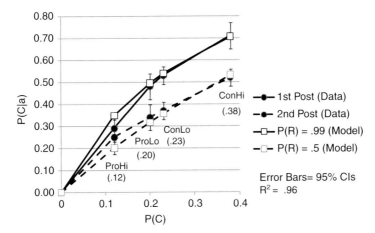

Fig. 2 Fit of the model to the data aggregated across ad hominem argument type (data) showing the Bayesian source reliability models predictions (model) at two levels of $P(R)$ fixed to .99 and .50 (as in Fig. 1) with only $P(C)$ free to vary (*Note*. The fitted value of $P(C)$ for the pro argument high initial degree of belief condition (ProHi) was .12; for the pro argument low initial degree of belief condition (ProLo), it was .20; for the con argument low initial degree of belief condition (ConLo), it was .23; and for the con argument high initial degree of belief condition (ConHi), it was .38. 1st post = 1st posterior judgement and 2nd post = 2nd posterior judgement; CIs = confidence intervals; R^2 is the coefficient of determination which indicates the proportion of variance in the data accounted for by the model)

was set to .99 for the 1st posterior and to .5 for the 2nd posterior. As we argued in the introduction, with these factors fixed then the differences between the 1st posterior for the different conditions—pro argument high initial degree of belief condition (ProHi), pro argument low initial degree of belief condition (ProLo), con argument low initial degree of belief condition (ConLo), con argument high initial degree of belief condition (ConHi)—must be due to differences in the prior, $P(C)$. $P(C)$ was the only parameter varied to capture the data in each of the four conditions. As it took on four different values, there were effectively four degrees of freedom against which to assess the model fit. In Fig. 2, we have plotted the best fit values of the prior $P(C)$ on the x-axis and the 1st and 2nd posteriors on the y-axis, for the data and for the model. Figure 2 shows good eye-ball fits, which were confirmed using the coefficient of determination, R^2, which indicates the proportion of variance in the data accounted for by the model. We have not attempted to formally optimise these fits but nonetheless an R^2 value of .96 was easily obtained by adjusting $P(C)$ by hand to get as close as possible to the 1st posterior and then using this value to calculate the 2nd posterior and then iterating once or twice. This R^2 value indicates that at least 96% of the variance in the data can be accounted for by the model. Figure 2 also shows that each predicted value fell within the 95% confidence interval for the data. In sum, the Bayesian source reliability model can account for most of the variation in our data on how convincing people find the ad hominem argument.

7 Conclusion

In this chapter, we have presented a Bayesian source reliability model of how the argumentum ad hominem should modify people's degrees of belief in a conclusion. According to this model, someone judges how convinced they are by an argument by initially assuming a principle of charity, that is, they assume that their informant is maximally reliable. The Bayesian model separates out the contribution of the argument and the reliability of the informant so that the likelihood ratio that maps their prior degree of belief into their posterior degree of belief is sensitive to both factors. The ad hominem argument represents a direct attack on the charity assumption, suggesting that the informant is unreliable. The effect on the Bayesian model is to reduce the likelihood ratio, so reducing someone's posterior degree of belief in the conclusion. We presented an experiment that tested this model using both pro and con versions of the argumentum ad hominem and materials derived from van Eemeren et al. (2009). That experiment revealed most of the effects predicted by the Bayesian model, which moreover provided excellent overall fits to the data.

This was also the first experiment we can find directly testing the effects of the argumentum ad hominem on people's degrees of belief in an argument, that is, on argument convincingness. While van Eemeren et al. (2009) showed that judgements of reasonableness appeared sensitive to violations of the pragma-dialectical freedom rule, they also speculated that how convincing people found the argumentum ad hominem would be sensitive to a variety of other factors. Our experiment seems to show that it is these other factors related to the content of the argument that primarily drive how convincing people find the argumentum ad hominem. We found no differences between different types of the argumentum ad hominem, where the freedom rule was violated, and a control, which introduced no violation of the freedom rule. However, consistent with the pragmatics of politeness we did find a trend over the different types of the argumentum ad hominem consistent with van Eemeren et al's (2009) results on reasonableness judgements and a difference between the abusive type and the other types of ad hominem argument. Further experiments are of course needed to determine what role if any pragma-dialectical discourse rules may have in determining how convincing we find this and a variety of other arguments.

Appendix: Experimental Materials

Abusive

(A) (Even) After listening to him, I *think it's possible* (strongly believe) that Ford cars *simply* (don't) drive better.
(B) Actually, you should be certain that they don't drive any better.
(A) Why do you think that?
(B) Because how would he know? He doesn't know the first thing about cars.

Circumstantial

(B) I *think it's possible* (highly likely) that her recommendation to use Stelcom Ltd is (not) a good one; (even though) she says that they are the only contractor in the Netherlands that can handle such an enormous job.

(B) Well, you should be absolutely certain that her recommendation isn't a good one.

(A) Why do you say that?

(B) How can we really believe her? Surely, it's no coincidence that the company is owned by her father-in-law.

Tu Quoque

(A) It's *possible* (highly likely) he *was* (wasn't) right to criticise the way in which they processed the data statistically.

(B) Well, you should be convinced that he wasn't right to criticise them.

(A) What do you mean?

(B) Because he said they should have expressed the figures as percentages. But how can he say that when his own statistics are not up to the mark.

Control

(A) I *think it's possible* (strongly believe) that her scientific integrity *is* (isn't) impeccable. She says her research has always been honest and sound.

(B) Well, you should be convinced that her integrity isn't impeccable.

(A) Why do you say that?

(B) Well, how can you really believe her? She has already been caught twice tampering with her research results.

References

Anderson, J. R. (1990). *The adaptive character of thought*. Hillsdale: Erlbaum.

Bovens, L., & Hartmann, S. (2003). *Bayesian epistemology*. Oxford: Oxford University Press.

Brinton, A. (1995). The *ad hominem*. In H. V. Nansen & R. C. Pinto (Eds.), *Fallacies: Classical background and contemporary developments* (pp. 213–222). University Park: Pennsylvania State University Press.

Cherniak, C. (1986). *Minimal rationality*. Cambridge, MA: MIT Press.

Coady, C. A. J. (1992). *Testimony: A philosophical study*. Oxford: Oxford University Press.

Davidson, D. (1974). On the very idea of a conceptual scheme. In D. Davidson (Ed.), *Inquiries into truth and interpretation* (pp. 183–198). Oxford: Oxford University Press.

Eagly, A. H., & Chaiken, S. (1993). *The psychology of attitudes*. Belmont: Thompson Wadsworth.

Gillies, D. (2000). *Philosophical theories of probability*. London: Routledge.

Hahn, U., & Oaksford, M. (2006). A Bayesian approach to informal argument fallacies. *Synthese, 152*, 207–236.

Hahn, U., & Oaksford, M. (2007). The rationality of informal argumentation: A Bayesian approach to reasoning fallacies. *Psychological Review, 114*, 704–732.

Hahn, U., Harris, A. J. L., & Corner, A. (2009). Argument content and argument source: An exploration. *Informal Logic, 29*, 337–367.

Harris, A.J.L., & Hahn, U. (2009). Bayesian rationality in evaluating multiple testimonies: Incorporating the role of coherence. *Journal of Experimental Psychology: Learning, Memory and Cognition, 35*, 1366–1373.

Ikuenobe, P. (2004). On the theoretical unification and nature of the fallacies. *Argumentation, 18*, 189–211.

Johnson, B. T., Maio, G. R., & Smith-McLallen, A. (2005). Communication and attitude change: Causes, processes, and effects. In D. Albarracin, B. T. Johnson, & M. P. Zanna (Eds.), *The handbook of attitudes and attitude change: Basic principles* (pp. 617–669). Mahwah: Erlbaum.

Olsson, E. J. (2005). *Against coherence: Truth, probability and justification*. Oxford: Oxford University Press.

Perelman, C., & Olbrechts-Tyteca, L. (1969). *The new rhetoric: A treatise on argumentation*. Notre Dame: University of Notre Dame Press.

Shogenji, T. (1999). Is coherence truth-conducive? *Analysis, 59*, 338–345.

van Eemeren, F. H., & Grootendorst, R. (2004). *A systematic theory of argumentation. The pragma-dialectical approach*. Cambridge: Cambridge University Press.

van Eemeren, F. H., Grootendorst, R., & Snoeck Henkemans, F. (1996). *Fundamentals of argumentation theory*. Mahwah: Erlbaum.

van Eemeren, F. H., Garssen, B., & Meuffels, B. (2009). *Fallacies and judgements of reasonableness*. Dordrecht: Springer.

Voss, J. F., & Van Dyke, J. A. (2001). Argumentation in psychology: Background comments. *Discourse Processes, 32*, 89–111.

Walton, D. N. (1990). What is reasoning? What is argument? *Journal of Philosophy, 87*, 399–419.

Walton, D. N. (2000). Case study of the use of a circumstantial *ad hominem* in political argumentation. *Philosophy and Rhetoric, 33*, 101–115.

Walton, D. N. (2009). *Ad hominem arguments*. Tuscaloosa: University of Alabama Press.

Wilson, N. L. (1959). Substance without substrata. *The Review of Metaphysics, 12*, 521–539.

Part II
The Legal Domain

A Survey of Uncertainties and Their Consequences in Probabilistic Legal Argumentation

Matthias Grabmair and Kevin D. Ashley

Abstract In this chapter, we present a survey of different sorts of uncertainties lawyers reason with and connect them to the issue of how probabilistic models of argumentation can facilitate litigation planning. We briefly survey Bayesian Networks as a representation for argumentation in the context of a realistic example. After introducing the Carneades argument model and its probabilistic semantics, we propose an extension to the Carneades Bayesian Network model to support probability distributions over argument weights, a feature we believe is desirable. Finally, we scout possible future approaches to facilitate reasoning with argument weights.

1 Introduction

Formal models of argument can be considered as qualitative alternatives to traditional quantitative graphical probability methods for reasoning about uncertainty, as has been observed by Parsons et al. (1997). We understand a *formal model of argument* as a description of a dialectical process in formal mathematical terms. It typically contains entities such as arguments and/or propositions in some language as well as (possibly typed) relations between those elements. *Probabilistic graphical models* is a summary term for graph structures encoding dependencies between a set of random variables.

In other words, discourse about what is likely to be true in an uncertain domain becomes a question of persuasion and proof rather than a subject of a supposedly objective probability. For a proposition of interest, the answer given by the system

M. Grabmair (✉) • K.D. Ashley
University of Pittsburgh, Pittsburgh, PA, USA
e-mail: mag134@pitt.edu

F. Zenker (ed.), *Bayesian Argumentation: The practical side of probability*,
Synthese Library 362, DOI 10.1007/978-94-007-5357-0_4,
© Springer Science+Business Media Dordrecht 2013

as to its truthfulness is hence no longer a number but a qualitative label assigned to it according to some formal model of dialectic argumentation.

One task that combines argumentation and the need to deal with uncertainty is litigation planning, that is, planning whether to commence a lawsuit and what kinds of legal claims to make. The task of a lawyer in litigation planning is unique in that she is professionally engaged in argumentation to convince an audience of the truthfulness of certain assertions. For her, however, argumentation takes place in a planning context, and she needs decision support for the uncertainty she faces *in* argumentation. Her utility is the degree of persuasiveness of the arguments, and she has to plan her litigation strategy and research according to what will give her the maximum payoff in the task of convincing her audience.

The nature of this task, that is, systematizing uncertainty about the outcome of an argument, is a kind of practical reasoning. It is hence a promising step to bring quantitative models of uncertainty inside qualitative argument models with the goal of obtaining utility information for purposes of planning ones moves and allocating resources. In litigation, lawyers must view their case from multiple angles. They can argue about the facts playing in their favor, about the law rendering the established facts favorable for ones side, about the ethical or policy concerns given the facts, and, finally, about relating the case at bar to previous decisions in a way that helps their client. Motivated by the search for a promising systematization in which to invest further research and development resources, we survey how these four kinds of uncertainties interrelate using a realistic trade secret law case. We distill a set of criteria for the suitability of a probabilistic graphical representation to model legal discourse and present the Carneades argument model as well as its probabilistic interpretation using Bayesian Networks [BN] as our running example model. Finally, we explain and emphasize the role of argument weights in the process and suggest promising extensions to the model.

2   Survey of Relevant Uncertainties

In planning for litigation, lawyers take account of uncertainties both in the facts themselves and in how the law applies to the facts. They address uncertainty about the facts through evidence and evidential argument and uncertainty about the application of the law through dialectical argumentation.

In so doing, we believe that litigators need to address four main types of uncertainties:

- *Factual*: evidence and the plausibility of factual assertions
- *Normative*: dealing with the application of the law to facts
- *Moral*: dealing with an ethical assessment of the conflict
- *Empirical*: relating to prior outcomes in similar scenarios

2.1 The Example Case

We illustrate these in the context of a real lawsuit, ConnectU versus Zuckerberg,[1] in which plaintiffs C. and T. Winklevoss and D. Narendra sued defendant Mark Zuckerberg. The plaintiffs founded ConnectU while at Harvard University in 2002–2003; they allegedly developed a business plan for a novel institute-specific website and network for online communication and dating. According to the plan, ConnectU was to expand to other institutions and generate advertising revenue. To develop software for the website, the plaintiffs hired two students. They engaged Zuckerberg to complete the code and website in exchange for a monetary interest if the site proved successful. They gave him their existing source code, a description of the website's business model and of the functionality and conceptual content, and the types of user information to be collected. They alleged that the defendant understood this information was secret and agreed to keep it confidential. The plaintiffs averred that they had stressed to the defendant that he needed to complete the code as soon as possible and that he assured them he was using his best efforts to complete the project. As late as January 8, 2004, he confirmed via email that he would complete and deliver the source code. On January 11, however, the defendant registered the domain name "thefacebook.com" and a few weeks later launched a directly competing website. By the time plaintiffs could launch ConnectU.com, Zuckerberg had achieved an insurmountable commercial advantage.

An initial decision is what kind of legal claim to bring such as trade secret misappropriation or breach of contract. In considering a claim of trade secret misappropriation, an attorney would be familiar with the relevant law and might even have in mind a model of the relevant legal rules and factors like the one employed in IBP (Ashley and Brüninghaus 2006) and shown in Fig. 1. Factors are stereotypical patterns of facts that strengthen a claim for one side or the other.

2.2 Factual Uncertainty

Regarding factual uncertainty, the attorney knows that showing the factual basis for some factors will be easier than others. In the diagram, easy to prove factors are underlined. Clearly, the information has commercial value; the social network model was a unique product at the time. And, the information may have given Zuckerberg a competitive advantage. On the other hand, to those in the know, the database is fairly straightforward and likely to be reverse-engineerable by a competent internet programmer in a reasonable amount of time. In addition, it is not clear whether the Winklevosses took security measures to maintain the secrecy of the information. They allege Zuckerberg knew the information was confidential,

---

[1] *ConnectU, Inc. v. Facebook, Inc. et al.*, Case-Number 1:2007cv10593, Massachusetts District Court, filed March 28, 2007.

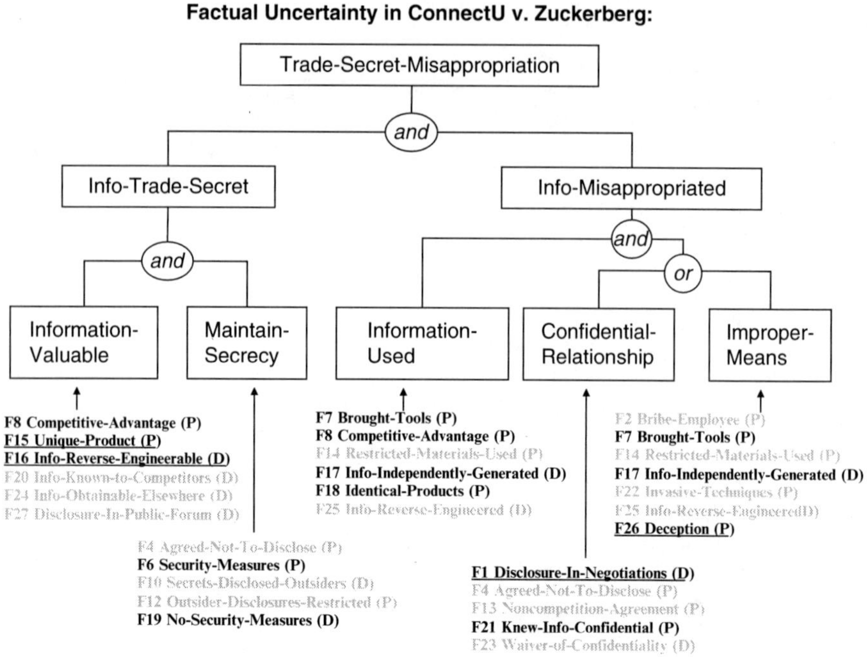

Factual Uncertainty in ConnectU v. Zuckerberg:

Fig. 1 IBP's domain model of trade secret law with the applicable factors for plaintiff (P) and defendant (D) in ConnectU versus Zuckerberg. Inapplicable factors are grayed out. Easy to prove factors are underlined

but there was no agreement not to disclose, or they would have said. As to a breach of confidential relationship, it was the Winklevosses who gave the information to Zuckerberg, presumably in negotiations to get him to agree to be their programmer on this project. Another question mark concerns whether Zuckerberg used improper means to get the information. It seems clear that he never intended to actually perform the work the Winklevosses wanted him to perform; that was deceptive. Though he had access to the ConnectU source code (i.e., tools), he very may well have developed the Facebook code completely independently, not using the plaintiff's information at all, and it may have been quite different from the ConnectU code.

2.3 Normative Uncertainty

Normative uncertainty refers to uncertainty in the application of legal concepts to facts based on dialectical argumentation involving two kinds of inferences: subsumption (i.e., the fulfillment of sets of conditions) or analogy (i.e., a kind of statutory interpretation based on similarity to some precedent or rule). For example, a normative issue is whether ConnectU's knowledge or expertise constitutes a trade secret. Subsumption does not work too well in this example since Sec. 757 Comment b disavows "an exact definition of a trade secret,"[2] listing six relevant factors, instead. Analogy fills the gap, however. If a prior court has held it sufficient to establish a trade secret that the plaintiff's product was unique in the marketplace even though it could be reverse-engineered, that is a reason for finding a trade secret in ConnectU versus Zuckerberg. There is uncertainty, however, due to questions like whether the present case is similar enough to the precedent to warrant the same outcome. If one were fairly sure that the factors relating to an element (or legal concept) apply and uniformly support one side, then one could tentatively decide the element is satisfied. But here, since the factors are only fairly certain or doubtful and have opposing outcomes, a litigator will probably decide that the various elements are still open (indicated in bold in Fig. 1).

2.4   Moral Uncertainty

Moral uncertainty is involved in assessing if a decision is "just," "equitable," or "right" based on whether applicable values/principles are in agreement with or in conflict with the desired legal outcome of the case. For instance, in trade secret law, considerations of unfair competition, breach of confidentiality, or innovation all favor a decision for the plaintiff, while access to public information and protecting employees' rights to use general skills and knowledge favor the defendant. Most of these values are at stake in the ConnectU scenario and they conflict. If the allegedly confidential information is reverse-engineerable, that would undermine a trade secret claim or limit its value. On the other hand, if Zuckerberg obtained the information through deception, that would support the claim. Thus, there are questions about the nature of the trade-off of values at stake and which critical facts make the scale "tip over." It makes sense to consider the balance of values at the level of the individual elements as well as of the claim; the values at stake and the facts that are critical will differ at these levels.

2.5   Empirical Uncertainty

Finally, there is empirical uncertainty relating to prior outcomes in similar scenarios. In common law jurisdictions, precedents are recorded in detail, including information about the cases facts, outcome, and the courts normative and moral reasoning. In the United States and elsewhere, this case data may be retrieved manually and electronically with the result that attorneys can readily access relevantly similar cases. The precedents are binding in certain circumstances (stare decisis), but even if

---

[2] Restatement of Torts (First) Section 757, Comment b.

not binding, similar cases provide a basis for predicting what courts will do in similar circumstances. Given a problem's facts, a litigation planner can routinely ask for the outcomes that similar cases predict for claims, elements, and issues in the current case. The degree of certainty of these predictions (or, respectively, the persuasiveness of an argument based on prior decisions) depends on the degree of factual, normative, and moral analogy among the problem and the multiple, often competing precedents with conflicting outcomes.

2.6   Interdependencies

The four types of uncertainty are clearly not independent (e.g., normative and empirical, both involve questions of degree of similarity.) There interactions can be quite complex, as illustrated by the role of narrative. At a factual level, narrative and facts may mutually reinforce or be at odds. A narrative that is plausible in light of specific facts may enhance a jury's disposition to believe those facts; it also raises expectations about the existence of certain other facts. For instance, if an attorney tells a "need code" story (i.e., Zuckerberg really needed to see ConflictU's code to create Facebook), one would expect to find similarities among the resulting codes. If it is a "delaying tactic" story, the absence of similarities between codes supports a conclusion that Zuckerberg may simply have been deceiving the Winklevosses to get to the market first. At the normative and moral levels, the narrative affects trade-offs among conflicting values that may strengthen one claim and weaken another. Trade secret misappropriation does not really cover the Delaying Tactic story for lack of interference with a property interest in confidential information.

3   Desirable Attributes for a Probabilistic Argument Model to Assist Litigation Planning

The prior work and literature on evidential reasoning using Bayesian methods as well as BNs is extensive (see prominently, e.g., (Kadane et al. 1996)). This chapter, however, focuses more narrowly on how probabilistic graphical models can enrich the utility of qualitative models of argument for litigation planning. This section will explain a list of desirable attributes that a probabilistic graphical argument model should provide in order to be useful for the task. We believe that there are four such attributes, namely, (1) the functionality to assess argument moves as to their utility, including (2) the resolution of conflicting influences on a given proposition, (3) easy knowledge engineering, as well as (4) the functionality to reason with and *about* argument weights.

3.1 Assessment of Utilities

As a starting point, the model should provide for a way to assess the effect of argument moves on the expected outcome of the overall argument. In other words, for every available argument move, one would like to know its expected payoff in probability to convince the audience. Quantitative probabilistic models allow for changes in the model's configuration/parameters to be quantified by calculating the relevant numbers before and after the change.

Similarly, Roth et al. (2007) have developed a game theoretical probabilistic approach to argumentation using defeasible logic. There, players introduce arguments as game moves to maximize/minimize the probability of a goal proposition being defeasibly provable from a set of premises, which in turn are acceptable with some base probability. Riveret et al.'s game theoretical model of argumentation additionally takes into account costs that certain argument moves may entail, thereby assessing an argumentation strategy as to its overall "utility" (Riveret et al. 2008). As Riveret et al. point out, the concept of a quantitative "utility" is complex and needs to take into account many factors (e.g., risk-averseness of a player) and does not necessarily need to be based on quantitative probability. We do not take position with regard to these questions in this survey chapter. Rather, we observe that quantitative probabilistic models enable an argument formalism to be used for utility calculations in litigation planning. We then suggest how this combination of models can also take account of certain phenomena in legal reasoning, for example, through probability distributions over argument weights (see Sect. 6).

3.2 Easy Knowledge Engineering

One of the difficulties in probabilistic models is the need to gather the necessary parameters, that is, probability values. This problem has been of particular importance in the context of BNs, where a number of approaches have been taken. For example, Díez and Druzdzel have surveyed the so-called "canonical" gates in BNs, such as noisy/leaky "and," "or," and "max" gates (see Díez et al. 2006 with further references) which allow for the uncertainty to be addressed in a clearly delimited part of the network with the remaining nodes behaving deterministically. This greatly reduces the number of parameters that need to be elicited. In furtherance, the BN3M model by Kraaijeveld and Druzdzel (Kraaijeveld et al. 2005) employs canonical gates as well as a general structural constraint on diagnostic BNs, namely, the division of the network into three layers of variables (faults, evidence, and context). A recent practical evaluation of a diagnostic network constructed under such constraints is reported in (Agosta et al. 2008; Ratnapinda et al. 2009).

We believe that a formal model of argument lends itself well to the generation of BNs from metadata (i.e., from some higher level control model using fewer or easier-to-create parameters). Specifically for the Carneades model, this route has previously been examined in (Grabmair et al. 2010). We will give an overview of it in Section 5.3 and will build on it in Sections 6 and 7. This is conceptually related to the works on translation of existing formal models into probabilistic graphical models. For an example of such a translation, namely, of first-order logic to BNs, and a survey of related work on so-called probabilistic languages, see (Laskey 2008).

An example of a law-related BN approach that appears not to support easy knowledge engineering is the decision support system for owner's corporation (i.e., housing co-op) cases of Condlie et al. (2010). There, a BN was constructed using legally relevant issues/factors as its random variables. A legal expert was entrusted with the task of determining the parameters. The overall goal was to predict the outcome of a given case in light of prior cases in order to facilitate pre-litigation negotiation efforts. While this is a good example of a legal decision support system, it employs no argumentation-specific techniques or generative meta-model. From the example BN in the article, it appears that the domain model is essentially "hardwired" into a BN and would need major knowledge engineering efforts to maintain if relevant legislation/case law (or any other kind of applicable concerns) were to change and the complexity of the network would increase. We believe that the construction of decision support BNs under the structural constraints, and control of a qualitative argument model provides a more efficient and maintainable way to knowledge engineer such systems. By contrast, admittedly, our approach still requires validation.

3.3 Conflict Resolution and Argument Weights

The argument model needs to account for pro and con arguments as it resolves conflicts in supporting and undermining influences on a given proposition. Since conflicting arguments are very common in legal scenarios, it is critical for a system to be able to tell how competing influences outweigh or complement each other. In a quantitative model, this can be done straightforwardly, for example, by computing an overall probability based on some weighting scheme. In this way, a strong pro argument will outweigh a weak con argument with some probability. In qualitative models, to the best of our knowledge, such conflict resolution needs to be established in a model-specific way. For example, in a qualitative probabilistic network (Wellman 1990), one could introduce a qualitative mapping for sign addition where a strong positive influence (++) outweighs a weak negative influence (−), leading to an overall weaker positive influence (+) (Renooij et al. 1999). Also, Parsons (Parsons et al. 1997) has produced a qualitative model which allows for some form of defeasibility in combining multiple arguments into a single influence.

Dung's prominent work on argumentation frameworks (Dung 1995) only uses only one kind of attack relation and thereby abstracts away the precise workings which lead one argument to attack/defeat another (explained, e.g., in Baroni et al. 2009). There, arguments are equally strong, and resolving the argument means finding certain kinds of extensions in the argument graph. For a brief probabilistic interpretation and ranking of different extensions by likelihood, see Atkinson and

Bench-Capon (2007). Value-based argumentation frameworks (Bench-Capon 2003) expand upon this model and implement conflict resolution not through weights but through a hierarchy of values which prioritize conflicting arguments depending on which values they favor.

Whether conflict resolution is undertaken through a hierarchy of values or numerical argument weights (such as in Carneades (Gordon and Prakken 2007)) or in some way, two major conceptual challenges need to be addressed in the legal context. First, the notion of conflict resolution or degrees of persuasion needs to interface with the concepts of a standard and burden of proof. There is ample literature on the topic both in formal models of argument (e.g., in argumentation frameworks (Atkinson and Bench-Capon 2007) including a general survey and specifically in Carneades (Gordon et al. 2009)) and elsewhere, such as in the work of Hahn and Oaksford (2007), who (in our opinion, correctly) point out that proof standards may be relative to the overall utility at stake.

For example, in ConnectU versus Zuckerberg, a judge may be more likely to grant the plaintiffs' request for injunctive relief if it were claimed only for a limited duration such as the time it would reasonably take for a competent programmer to reverse engineer the information once the plaintiffs' program was deployed. Such a solution would possibly maximize the realization of the values protected, protecting property interest in the invention for a limited time while allowing access to public information afterward.

Second, an argument model should allow for meta-level reasoning about the conflict resolution mechanism, that is, arguments about other arguments (e.g., about their weight/strength). This is our main motivation for the extensions suggested in Sect. 6.

4 Sample Assessment of Graphical Models

This section will lead through a comparison of graphical models and their capabilities in the context of modeling the ConnectU versus Zuckerberg case. Connecting to our previous explanations of uncertainty, we systematize our legal problem by distilling it into the three major uncertainties: normative, moral, and factual. Empirical uncertainty is not explicitly represented, but rather affects both normative and moral uncertainty, where it flows into how decisions about precedents affect the argument. The overall outcome is influenced both by normative and moral assessments of the facts (Fig. 2). We will now expand this basic framework into a more detailed reflection of arguments.

4.1 A Graphical Structure of the Analysis

As we have seen in the IBP domain model sketched above, in order for a trade secret misappropriation claim to be successful, the information in question would

Fig. 2 A basic graph for a
legal decision problem

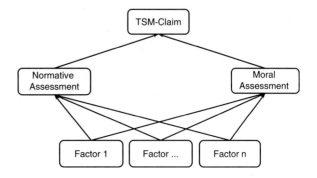

need to constitute a trade secret, and the information would need to have been misappropriated in some way. Assume that the primary legal issue before the court is just the former, that is, whether the source code and business documentation obtained by Zuckerberg constitute a trade secret.

A factor in the affirmative is that the code is part of a hitherto *unique product* (compare factors in Fig. 1). There is no service on the market yet with comparable prospects of success. The value underlying this factor is the *protection of property*, as the inventor of a unique product has an ownership interest in the information that is protected by the legal system.

On the other hand, a factor speaking against the trade secret claim could be the fact that the product is easily *reverse-engineerable*. After all, ConnectU (functionally similar to Facebook) is a straightforward online database-driven website application. After seeing it work, an internet programmer of average competence could recreate the functionality from scratch without major difficulty within a reasonable amount of time. The value underlying this conflicting factor is the protection of *public information*. The policy is that trade secret law shall not confer a monopoly over information that is publicly available and easily reproduced and hence in the public domain.

The two conflicting concerns influence both the normative and the moral assessments. In the normative part, *unique product* and *reverse-engineerable* essentially become two arguments for and against the legal conclusion that there is a trade secret. They, in turn, can be established from facts in an argumentative way. In the moral part, we have the conflicting interests behind these factors, namely, the desire to protect one's property and the goal to protect public information. However, these interests are not *per se* arguments in the debate of whether a moral assessment of the situation speaks for or against a trade secret misappropriation claim. Rather, they are *values* which are to be weighed against each other in a balancing act. Again, this determination is contingent on an assessment of the facts.

The overall structure just presented can be visualized as a directed graph model in Fig. 3. It shall be noted that this graph is an incomplete and coarse-grained representation of the concerns. Our intention is only to expand parts of the normative and moral layer in order to illustrate certain features of graphical probabilistic argument models in the subsequent sections.

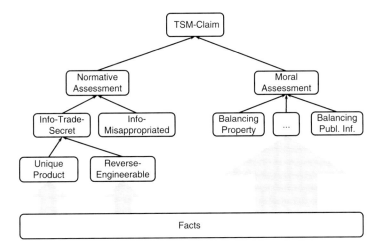

Fig. 3 The decision graph with moral and normative assessments expanded

4.2 Casting the Example into a Graphical Model

Figure 3 provides a basic graphical model of the decision problem in ConnectU versus Zuckerberg. On the normative side, there are two conflicting arguments (*unique product* and *reverse-engineerable*), each stemming from a certain factor and conflicting values, which underlie these factors. Overall, the two components are framed by the factual layer of the graph (shown as a single large node standing in for a set of individual facts nodes) feeding into the normative and moral parts, as well as the overarching conclusion, that is, the success of the trade secret misappropriation claim. A probabilistic interpretation of the graph implies that, for every arrow, our belief in the target proposition is influenced by our belief in the propositions that feed into it. Our belief in certain facts influences our belief in the status of the intermediate concepts involved. The way in which this influence takes place varies across the different kinds of uncertainty. For example, in factual uncertainty, a significant part of the reasoning may concern evidential questions of whether a certain fact is true (or not) and what its causal relations are to other uncertain facts. Here, and probably to a greater extent in normative uncertainty, multiple conflicting arguments are a typical occurrence and need to be resolved by some functionality of conflict resolution, as will be addressed further below.

4.3 Generic Bayesian Networks

This section will give a brief overview of Bayesian Networks (as introduced in Pearl et al. 1985) and a brief survey of how they can be used to model argumentation.

Fig. 4 Pro and con
arguments for trade secret
issue

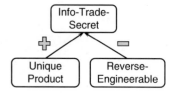

A Bayesian Network [BN] is a probabilistic graphical model based on a directed
acyclic graph whose nodes represent random variables and whose edge structure
encodes conditional dependencies between the variables. Each variable has a
conditional probability function (typically represented as a table of conditional
probabilities) defining the probability of the given node having a certain value
conditioned on the values of its immediate parent variables. One can then compute
a probability value of interest in the network by multiplying respective probabilities
along a corresponding path. BNs are capable of both forward reasoning (i.e.,
determining the probability of effects given causes) and diagnostic reasoning
(i.e., determining the probability of causes given effects). In the context of this
chapter and at the current state of our research of applying BNs to argumentation,
we only discuss the former.

From now on, we shall assume that the graph is completed in the interface of the
facts layer to the assessment layer. One can take a straightforward approach and
translate the graph in Fig. 3 into a BN. While the node and edge structure can be
mapped over identically, one needs to define conditional probability tables. In our
example, the main instances of interest are the conflicting arguments for *unique
product* and *reverse-engineerability* (see Fig. 4).

Using a BN for representing argument graphs has a number of desirable features.
First, it allows the calculation of probability values given its parameters, while
qualitative models provide this functionality only to a very limited extent. In the
context of argument models, this means that by changing the parameters or altering
the graph in certain ways, one can calculate the increase or decrease in persuasiveness of a conclusion statement of interest. Second, probabilities are propagated
through the network, thereby leading to a quantitative synthesis of pro and con
influences on a given proposition. This is because, through the conditional
probabilities, relative strength among competing arguments is expressed via the
probability with which one set of arguments defeats another. This aspect of BNs as
a representation technique addresses the first two of our desired attributes for an
argument-based litigation support system (see Sect. 3).

An example of a system combining argument graphs and BNs is the work of
Muecke and Stranieri (2007), who use a combination of a generic argument model
and expert-created BNs to provide support for the resolution of property issues in
divorce cases. The resulting system was intended to reflect the judicial reasoning to
be anticipated if the case were to be litigated, also taking into account precedent
cases in designing the argument graphs. However, our approach is not to be
confused with work aiming to construct argument graphs from existing BNs (see,
e.g., Keppens et al. 2012) for an approach to extracting an argument diagram from

BNs in order to scrutinize and validate evidential reasoning with the BN). Zukerman et al. (1998) developed a system which uses a combination of multiple knowledge bases and semantic networks to construct two BNs, one normative model and a user model. These are then used to gradually expand a goal proposition of interest into an argument graph (with premise propositions and inference links) until a desired level of probabilistic belief in the goal is established.

However, a difficulty is that BNs traditionally have proven to be difficult in terms of the required knowledge engineering. This is particularly true with regard to the elicitation of the necessary conditional probabilities (compare Díez et al. 2006). Also, although BNs reduce in parametric complexity compared to a full joint distribution, exact inference is still NP hard (see Cooper 1987), and individual conditional probability tables can become quite large very easily. We will now illustrate this rapid growth in the context of our example.

Let us assume, similar to Carneades (Gordon and Prakken 2007; Gordon et al. 2009), that statements can have three possible statuses: *accepted* (where the audience has accepted a statement p as true), *co-acceptable* (where the audience has accepted the statement's complement $\bar{p}$ as true), and *questioned* (where the audience is undecided about whether to accept or reject a statement). If one applies this triad of possible statuses to the three statement sub-issues in Fig. 4, then we need to define $3^3 = 27$ possible statuses (called "parameters") in the conditional probability table of *info-trade-secret*. For each of the possible three statuses of the conclusion *info-trade-secret*, we need to determine the probability of said status conditioned on every possible combination of the three statuses of each of *unique product* and *reverse-engineerable*.

A domain expert would need to provide all these probabilites and tackle the challenges this task entails, for instance:

- What is the probability of the conclusion being accepted if both the pro and con arguments are accepted by the audience and hence conflict? Which one is stronger and how much stronger?
- If neither argument is acceptable, is there a "default" probability with which the audience will accept the statement?
- If only the pro argument is accepted, what is the probability of the conclusion being accepted? Is this single accepted pro argument sufficient? Is there some threshold of persuasion to be overcome?
- Similarly, if only the con argument is accepted, is this sufficient to make the audience reject the conclusion? Does it make a difference whether the audience is undecided over a pro argument or whether it explicitly rejects it?

It is difficult for domain experts to come up with exact numbers for all these scenarios, irrespective of which argument model or which precise array of possible statuses is used. One may argue that the use of three statuses as opposed to a binary true/false scheme artificially inflates complexity to a power of three as opposed to a power of two (thereby leading to only $2^3 = 8$ required probabilities). In scenarios where there are more than two arguments, however, the number of required probabilities outgrows the feasible scope very quickly. Also, once a table of probabilities has been created, modifications like adding or removing arguments require significant effort.

In light of this difficulty, it is desirable to have a simpler mechanism for knowledge engineering when using BNs as a representation. One solution is to use an existing qualitative model of argumentation to generate BNs including their parameters. In such an approach, the superior "control" model (in our case, an argument model) steers the construction of the networks and the determination of its parameters. In argumentation, previous work on probabilistic semantics for the Carneades argument model (Grabmair et al. 2010) produced a formalism with which an instance of a Carneades argument graph can be translated into a BN. This method may resolve at least some of the issues enumerated above or, at least, provide a more usable representation.

5   Carneades

5.1   A Brief Introduction to the Carneades Model

This section gives a brief overview of the Carneades argument model as well as its BN-based probabilistic semantics and explains the benefits it provides over a generic BN model.

The Carneades argument model represents arguments as a directed, acyclic graph. The graph is bipartite, that is, both statements and arguments are represented as nodes in the graph. An argument for a proposition p (thereby also being an argument con $\neg p$) is considered *applicable* if its premises hold, that is, if the statements on which it is based are *acceptable*. This acceptability is in turn computed recursively from the assumptions of the audience and the argument leading to a respective statement. For each statement, applicable pro and con arguments are assessed using formally defined *proof standards* (e.g., preponderance of the evidence, beyond a reasonable doubt), which can make use of numerical weights (in the zero to one range) assigned to the individual arguments by the audience.

In recent work on Carneades (Ballnat et al. 2010), its concept of argumentative derivability has been extended to an additional labeling method using the statuses of *in* and *out*, which we will use occasionally throughout this chapter. So far, we have spoken of a literal p being *acceptable*, which can alternatively be labeled as p being *in* and $\neg p$ being *out*. In the opposite case, if $\neg p$ can be accepted (i.e., is *in*), p is labeled *out*, whereas $\neg p$ is labeled *in*. Finally, if p remains questioned, both p and $\neg p$ are *out*. One can see that the new method is functionally equivalent to the original one yet entails a clearer separation of the used literals into positive and negated instances. This has been taken over into the BN-based probabilistic semantics for Carneades in (Grabmair et al. 2010).

Fig. 5 A Carneades graph for
the trade secret issue

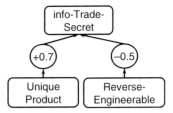

Figure 5 recasts our trade secret example into a Carneades graph. Similar to the previous Fig. 4, three rectangular nodes represent the statements. The circular nodes stand for the arguments which use these statements as premises and are labeled with exemplary argument weights. Now, assume that the trade secret issue shall be decided based on a *preponderance of evidence* proof standards. Verbalized, this means that the side shall win who provides the strongest applicable argument. A statement is acceptable under the Carneades implementation of the preponderance of evidence standard if the weight of the strongest applicable pro argument is greater than the weight of the strongest applicable con argument (for a full formal definition, see Gordon et al. 2009). The inverse condition needs to be fulfilled for the statement to be rejected. If neither side can provide a trumping applicable argument, the statement remains questioned. The only constraint is that each weight is within the [0, 1] range. They represent a quantitative measure of the subjective persuasiveness assigned to the arguments by the audience, not probabilities, and hence do not need to sum to 1. Carneades makes the assumption that such numbers can be obtained and uses the set of real numbers as its scope, that is, there is no minimum level of granularity for the precision of the number.

Hence, in our example (Fig. 5), if both *unique product* and *reverse-engineerable* are acceptable or assumed true by the audience, the pro argument with a weight of 0.7 trumps the con argument with a weight of 0.5, and hence the statement *info-trade-secret* is acceptable.

5.2 *Carneades Bayesian Networks*

From the graphical display in Fig. 5, we can easily conceptualize a corresponding Carneades Bayesian Network [CBN] quantitatively emulating the same qualitative inferences. The structure would be identical, and we only would need to define probability functions/tables. These probabilities basically emulate the deterministic behavior of the Carneades model. Later, the model can be extended to support new phenomena of uncertainty, for example, probability distributions over assumptions. The following explanations are essentially a verbalized summary of the formalism given in (Grabmair et al. 2010), to which we refer the interested reader for greater detail.

First, we determine the probability parameters of the leaf nodes. Depending on whether our audience assumes *unique product* and/or *reverse-engineerability* as accepted or rejected, or has no assumptions about them, the respective probability will be either 0 or 1 for the positive and negated versions of the respective statements. Second, the probability for each of the arguments being applicable will be equal to 1 if their incoming premise statement is acceptable and 0 otherwise. Third, the conditional probability table for *info-trade-secret* contains the probability of the statement being acceptable conditioned on the possible combinations of in/out statuses of the two arguments (i.e., $2 \times 2 = 4$ parameters). Here, the probability of the presence of a trade secret being acceptable for the audience is equal to 1 for the two cases where the pro argument based on *unique product* is applicable and 0 otherwise because the pro argument is required for acceptability and always trumps the con argument (based on *reverse-engineerable*) because $0.7 > 0.5$.

Notice that the just explained probabilities change once the Carneades argument graph changes. For example, if the weights of the arguments are changed such that the con argument strictly outweighs the pro argument, then the conditional probability table for *info-trade-secret* would need to be changed to assign a probability of 0 to the statement being *in* (or, more generally, the statement's acceptability) in case of conflicting applicable arguments.

This simple example illustrates how one can translate instances of a qualitative model of argumentation into a BN. Notice, however, that all probabilities we have defined so far are deterministic, that is, they are either equal to 1 or equal to 0. This makes the BN function exactly like the original Carneades argument graph. Once some part of the configuration changes, this change can be taken over into the BN by modifying the structure or conditional probability tables of the network. In this way, our qualitative model of argument becomes a control structure which takes care of constructing an entire BN. The required knowledge to be elicited from domain experts is hence limited to the information necessary to construct the Carneades argument graph, such as the assumptions made and the weights assigned by the audience.

Finally, the probabilistic semantics of Carneades allow for a conceptual distinction between the subjective weight of an argument (to the audience) and the probability of the argument being *applicable* given the probability of the argument's premises being fulfilled. For detail and related work, we refer the reader to (Grabmair et al. 2010).

5.3 Carneades Bayesian Networks with Probabilistic Assumptions

Probabilistic semantics for a qualitative argument model provide little benefit if their parameters make the BN behave deterministically. A first extension introduces probabilistic assumptions and has been formally defined and illustrated in an example context in (Grabmair et al. 2010). Therefore, it shall only be explained briefly in this chapter.

Carneades allows for an audience to assume certain propositions as *in* or *out*. In realistic contexts, one might not be able to make such a determination about the

Fig. 6 Example CBN with
priors for arguments weights

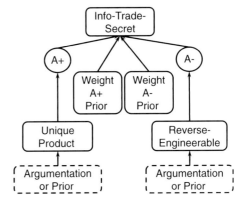

audience. Instead, one may characterize an audience as being more or less likely to
accept a certain statement than to reject it by some degree of confidence, or vice
versa. One can capture this into a Carneades BN by allowing for prior probability
distributions over the leaf node literal statements that the foundations of the argument and which may be assumptions. From there upward, the network propagates
these values and provides for means to calculate the probability of success in
the overall argumentative goal given the knowledge about the assumptions of the
audience (see Fig. 6). The remaining parts of the network still are deterministically
parametrized. This means that changes to the model graph (such as the introduction
of new arguments or the alteration of weights) are still straightforward to reflect in
the BN and can be assessed in terms of their impact on the probability of the success
of the overall argument.

In a practical application, one can use available knowledge about the audience
(e.g., the composition of a jury or a particular judge in a legal proceeding) to model
these prior distributions.

5.4   Introduction to Argument Weights

Besides the assumptions about statements, Carneades associates with the audience
the weights of the arguments employed in order to be able to resolve conflicting
arguments using proof standards. Similar to probabilistic assumptions, one might
not be able to determine that the audience will definitely prefer argument $A +$ over
argument $A-$ (compare Fig. 6) by some margin. Instead, one may be able to say that
the audience is more likely to assign high weight to an argument than a low one. Or
one may say that the audience is so mixed that it is just as likely to give great weight
to the argument as it is to disregard it. It is hence useful to model argument weights
using prior probability distributions as well. Figure 6 displays our example network
in such a structure. Notice that the statements *unique product* as well as *reverse-
engineerable* can either be subject to further argumentation or assumed by the

audience to be *in, out,* or questioned according to some prior probability. For example, the audience can either assume the reverse-engineerability *as such* or it can be convinced to believe in it because of, for example, an IT expert testifying that an average programmer can reverse-engineer the database. In the latter case, one could expand *reverse-engineerable* into a subtree containing all arguments and statements related to this expert testimony.

6   Extension of Carneades to Support Probabilistic Argument Weights

We now formally define an extension/modification of the CBN model to support probability distributions over argument weights. We build on the formalism published in (Grabmair et al. 2010), which we have not reproduced in its entirety here. To make this chapter stand alone, we present slightly altered versions of three definitions used in (Grabmair et al. 2010) and accompany them with explanations about the symbols and constructs. These are the new argument weight random variable (representing the actual weights), the modified audience (with distributions over argument weights instead of static ones), and the enhanced probability functions (determining the probability of an argument having a certain weight and of its conclusion being acceptable). All other modifications are straightforward and have been omitted for reasons of brevity.

Definition 1. (argument weight variables). *An **argument weight variable** w_a is a random variable with eleven possible values: $\{0, 0.1, 0.2, \ldots, 0.9, 1.0\}$. It represents the persuasiveness of an argument a.*

By contrast to the original Carneades models, we have segmented the range of possible weights using 0.1 increments. While the granularity of the segmentation is arbitrary, we consider a segmentation useful for purposes of this extension because (1) it is flexible yet allows to reasonably model a tie among weights of conflicting arguments (which would be harder if one were dealing with a continuous distribution) and (2) it allows the probabilities to be displayed in table form. This latter feature will become relevant in the next section, where we survey the possibility of yet another extension, subjecting the weight distributions to further argumentation. Next is our enhanced definition of an audience (compare to def. 12.3 in Gordon et al. 2009). For understanding, L stands for the propositional language in which the statements have been formulated.

Definition 2. (audience weight distributions). *An **audience with weight distributions** is a structure $\langle \phi, f' \rangle$, where $\Phi \in L$ is a consistent set of literals assumed to be acceptable by the audience and f' is a partial function mapping arguments to probability distributions over the possible values of argument weight variables. This distribution represents the relative weights assumed to be assigned* *by the audience to the arguments. For a given set of weight values $w_{a_1}, \ldots, w_{a_n}$, let $f''(w_{a_1}, \ldots, w_{a_n})$ be a partial function mapping the arguments $a_1, \ldots, a_n$ onto these values.*

The main aspect of the extension is the modified probability functions given in the next definition. In the original definitions in (Grabmair et al. 2010), weights were not explicitly represented as random variables in the network. As we introduce them now, we alter the probability functions for arguments by making them conditioned on the values of their argument weight parent variables. We further assign probability functions for the weight variables themselves.

Carneades conceptualizes argumentation as an *argumentation process* divided into *stages*, which in turn consist of a list of arguments, each connecting premise statements to a conclusion statement. The central piece of the formalism is the *argument evaluation structure*, which contains the elements necessary to draw inferences, namely, the stage containing the arguments, the proof standards of the relevant statements, and, finally, an audience holding assumptions and assigning argument weights. Carneades features *in-out* derivability in (Ballnat et al. 2010) as explained above. When verbalized, $(\Gamma, \phi) \vdash_{f''(w_{a_1}, \ldots, w_{a_n}), g} p$ means that the arguments contained in the stage Γ and the set of assumptions by the audience $\phi\Phi$ argumentatively entail statement p (i.e., p is *in*) given the argument weights determined by the partial function f' and the proof standards of the statements determined by the function g.

Definition 3. (modified probability functions). *If $\mathcal{S} = \langle \Gamma, \mathcal{A}, g \rangle$ is an argument evaluation structure with a set of arguments Γ (called a "stage" in an "argumentation process"), a function g maps statements to their respective proof standard, $\mathcal{A} = \langle \phi, f' \rangle$ is the current audience, the set of random variables $V_S = S \cup A \cup W$ consists of a set of statement variables S, a set of argument variables A as well as a set of weight variables W, and D_S is the set of connecting edges, then $\mathcal{P}_S = \mathcal{P}_a \cup \mathcal{P}_s \cup \mathcal{P}_w$ is a set of probability functions defined as follows:*
Definitions of $\mathcal{P}_a = \{P_a | a \in A\}$ have been omitted for brevity reasons. See def. 13 in (Grabmair et al. 2010). It states that arguments are applicable with a probability of 1 if their premises hold.
If $s = S$ is a statement variable representing literal p and $a_1, \ldots, a_n$ are its parent argument variables with corresponding weights variables $w_{a_1}, \ldots, w_{a_n}$, then P_s is the probability function for the statement variable s:

$$P_s(s = \text{in}|a_1, \ldots, a_n, w_{a_1}, \ldots, w_{a_n}) = \begin{cases} 1, & \text{if } (\Gamma, \Phi) \vdash_{f''(w_{a_1}, \ldots, w_{a_n}), g} p, \\ 0, & \text{if } (\Gamma, \Phi)_{f''(w_{a_1}, \ldots, w_{a_n}), g} p. \end{cases}$$

$$P_s(s = \text{out}|a_1, \ldots, a_n, w_{a_1}, \ldots, w_{a_n}) = 1 - P_a(s = \text{in}|a_1, \ldots, a_n).$$

We further add probability functions for weight variables:

$$P_{w_a}(w_a = v) = f'(a, v).$$

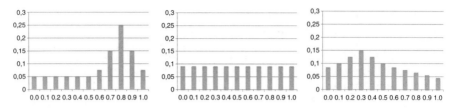

Fig. 7 Example probability distributions over weights (high peak, uniform, low shallow). The horizontal axes show argument weight values for an argument whose probabilities are displayed on the vertical axes

Finally, the total set of probability functions consists of one such function for each statement, argument, and weight:

$$\text{Let } \mathcal{P}_a = \{P_a | a \in A\}, \ \mathcal{P}_s = \{P_s | s \in S\} \text{ and } \mathcal{P}_W = \{P_{w_a} | a \in A\}.$$

In our example, we can use this function to automatically construct a conditional probability table for the statement *info-trade-secret*. Because there are 11 possible argument weights, its conditional side would contain $11 \times 11 \times 2^2 = 484$ possible combinations of argument applicability and argument weights for both $A+$ and $A-$. The literal is *in* with a probability of 1 in all combinations where (1) $A+$ is applicable and $A-$ is either not applicable or, in case, both arguments are applicable and (2) its weight w_{A-} is less than w_{A+}. This second case is new in this extension; in the basic model weights (and hence the outcomes of the aggregation of the arguments using the proof standard) are static. For example, using this extension, in Fig. 6, the probability of *info-trade-secret* being *in* would be determined by not only taking into account the probability of the audience accepting or rejecting reverse-engineerability or uniqueness of the product but also the possibility of either of the two arguments outweighing the other with some probability. Without the extension, one could only calculate the probability of the outcome given some static weights (e.g., $0.7 > 0.5$ as above).

For example, one can use a discretized bell-curve-like distribution over the 11 intervals (assuming it holds that $\sum_{i=0}^{10} P\left(w = \frac{i}{10} = 1\right)$, depending on what one believes to be true about the audience). For example, in ConnectU versus Zuckerberg, we may be fairly certain that the uniqueness of the product is a persuasive argument and hence model a narrow bell-curve-like segmentation of probabilities with a high center (see Fig. 7 left). The reverse-engineerability, on the other hand, may only be low in weight, resulting in a shallow discrete curve-like distribution (see Fig. 7 middle). In a litigation planning context, these distributions correspond to the attorney's assumption about the audience. The narrower and higher the curve, the more certain she will be about exactly how persuasive an argument is. The more uncertain she is, the flatter the curve will become. If she cannot tell at all how strong her jury/judge will deem an argument, a uniform distribution can be employed (see Fig. 7 right).

The benefit of using probability distributions over argument weights as opposed to static weights is that the system can compute the probability of a statement being acceptable in the argument model by taking into account the probabilities with which conflicting arguments defeat each other under the different proof standards. For example, a strong argument may no longer deterministically defeat a weaker one, but only by some relatively high probability that can be determined by computing both weight prior distributions of the two arguments. Or an argument may fall below a minimum relevance threshold or not with some probability. These implicit computations can take place through Carneades' existing proof standard functions and the basic conditional probability functionality of BNs. Notice that this extension is set on top of the core formalism for CBNs in (Grabmair et al. 2010) and does not include prior probabilities over assumptions (compare Sect. 5.3). A comprehensive formalism including multiple extensions is intentionally left for future work.

7 Desiderata for Future Developments

In this section, we suggest two further extensions, namely, to influence argument weights by (a) making the argument weights subject to argumentation and, in order to connect to our previous explanations about moral uncertainty, (b) making the argument weights subject to influence from the results of the moral assessment of the case, that is, the results of the balancing of the principles involved. We will outline these extensions conceptually, justify why we consider them relevant, and hint at possible ways to implement them.

The common idea underlying the just suggested extensions as well as the following explanations is that argument weights are a crucial part of an argument model as they potentially enable the system to give definite answers in instances of conflicting arguments. Also, the weights stand for the realization that arguments differ in persuasiveness and are relative to a factual context and to abstract values. We do not take a position with regard to the philosophical and argument-theoretical implications of these notions, but only explore their ability to be modeled in this formal context.

7.1 Weights Subject to Argumentation

Arguments can be abstracted from and reasoned about. One can argue about how heavily a certain argument weighs in comparison to others and in light of the context in which it is employed. For example, in ConnectU versus Zuckerberg, if the plaintiff argumentatively establishes that the database is really difficult to reverse engineer and requires considerable skill, then the defendant's argument based on reverse-engineerability becomes weaker, despite still being applicable.

Once weights are represented explicitly in the argument graph, one can make them subject to argumentation. This presupposes the model's ability to express in its proposition information about the weights. What this information specifically means is dependent on how the argument model represents weights. In the Carneades-BN derivative, we have been describing in this chapter, this information about the weights takes the shape of normalized real numbers or, in the case of the extension, a prior probability distribution over a discretized range of weights.

As has been proposed above, a very strong argument could, for example, be modeled as a narrow bell-curve-like prior weight distribution with its peak centered at 0.8. On the other hand, a weak argument might be a similar bell curve but with its maximum probability located at only 0.3. Finally, an argument of average weight would be situated at 0.5. If one attempts to represent as a graph a meta-argument that a certain argument is either strong, weak, or average, the discourse essentially becomes an argument about a potentially unconstrained number of alternative choices as opposed to an argument about the acceptance of a certain statement as true. Carneades, with its current qualitative semantics, does not provide for such functionality.

In a generic BN representation, however, these choices can be represented as probability distributions conditioned on the status of the parent variables, where the parent variables here would represent, for example, the nodes in the fact layer or normative layer informing the weights. This essentially leads to an interdependence of argument formation and argument weights. We have just scouted the possibility of informing a choice of argument weights from fact patterns, which in turn can be argumentatively established. This can be considered as in part conceptually reminiscent of arguing from *dimensions* (Ashley et al. 1991). For example, in a trade secret misappropriation case, imagine that the manufacturer of a unique product has communicated production informations of the product to outsiders. This forms an argument against a trade secret claim because the manufacturer himself has broken the secrecy. However, it arguably makes a difference to whom he has communicated the secret (e.g., his wife, his neighbor, or a competitor's employee) and, in a second dimension, to how many people he has done so. This small example shows that the weight of an existing argument may be subject to argumentation itself based on the facts and the values at stake in the dispute. This leads over to our final suggested extension.

7.2   Inform Weights from Values

The values underlying the legal issues are another source of information for the question of which weights certain arguments shall carry. In ConnectU versus Zuckerberg, we have an argument based on the product's uniqueness furthering the protection of intellectual property interests, whereas an argument based on the product's reverse-engineerability goes against property interests in public information. This mechanism of arguments furthering values has been debated in

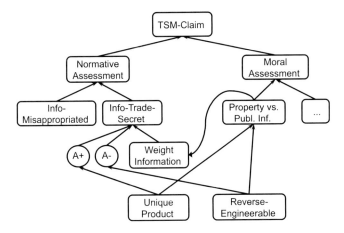

Fig. 8 Conceptual argument graph with values informing weights of legal arguments

computational models of argument, perhaps most prominently in the context of the already mentioned value-based argumentation frameworks (Bench-Capon 2003), where a hierarchy of values resolves conflicts among arguments. In further work (Modgil 2006), this hierarchy can be made subject to argumentation as well, lifting the argument framework into a meta-representation. Feteris (2008) presents a pragma-dialectical model for how legal arguments for and against the application of rules can be weighted by underlying values and the factual context, connecting to prominent legal theories which we do not reference here for reasons of brevity.

One can adapt this notion in the context of probabilistic semantics for argument weights, by allowing the moral assessment of a case to influence the probability with which certain legal arguments will prevail over others. In other words, if a judge in ConnectU versus Zuckerberg, after considering the given facts, is of the opinion that property interests outweigh the interest in protecting public access (because, e.g., the evidence indicates that the social network idea is so unique and new that its farsighted inventor deserves a head start on its marketing), she might be more likely to accord greater weight to the legal arguments about the controversial issues which favor the property interest value (Fig. 8).

From a technical point of view, one can imagine that the decision about which principle is more important can determine a choice among different prior probabilities for the argument weights. A more satisfying solution, however, would be to not choose among predefined priors, but to have the priors of the weights be a qualitative outflow of the balancing decision between the two principles. If one value outweighs another by a larger or smaller margin, this margin should be reflected in the shape of the prior distribution of the argument weights. We are presently researching ways of modeling legal argumentation with values and have not yet conceived how to integrate it with a probabilistic argument model as described. Still, the idea of a value-based approach coheres with the intuitions of legal experts and has the potential of enriching the expressivity of probabilistic argument models.

8   Conclusions and Future Work

We have presented a survey of four kinds of uncertainties lawyers reason about and plan for in litigation and presented a realistic case example in trade secret law. Systematizing the uncertainties into a graphical model, we explained desirable attributes for probabilistic models of argument intended for litigation planning. Generic BNs as well as a probabilistic semantics for the Carneades model have been used as examples, and we have suggested extensions to the latter that allow more sophisticated reasoning with argument weights. We see great potential in combining quantitative models of uncertainty with qualitative models of argument and consider legal reasoning as an ideal testing ground for evaluating how qualitative models can be used most effectively to create quantitative models and how quantitative methods can provide steering heuristics and control systems for qualitative argumentation.

Acknowledgments We wish to thank the organizer Frank Zenker and the participants of the Workshop on Bayesian Argumentation at the University of Lund for the very inspiring discussion and all the feedback and questions we received in the context of our presentations and the workshop as a whole. We further thank Prof. Marek Druzdzel (Intelligent Systems Program, School of Information Science, University of Pittsburgh) and Collin Lynch (Intelligent Systems Program, University of Pittsburgh) for very helpful suggestions in the preparation of this chapter.

References

Agosta, J. M., Gardos, T. R., & Druzdzel, M. J. (2008). Query-based diagnostics. In M. Jaeger & T. D. Nielsen (Eds.), *Proceedings of the fourth European workshop on probabilistic graphical models (PGM-08), Hirtshals, Denmark, September 17–19* (pp. 1–8).

Ashley, K. D. (1991). *Modeling legal arguments: Reasoning with cases and hypotheticals.* Cambridge, MA: MIT Press.

Ashley, K. D., & Brüninghaus, S. (2006). Computer models for legal prediction. *Jurimetrics Journal, 46,* 309–352.

Atkinson, K., & Bench-Capon, T. (2007). Argumentation and standards of proof. In *ICAIL 2007* (pp. 107–116). New York: ACM Press.

Ballnat, S., & Gordon, T. F. (2010). Goal selection in argumentation processes: A formal model of abduction in argument evaluation structures. In *Computational models of argument proceedings of COMMA 2010* (pp. 51–62). Amsterdam: IOS Press.

Baroni, P., & Giacomin, M. (2009). Semantics of Abstract Argument Systems. In I. Rahwan & G. Simari (Eds.), *Argumentation in Artificial Intelligence* (pp. 25–44). Berlin: Springer-Verlag.

Bench-Capon, T. J. M. (2003). Persuasion in practical argument using value-based argumentation frameworks. *Journal of Logic and Computation, 13*(3), 429–448.

Condliffe, P., Abrahams, B., & Zeleznikow, J. (2010). A legal decision support guide for owners corporation cases. In R. G. F. Winkels (Ed.), *Proceedings of Jurix 2010* (pp. 147–150). Amsterdam: IOS Press.

Díez, F. J., & Druzdzel, M. J. (2007). Canonical probabilistic models for knowledge engineering (Technical Report CISIAD-06-01). UNED, Madrid (2006), Version 0.9, April 28 (2007), Available at http://www.ia.uned.es/fjdiez/papers/canonical.pdf

Dung, P. M. (1995). On the acceptability of arguments and its fundamental role in nonmonotonic reasoning, logic programming and n-person games. *Artificial Intelligence, 77*(2), 321–358.

Feteris, E. T. (2008). Weighing and balancing in the justification of judicial decisions. *Informal Logic, 28*, 20–30.

Cooper, G. F. (1987). *Probabilistic inference using belief networks is Np-hard* (Paper No. SMI-87-0195). Stanford: Knowledge Systems Laboratory, Stanford University.

Gordon, T. F., & Walton, D. (2009). Proof burdens and standards. In I. Rahwan & G. Simari (Eds.), *Argumentation in artificial intelligence*. Berlin: Springer.

Gordon, T. F., Prakken, H., & Walton, D. (2007). The Carneades model of argument and burden of proof. *Artificial Intelligence, 171*(10–11), 875–896.

Grabmair, M., Gordon, T. F., & Walton, D. (2010). *Probabilistic semantics for the Carneades argument model using Bayesian networks: Proceedings of the third international conference on computational models of argument (COMMA)* (pp. 255–266). IOS Press: Amsterdam.

Hahn, U., & Oaksford, M. (2007). The burden of proof and its role in argumentation. *Argumentation, 21*, 39–61.

Kadane, J. B., & Schum, D. A. (1996). *A probabilistic analysis of the Sacco and Vanzetti evidence*. New York: Wiley.

Keppens, J. (2012). Title: Argument diagram extraction from evidential Bayesian networks. *Artificial Intelligence and Law, 20*(2), 109–143.

Kraaijeveld, P., & Druzdzel, M. (2005). GeNIeRate: An interactive generator of diagnostic Bayesian network models. In *16th international workshop on principles of diagnosis* (pp. 175–180).

Laskey, K. B. (2008). MEBN: A language for first-order Bayesian knowledge bases. *Artificial Intelligence, 172*(2–3), 140–178.

Modgil, S. (2006). Value based argumentation in hierarchical argumentation frameworks. In P. E. Dunne & T. Bench-Capon (Eds.), *Computational Models of Natural Argument, Proceedings of COMMA 2006* (pp. 297–308). IOS Press.

Muecke, N., & Stranieri, A. (2007). An argument structure abstraction for Bayesian belief networks: Just outcomes in on-line dispute resolution. In *Proceedings of the fourth Asia-Pacific Conference on Conceptual Modeling* (pp. 35–40). Darlinghurst: Australian Computer Society, Inc.

Parsons, S., Gabbay, D., Kruse, R., Nonnengart, A., & Ohlbach, H. (1997). Normative argumentation and qualitative probability. In *Qualitative and quantitative practical reasoning* (LNCS, Vol. 1244, pp. 466–480). Berlin/Heidelberg: Springer.

Pearl, J. (1985, August 15–17). *Bayesian networks: A model of self-activated memory for evidential reasoning* (UCLA Technical Report CSD-850017). Proceedings of the 7th Conference of the Cognitive Science Society, University of California, Irvine, pp. 329–334.

Ratnapinda, P., & Druzdzel, M. J. (2009). Passive construction of diagnostic decision models: An empirical evaluation. In *Proceedings of the international multiconference on computer science and information technology (IMCSIT-2009), Mragowo, Poland, October 12–14* (pp. 515–521). Piscataway: IEEE.

Renooij, S., & van der Gaag, L. (1999). Enhancing QPNs for trade-off resolution. *Proceedings of the fifteenth conference annual conference on uncertainty in artificial intelligence (UAI-99)* (pp. 559–566). San Francisco: Morgan Kaufmann.

Riveret, R., Prakken, H., Rotolo, A., & Sartor, G. (2008). Heuristics in argumentation: A game-theoretical investigation. In *Proceedings of COMMA 2008* (pp. 324–335). Amsterdam: IOS Press.

Roth, B., Riveret, R., Rotolo, A., & Governatori, G. (2007). Strategic argumentation: A game theoretical investigation. In *Proceedings of the 11th international conference on artificial intelligence and law* (pp. 81–90). New York: ACM.

Wellman, M. P. (1990). Fundamental concepts of qualitative probabilistic networks. *Artificial Intelligence, 44*, 257–303.

Zukerman, I., Mcconachy, R., & Korb, K. (1998). Bayesian reasoning in an abductive mechanism for argument generation and analysis. In *Proceedings of the fifteenth national conference on artificial intelligence* (pp. 833–838). Menlo Park: AAAI.

Was It Wrong to Use Statistics in *R v Clark*? A Case Study of the Use of Statistical Evidence in Criminal Courts

Amit Pundik

Abstract This chapter discusses the use of statistical evidence to prove the material fact of causation in criminal courts. It focuses on *R v Clark*, in which a mother was wrongfully convicted of murdering both her babies. In order to disprove a potential defence claim that the babies died of SIDS (aka cot death), the prosecution adduced statistics that allegedly showed that the probability of two SIDS deaths in a family similar to the Clarks was 1 in 73 million. This chapter considers the question of whether it was wrong to use such statistical evidence in *Clark*. Four common explanations of why it was wrong, each of which attributes the wrongful convictions to the use or misuse of the statistical evidence, are scrutinised and rejected. However, drawing on the theory of contrastive explanation, it is argued that it was still wrong *in principle* to use the SIDS statistics in Clark, because using them properly would require another piece of evidence which is clearly objectionable: statistical evidence on the rate of smothering among mothers who are similar to Clark. Regardless of whether the exercise of comparing probabilities of SIDS and smothering is feasible, such an exercise should not be conducted as part of criminal proceedings. This chapter thus concludes that *Clark* should serve as a warning against any attempt to prove the fact of causation using statistical evidence about the rate of potential exonerating causes.

I would like to thank Mike Redmayne for his helpful and constructive comments on an early version of this chapter. I would also like to thank Asaf Wiener and Maya Ben-Meir, who have provided me with excellent research assistance and helpful comments. The research leading to these results received funding from the European Community's Seventh Framework Programme (FP7/2007–2013) under grant agreement n° 299653.

A. Pundik (✉)
Buchmann Faculty of Law, Tel Aviv University, Tel Aviv, Israel
e-mail: amitp@post.tau.ac.il

F. Zenker (ed.), *Bayesian Argumentation: The practical side of probability*,
Synthese Library 362, DOI 10.1007/978-94-007-5357-0_5,
© Springer Science+Business Media Dordrecht 2013

1   Introduction

Sally Clark's two baby boys, Christopher and Harry, were found dead on separate occasions.[1] Christopher's death was at first treated as sudden infant death syndrome ('SIDS', also known as cot death).[2] However, when Harry died two years later, the autopsy revealed suspicious injuries and the findings from Christopher's autopsy were re-evaluated. Clark was then charged with and convicted of the murder of both babies. At the trial, the prosecution called Professor Meadow, an expert paediatrician, to counter a potential defence claim that both deaths were natural as due to SIDS. In his testimony, Professor Meadow said that the probability of two occurrences of SIDS in a family similar to the Clarks was 1 in 73 million. This calculation was found to be flawed, but the Court of Appeal upheld the two murder convictions after finding the case against Clark still 'overwhelming' on each account (*Clark-I*: [254], [272]). A few years later, Clark's husband found evidence in the hospital archives of microbiological results indicating that Harry had died from natural causes. A second appeal was allowed, and Clark was set free on 29 January 2003 after serving more than three years in prison.[3] Sadly, four years later, she was found dead in her home as a result of alcohol poisoning (BBC 2007).

While the wrongful convictions[4] of Clark raise various issues,[5] much of the public and scholarly attention given to this case focused on the use of the SIDS statistics (the probability of two cases of SIDS in the same family).[6] The SIDS statistics were commonly regarded in the public media as somehow responsible, at least in part, for the wrongful convictions of Clark.[7] One newspaper even went

---

[1] *R v Clark* (Crown Court Chester 9 November 1999), R v Clark (No 1) [2000] EWCA Crim 54 (hereafter '*Clark-I*'), *R v Clark (No 2)* [2003] EWCA Crim 1020 (hereafter '*Clark-II*')

[2] SIDS (sudden infant death syndrome) is defined as 'the sudden death of a baby that is unexpected by history and in whom a thorough necropsy examination fails to demonstrate an adequate cause of death' (*Clark-I*: [104]).

[3] The convictions were quashed and Clark was released after the Crown decided not to seek a retrial (*Clark-II*: [5]). The Court of Appeal commended this decision (*ibid.*: [181]).

[4] The term 'wrongful convictions' is used because it is assumed that the admissible evidence available today, including the microbiological results found later by the husband, is insufficient to prove beyond reasonable doubt that Clark murdered Christopher and Harry (this assumption is made explicitly in the second appeal, *Clark-II*: [179]). It should be noted that this assumption is weaker than the claim that Clark is in fact innocent (though this is also probably true), but none of the points made in this chapter requires the stronger claim of actual innocence.

[5] For example, the duties of expert witnesses repeatedly received scholarly attention. See Wilson (2005), Dwyer (2003), Blom-Cooper (2006).

[6] For the centrality of the SIDS statistics in the discussion of *Clark*, see, for example, Editorial (2000) and Nobles and Schiff (2005).

[7] 'The statistic was quoted in every headline and is widely believed to have led to Sally Clark's conviction' (Barraclough 2004); '[t]he jury at Sally Clark's trial, however, was apparently persuaded by the evidence of a leading expert called by the prosecution, Professor Sir Roy Meadow, who maintained that the probability of two cot deaths occurring in a single affluent family was "one in 73 million"' (Telegraph 2007).

as far as to assert that the statistical evidence was almost the only evidence against Clark.[8] The existence of some causal connection between the (mis)use of the SIDS statistics and the wrongful convictions not only appeared in the public media but was also hinted at by expert statisticians, such as Professor Donnelly[9] and Professor Dawid.[10]

This chapter examines whether it was wrong to use the SIDS statistics in *Clark*, and if so, why. After providing a more detailed factual description of *Clark* in Section 2, in Section 3 the chapter scrutinises and rejects four common explanations, each of which draws a connection, either explicitly or implicitly, between the SIDS statistics and the wrongful convictions. The first explanation concentrates on the flaws in the calculation made by Meadow that led to the 1 in 73 million figure. The second holds that the SIDS statistics had an overwhelming psychological effect which overshadowed other evidence more favourable to Clark. The third explanation focuses on a logical mistake called the 'prosecutor's fallacy' (explained below). The last explanation considers the courts' refusal to use Bayes' Theorem (also explained below). This chapter seeks to show that each of these explanations suffers from its own specific weaknesses. More generally, it is shown that these explanations are unpersuasive, taken either separately or jointly, since any connection between the SIDS statistics and the wrongful convictions is hard to establish. This is because it is difficult to accept that the wrongful convictions could have been prevented if the SIDS statistics had been used correctly, or even if they had not been used at all.

Section 4 suggests an alternative explanation of why it was wrong to use the SIDS statistics in *Clark*. Drawing on the theory of contrastive explanation from the philosophy of science (van Fraassen 1980: 97–157; Lipton 1990), this chapter shows that the use of SIDS statistics in *Clark* was wrong *in principle*. This is because the only way to make the SIDS statistics meaningful is to compare them, even implicitly, to another piece of statistical evidence: in this case, the rate of mothers who smothered to death both of their babies among the population of mothers who are similar to Clark. Using this second piece of statistical evidence is clearly objectionable. Hence, even if all the difficulties highlighted by the existing explanations were rectified, it would still have been wrong to use the SIDS statistics in *Clark*.

---

[8] 'You are incarcerated for their killing – *for almost no other reason* than that a leading paediatrician, Sir Roy Meadow, was permitted to tell the jury that the likelihood of there being two infant deaths in the same family was one in 73 million' (Wansell 2007), my emphasis. See also Shaikh (2007).

[9] In a public presentation, Professor Donnelly stated that '[the mistaken conviction] happened in large part here because the expert [Professor Meadow] got the statistics horribly wrong'. He concluded his presentation of the case with the statement that 'there is a situation where errors in statistics had really profound and really unfortunate consequences' (Donnelly 2005).

[10] 'Although we cannot know how the jury regarded the statistical evidence, it is reasonable to speculate that it was strongly influenced by the extremely small probability value of 1 in 73 million that both deaths could have arisen from SIDS, regarding this as ruling out the possibility of death by natural causes' (Dawid 2002: 75).

This explanation provides a principled reason that does not hinge on the actual consequences of the use of statistics in the specific case of *Clark*. It is thus not limited to *Clark* and can be applied to any similar case in which such statistics are adduced to eliminate potential natural, accidental, or other types of non-culpatory causes. It is argued here that even when the statistical evidence is gathered, analysed, and presented in the utmost professional manner by experienced expert statisticians and interpreted correctly by the judges and jurors, it is still wrong in principle to use it in cases such as *Clark*. This chapter thus concludes that such statistics should not be used in criminal proceedings to prove the material fact of causation (i.e. the fact that the harm was caused by the accused's misconduct).

This chapter focuses mainly on the decision of the first appeal to uphold the convictions, rather than on the initial trial or the second appeal, for several reasons. Firstly, trained and experienced judges, such as those who presided over the first appeal, are said to be less vulnerable to counsel's trial tactics, logical fallacies and so on, than lay juries, such as those who convicted *Clark* in the actual trial and who, most likely, were participating in a trial setting for the first time in their lives. Focusing on the first appeal thus reduces the importance of factors external to the available evidence and to the legal reasoning. Secondly, while the jury in the actual trial did not provide any detailed account of its reasoning,[11] the decision of the first appeal contains immense detail about the judges' reasons for upholding the convictions. Lastly, the convictions were upheld by the first appeal *despite* the immense attention to detail and argument.[12] It is the thoroughness of the judgment which makes its erroneous outcome so troubling and thus also makes it a more suitable source for analysis than the second appeal or the actual trial.

2   Factual Background

Before considering possible explanations, it is first necessary to provide a more detailed description of the case.[13] Clark, who was 35 years old at the time of the trial, was a solicitor with no previous criminal record. Christopher, her first child, was born healthy but died at the age of 11 weeks while her husband was out at an office party. Dr Williams, a pathologist, initially treated the death as a case of SIDS and considered the cause of death to be lower respiratory tract infection. He found bruises on the body and a small split in the frenulum, but he thought at the time that these were caused by resuscitation attempts. Before the body was cremated,

---

[11] In general, the jury is not required to provide reasoning for its 'guilty' or 'not-guilty' judgment (Roberts and Zuckerman 2010: 65–72).

[12] By way of illustration, this decision consists of over 35,000 words of detailed description of the facts, the witnesses' testimonies and the arguments of the parties, together with the judges' reasoning.

[13] The following background is based on the description in the first judgment of the Court of Appeal, in order to remain as close as possible to the standpoint of the judges of the first appeal.

Dr Williams took photographs and preserved slides of the lungs. Two years later, Harry, the second child, was also born healthy but was found dead at the age of 8 weeks by his mother when the husband was not in the room. The findings at the autopsy were indicative of nonaccidental injury, and Dr Williams determined the cause of death as shaking. He also revisited Christopher's case, conducted further tests, and altered his opinion, concluding that Christopher's death was also unnatural and that the evidence was suggestive of smothering (*Clark-I*: [2]–[3]).

The prosecution case was that Clark had murdered both babies (*Clark-I*: [6]–[7]). According to the prosecution, neither could be considered SIDS because of the existence of recent and old injuries that had been found in each case. There were several similarities between the cases: both babies were of similar age and found unconscious shortly after having been fed, in the same room, by Ms Clark, when she was alone with them, and when Mr Clark was absent or about to leave. Most importantly, in each case there was evidence of previous abuse and of deliberate injury recently inflicted. With regard to Christopher,[14] three pieces of medical evidence were adduced. Firstly, there was bleeding in his lungs, both old and fresh. The old bleeding is a marker for asphyxia and cannot be explained by the nosebleed Christopher had during a family trip to London because so much blood going into the lungs would have required urgent hospital treatment, but in fact Christopher recovered spontaneously. The nosebleed was also independently consistent with a prior attempt at smothering. Secondly, in the autopsy, Christopher's frenulum was found to be torn. The prosecution alleged that this was a result of deliberately inflicted injury rather than of resuscitation efforts and thus consistent with smothering. Lastly, Dr Williams had no doubt that he saw bruises on the body.

The defence case was that the evidence available was insufficient to prove beyond reasonable doubt that the babies' cause of death was unnatural (*Clark-I*: [10]–[15]). The defence therefore suggested that the babies must have died of natural causes, though it did not commit to any specific natural cause (including SIDS).[15] The defence emphasised that two of the prosecution's expert pathologists (Professor Green and Dr Keeling) gave the cause of death as unascertained and that therefore the prosecution's entire case hinged on the reliability of Dr Williams, who performed the autopsies. With regard to the medical evidence, the defence claimed that the marks on the body, which were interpreted by Dr Williams as bruises, were not examined under a microscope and were not seen at the hospital by other personnel who saw the baby. The injured frenulum could have been caused during insertion of the laryngoscope. As for the fresh bleeding, the defence claimed that it was only a marker for smothering and was often found both in suspicious cases and

---

[14] The description focuses on the prosecution case regarding Christopher, because the microbiological results that led to the second appeal and to Clark's release were relevant only to Harry, and the available medical and pathological evidence concerning Christopher's death remained more or less the same following Clark's conviction.

[15] In order to secure an acquittal, the defence did not need to provide a (natural) explanation for the babies' deaths but only to establish that there was a reasonable doubt in the (unnatural) explanation provided by the prosecution.

in cases of cot death. The old bleeding could have been a result of the nosebleed, the occurrence of which was not disputed. The defence argued that it was not caused by an attempted smothering because it was unlikely that Clark would have attempted to smother Christopher on the day she had brought him to London to show him to her friends.

3 Existing Explanations

3.1 The Flaws in Meadow's Calculation

A common explanation of why it was wrong to use the SIDS statistics in *Clark* focuses on the way the statistical evidence was used or, perhaps more precisely, misused. The statistical calculation used by Professor Meadow, which aimed to establish that the probability of two cases of SIDS occurring in the same family was 1 in 73 million, drew substantial criticism from the statistician community[16] and was even singled out as the cause of the wrongful convictions.[17] Meadow reached this figure by first calculating the probability of a SIDS death in a family similar to the Clarks (professional, non-smokers, and mother aged over 26) to be 1 in 8,543. He then multiplied this figure by itself to reach the probability of two cases of SIDS in the same family. This calculation was challenged on two grounds. Firstly, the probability of one case of SIDS (1 in 8,543) was contested (*Clark-I*: [138]), also with reference being made to another study (the CONI study, *ibid.*). Secondly, and more importantly, Meadow's calculation was flawed because it assumed independence between the two events of death.[18] In other words, Meadow assumed the probability of a second SIDS death to be equal to the probability of a first SIDS death.[19] However, there are numerous potential genetic and environmental reasons why a family which has already experienced SIDS is at higher risk of experiencing (another) SIDS death than a family which has never previously experienced SIDS (e.g. if the parents have certain genes which increase the risk of SIDS).[20] Had the

---

[16] See, for example, the official statement of the Royal Statistical Society, concluding that '[t]he well-publicised figure of 1 in 73 million thus has no statistical basis' (RSS 2001). See also Hill (2004).

[17] See Professor Donnelly's remarks, cited at footnote 9.

[18] Dawid states that 'this calculation is extremely dubious, being based on unrealistic assumptions of independence' (Dawid 2002: 75).

[19] In formal notation, if S1 is the first SIDS death and S2 is the second SIDS death, Meadow assumed that $p(S1) = p(S2 \mid S1) = p(S2 \mid \neg S1)$.

[20] Indeed, research has found a correlation between certain genes and SIDS. See Summers et al. (2000) and, more recently, Dashash et al. (2006).

calculation been accurate, the correct figure would have been less dramatic than 1 in 73 million.[21]

However, it remains questionable how the flaws in Meadow's calculation, serious as they may be, can explain why it was wrong to use the SIDS statistics in *Clark*. On their own, the most that these flaws can establish is that the calculation should have been done more carefully. However, that leaves open both the question of whether the wrongful convictions would have been prevented and the question of whether such statistics, even if calculated correctly, should have been used in *Clark*.

Furthermore, the flaws in Meadow's calculation were known and highlighted not only during the first appeal but also during the actual trial, before the involvement of the expert statisticians. During the trial, the defence referred to Professor Emery's study which showed cases of a second cot death to be more frequent than was argued by Sir Meadow (*Clark-I*: [116]). Professor Berry, one of the defence experts, emphasised the possibility of unknown factors, which further undermined Meadow's assumption of independence (*Clark-I*: [122]), as the court also noted (*Clark-I*: [155]). The jury was also warned by the trial judge that the 73 million figure should be treated with caution (*Clark-I*: [144]) and was reminded that the risks of SIDS were inherently greater in a family which had already experienced SIDS (*Clark-I*: [145]), a warning which undermined the assumption of independence made by Meadow in his calculation. Given that Meadow's calculation was strongly disputed from the outset, it is difficult to accept that the flaws in the calculation were responsible for the wrongful convictions. Therefore, while such calculations should be made more carefully, it is hard to see how the flaws in Meadow's calculation can offer an explanation of why it was wrong to use the SIDS statistics in *Clark*.

3.2 The Psychological Effect of the Statistical Evidence

Another related common explanation of why it was wrong to use the SIDS statistics in *Clark* refers to the psychological effect that the impressive figure of 1 in 73 million might have had on the jurors in Clark's trial or on the judges in the first appeal. According to this explanation, the figure of 1 in 73 million had such a strong psychological impact that it caused the suppression and underappreciation of the nonstatistical evidence that was more favourable to Clark. Stephen Clark, her husband, for instance, commented on the statistics as being 'an arrow through the fog' that gave the jury a compelling case against his wife.[22] According to this explanation, it was wrong to use the SIDS statistics because had they not been used,

---

[21] It was reported in the media that 'the odds are closer to 200 to one' (BBC 2005). See also Wansell (2007). But note that the grounds for this estimation are unclear.

[22] Sweeney and Law (2001). A similar comment was made by Dawid (2002), as cited in footnote 10.

other evidence would have received adequate attention and the wrongful convictions could have been prevented.[23]

However, this explanation relies on the empirical assumption that, when considering statistical evidence, people tend to discount other pieces of nonstatistical evidence which are available. By contrast, several commentators have pointed out that empirical research reveals the exact opposite (Shaviro 1989: 545). For example, the influential psychological experiments conducted by Kahneman and Tversky show that people tend to disregard statistical evidence ('background information') when other specific evidence is also available.[24] This empirical research is particularly relevant to *Clark*, since there, the fact-finder had immensely detailed *specific* evidence to consider, mostly about the pathological findings found in the autopsies.[25] The empirical research may thus suggest that it is unlikely that this specific evidence was suppressed by the general base-rate statistics presented by Meadow. Furthermore, if a hypothetical fact-finder in a similar case to *Clark* were presented with specific evidence which clearly showed a *natural* cause of death, it is difficult to accept that she would be so overwhelmed by the 1 in 73 million figure that she would convict in spite of such specific evidence. If anything, she would be more likely to fail to give this base-rate statistic the weight it deserved.[26] Hence, if there is a concern about the evaluation of the SIDS statistics, it is more likely to involve the unjustified *underweighting* of the statistics than any overwhelming effect.

---

[23] This explanation resonates with a more general point made by Tribe over 35 years ago: '[t]he problem of the overpowering number, that one hard piece of information, is that it may dwarf all efforts to put it into perspective with more impressionistic sorts of evidence' (Tribe 1971a: 1360).

[24] Kahneman and Tversky (1982). For similar findings about various types of circumstantial evidence when used in criminal proceedings, see Heller (2006: 250–252).

[25] For a detailed description of the prosecution's medical evidence, see *Clark-I*: [25]–[33] for Christopher and [50]–[63] for Harry.

[26] To illustrate this, Schoeman suggests the following example (Schoeman 1987: 180–181). A pellet dish was overturned in a rabbit pen. Among its 500 rabbits, only one was brown and the rest were white. A person who was watching the pen says it was the brown rabbit which overturned the pellet dish. Her colour identification ability is tested and found accurate in 95% of cases. On this evidence, what was the colour of the rabbit which overturned the pellet dish? Most people would believe the eyewitness and accept that the colour of the rabbit in question was brown rather than white. However, when the two pieces of evidence are properly combined, the probability of the rabbit's being brown is *only 4%*. If the eyewitness is presented with each of the 500 rabbits, she is very likely to identify the brown rabbit correctly (95%) but also would misidentify 25 white rabbits as brown (because her colour identification has a 5% error rate). Among the 500 rabbits in the pen, about 26 would be identified as brown, though only one of them is really brown. The probability that the rabbit which was identified as brown is indeed brown is therefore around 4% ($1/26 = {\sim}0.04$). The probability that the rabbit which overturned the dish is white *despite* the eyewitness testimony is 96%.

3.3 The Prosecutor's Fallacy

Yet another common attempt to explain why it was wrong to use the SIDS statistics in Clark, one which also refers to the psychological effects of the SIDS statistics, concerns the 'prosecutor's fallacy'.[27] The term 'prosecutor's fallacy' identifies the logical mistake of treating the probability of the occurrence of the available evidence given the innocence of the accused as if it were the probability of innocence given the available evidence.[28] In the first appeal, the defence argued that the probability of two deaths given Clark's innocence was confused with the probability of Clark's innocence given the occurrence of two deaths. The defence alleged that the jury fell prey to the prosecutor's fallacy by understanding the SIDS statistics as showing that the probability of Clark's innocence given these two deaths was 1 in 73 million, instead of understanding them as showing that the probability of two SIDS deaths given Clark's innocence was 1 in 73 million.[29]

However, to the extent that this explanation has strength, it is mainly with regard to the decision of the jury rather than of the judges of the first appeal.[30] In general, judges have more experience in dealing with complex and scientific evidence because such evidence appears in many cases and evaluating it is a frequent task in their day-to-day routine. More importantly, the judges of the first appeal were equipped with the expert opinions of two distinguished statisticians (Professor Phil Dawid and Dr Ian Evett).[31] Therefore, it is hard to accept that the judges of the first

---

[27] Nobles and Schiff (2005). For more about the prosecutor's fallacy, see Balding and Donnelly (1994). Concise explanations may be found in R v Doheny and Adams [1997] 1 Cr App R 369, 372–375 and in the Forensic Science Service's Guide to DNA, 27, accessible at http://www.cps. gov.uk/legal/assets/uploads/files/lawyers'%20dna%20guide%20kswilliams%20190208%20(i). pdf, accessed 22 June 2012.

[28] In a formal notation, where $p(x)$ stands for the probability that the proposition x is true, $p(x \mid y)$ for the probability of x given that proposition y is true, G for the proposition that the accused is guilty (and $\neg$G for the proposition that he is innocent) and E for the occurrence of the evidence, the prosecutor's fallacy means the confusion of $p(E \mid \neg G)$ with $p(\neg G \mid E)$. See also Balding and Donnelly (1994: 718–720).

[29] *Clark-I*: [162]. Interestingly, the court also refers (at [177]) to another known difficulty in using statistical evidence, which relates to the application of base-rate frequencies (indefinite probabilities) to an individual case (definite probabilities). For this difficulty, see Pollock and Cruz (1999: 92–111). They argue that none of the existing theories of probability can support a move from indefinite to definite probabilities.

[30] Yet even with regard to the jury, it is difficult to substantiate the concern that the jury might have fallen prey to the prosecutor's fallacy. See the detailed discussion, including extracts from the actual trial, in the judgment of the first appeal, *Clark-I*: [162]–[184].

[31] The fact that the statisticians were not called to give oral testimony does not mean that the court ignored their expert opinions or was unwilling to engage in the statistical issues at stake. The legal procedure allows expert opinion to be given in either oral or written testimony (Criminal Justice Act 1988 c. 33s. 30(1)). The court in the first appeal was satisfied with the experts' written reports and accepted the defence's point that in the initial trial 'the judge appeared to endorse the prosecution's erroneous approach' (*Clark-I*: [184]). The court therefore defined '[t]he ultimate question' to be 'whether the error of approach rendered the conviction unsafe' (*ibid.*), which is a question of law rather than of statistics, and hence there was no need for oral testimony.

appeal fell prey to the prosecutor's fallacy, especially since they had been warned about it specifically by the expert statisticians (even assuming such a warning was in any way necessary).

3.4 Bayes' Theorem

A further explanation for why it was wrong to use the SIDS statistics in *Clark* considers the courts' refusal to use Bayes' Theorem. Bayes' Theorem is a mathematical formula that aims to instruct an agent on how to rationally alter his or her initial (prior) probability in light of new evidence.[32] Several eminent statisticians support using Bayes' Theorem in situations where the jury faces both statistical and nonstatistical evidence.[33] It could be argued that it was wrong to use the SIDS statistics in *Clark* because the figure was adduced on its own. Instead, Bayes' Theorem should have been used to combine the statistical evidence with the nonstatistical evidence and to assess accurately the probability of Clark's guilt given all the available evidence.[34] It should be emphasised that such an explanation does not imply that using the SIDS statistics in *Clark* was wrong in principle. On the contrary, such critics tend to be sympathetic to the use of statistical evidence in court, as long as it is used correctly,[35] which means, *inter alia*, using Bayes' Theorem.[36]

---

[32] A good introduction to Bayes' Theorem can be found in Dawid (2002: 72–78), Fairley and Finkelstein (1970: 498–501), and Roberts and Zuckerman (2010: 153–159).

[33] In an unprecedented attempt, Professor Donnelly was allowed to take a jury through the application of Bayes' Theorem to determine the accused's guilt (R v Adams (No 1) [1996] 2 Cr App R 467, hereafter *Adams-I*). The Court of Appeal responded to this attempt by noting that 'to introduce Bayes' Theorem, or any similar method, into a criminal trial plunges the jury into inappropriate and unnecessary realms of theory and complexity deflecting them from their proper task' (*Adams-I*: 482). This unprecedented attempt proliferated scholarly debate on the issue, a summary of which can be found in Roberts and Zuckerman (2010: 153–163).

[34] Dawid, for example, holds that in order to incorporate the SIDS statistics into the body of other available evidence, '[i]t is necessary to make an assessment (formal or informal) of the probability of observing the medical evidence, under each of the two causes under consideration' (Dawid 2001: §21). He then concludes that '[e]ven though assessment of the relevant probabilities may be difficult, there is a clear and well established statistical logic for combining them and making appropriate inferences from them, which was not appreciated by the court' (Dawid 2001: Conclusion).

[35] Dawid even compares the current legal approach to statistics to the state of science before Galileo: '[t]he current state of legal analysis of evidence seems to me similar to that of science before Galileo, in thrall to the authority of Aristotle and loth to concede the need to break away from old habits of thought. Galileo had the revolutionary idea that scientists should actually look at how the world behaves. It may be equally revolutionary to suggest that lawyers might look at how others have approached the problem of interpretation of evidence, and that they might even have something to learn from them' (Dawid 2002: 71–72).

[36] See the sources at footnotes 33 and 34.

However, any explanation that refers to Bayes' Theorem faces various difficulties, most evidently the need to quantify the numerous pieces of complex medical evidence into precise probabilities. Furthermore, the legal literature has noted several general difficulties in applying Bayes' Theorem in criminal courts, and the question of whether this statistical method should be used in court is probably one of the most debated issues in the theory of evidence law.[37] It is worth mentioning some of the main difficulties in simplified form. Firstly, Bayes' Theorem requires an assignment of prior probability of guilt, before any evidence is introduced ($p(G)$). However, it is questionable how assigning prior probability of guilt could be consistent with the presumption of innocence.[38] Secondly, it is questionable whether jurors, lawyers, and judges, all of whom usually lack any statistical training, would be able to deploy this method accurately.[39] Thirdly, once the calculation has produced a figure, it is contentious as to whether and how this figure could or should be translated into a guilty/not-guilty verdict (Nesson 1985).

Given these difficulties in quantifying the complex medical evidence and in applying Bayes' Theorem in court, it is far from clear that using Bayes' Theorem would have assisted the administration of justice to avoid the wrongful convictions. While the applicability of Bayes' Theorem in court remains an important theoretical question, it is hard to see how the courts' refusal to use Bayes' Theorem can explain why it was wrong to use the SIDS statistics in *Clark*.

3.5 The Insignificance of the SIDS Statistics

All four explanations seem to assume, either explicitly or implicitly, that the use of the SIDS statistics in *Clark* was wrong because it was responsible, at least in part, for the wrongful convictions.[40] They mainly diverge on the details of exactly how the SIDS statistics led to the wrongful convictions: by exaggerating the rarity of two SIDS deaths in one family, by creating a psychological effect that overshadowed other exonerating evidence, by inducing the prosecutor's fallacy or by requiring the use of Bayes' Theorem, a method which the courts refused to adopt. However, all these common explanations seem to share the assumption that had the SIDS statistics been used correctly, or had they not been used at all, the wrongful convictions could have been prevented.

---

[37] For a good summary of this intensive and extensive debate, see Roberts and Zuckerman (2010: 153–159). In particular, in a controversial and challenging book, Cohen has provided six paradoxes which challenge the applicability of the mathematical theory of probability to the legal context (Cohen 1977).

[38] Tribe (1971a). Cohen also argues that giving the presumption of innocence its true meaning by assigning $p(G) = 0$ will render the formula useless (Cohen 1977: 107–109).

[39] This concern receives empirical support from the work of Kahneman and Tversky (1980).

[40] Remarks in that vein can be found both in the public media (see e.g. footnotes 7 and 8) and among the expert statisticians (see e.g. footnotes 9 and 10).

Contrary to this shared assumption, it is argued here that the role of the SIDS statistics in *Clark* is much overrated. Firstly, the prosecution had a strong case even without the SIDS statistics. In the *weaker* case of Christopher, the prosecution pointed to bruises, the torn frenulum and fresh bleeding in the lungs. The defence challenged the existence of each of these pieces of evidence, and they received thorough and repeated scrutiny both during the long trial and in the lengthy decision of the first appeal. Yet it is worthwhile to note that each of the defence medical experts 'agreed that if there was bruising, the injury to the frenulum and bleeding in the lungs, it suggested asphyxia' (*Clark-I*: [40]). The prosecution case about Christopher did not hinge on a single piece of medical evidence, while the evidence relating to Harry was even more worrying.[41] Even if the defence were successful in establishing a reasonable doubt about one of the pieces of evidence, the cumulative weight of these pieces of evidence was probably (and should have been) higher than the sum of its parts. It is therefore questionable whether using the SIDS statistics correctly, or not using them at all, would have, or should have, changed either the jury's decision to convict or the first appeal's decision to uphold the convictions. Given that the microbiological results which led to Clark's release were not yet known at that stage, the convictions would probably have been reached by the jury and upheld by the court in the first appeal, with or without the SIDS statistics.

Secondly, the SIDS statistics were inessential to the prosecution case, since the defence experts accepted the very fact that this evidence was adduced to prove: that SIDS was not the cause of death. This was most evident in Harry's case. Dr Whitwell, for the defence, testified that '[s]he would not classify this a SIDS death because a true SIDS death should be completely negative and would not normally occur at this time in the evening, after a feed, with the child in a bouncy chair' (*Clark-I*: [77]). Dr Rushton, also for the defence, went even further and 'agreed that there were features in both deaths that gave rise to very great concern and for that reason he would not class them as SIDS deaths' (*ibid.*). Little wonder that, when considering the fallacies of Meadow's statistics, the court concluded that:

> [The statistical evidence] was very much a side-show at trial. The experts were debating the incidence of genuine SIDS (unexplained deaths with no suspicious circumstances) in a case where both sides agreed that neither Christopher's death nor Harry's death qualified as such.[42]

---

[41] See a summary in *Clark-I*: [8] and a detailed description in *Clark-I*: [50]–[63].

[42] *Clark-I*: [142]. The defence experts' surprising concession that the deaths were not SIDS may be explained by a subtle yet crucial difference between how the experts used the term 'SIDS' and how the court used it. SIDS is defined as 'the sudden death of a baby that is unexpected by history and in whom a thorough necropsy examination fails to demonstrate an adequate cause of death' (*Clark-I*: [104]), and the court rightly noted that '[c]learly the accuracy of that definition depends on the pathologists' thoroughness in autopsy, and on his or her interpretation of the findings' (*Clark-I*: [105]). However, the first appeal also referred to SIDS as a basket classification for all unexplained natural deaths (including cases where the autopsy was insufficiently thorough). For example, when discussing the SIDS statistics, the court referred to SIDS as 'unexplained deaths with no suspicious circumstances' (*Clark-I*: [142]; another example appears at [170]). Perhaps this subtle difference in definition caused the court to misinterpret the defence experts as accepting that the babies' deaths could not be classified as 'unexplained deaths with no suspicious circumstances', while the defence experts probably agreed that the babies' deaths could not be classified as SIDS because of their concerns about the thoroughness of the autopsies.

4   The Contrastive Explanation

Having considered and rejected the existing common explanations of why it was wrong to use the SIDS statistics in *Clark*, this part proposes an alternative explanation. It is argued here that it was wrong in principle to use the SIDS statistics, regardless of their actual share in the responsibility for the wrongful convictions. The explanation here is also not connected to concerns regarding the correct use and presentation of statistics, which have been raised in relation to *Clark* and have been discussed more generally in the academic literature.[43] While objections to the use of statistical evidence which are based on such concerns are important, they are nevertheless practical in nature and may be overcome by better education and training of the legal profession[44] and/or by more assistance from expert statisticians.[45] Such concerns should be distinguished from the position that the use of the SIDS statistics in *Clark* was wrong in principle, which is what the following section seeks to establish.

The most appropriate point to begin is the way in which the expert statisticians in *Clark* thought the SIDS statistics *should have been used*. Consider the testimony of Professor Dawid, one of the two expert statisticians for the defence, who states that:

> The laws of probability now focus attention on, not the absolute values of these probabilities of the two deaths in one family arising from the different causes considered, but on their **relative** values.[46]

He then concludes that:

> [The probability of two SIDS deaths in the same family] could only be useful if compared with a similar figure calculated under the alternative hypothesis that both babies were murdered.[47]

---

[43] See, for example, the exchange between Tribe and Fairley and Finkelstein about the correct statistical analysis of an example brought by Fairley and Finkelstein (1970), Tribe (1971a, b), and Fairley and Finkelstein (1971).

[44] Various scholars have rightly called for such training. See, for example, Koehler (1992: 148–149).

[45] Dawid, for example, states that 'statisticians   have much to contribute towards identifying and clarifying many delicate issues in the interpretation of legal evidence' (Dawid 2002: 71–72). Dawid refers to both statistical and nonstatistical evidence. These remarks resonate with similar suggestions made decades ago in the United States. See, for example, Good (1950: 66–67) and Fairley and Finkelstein (1970: 502, 516–517). See also the official statement of the Royal Statistical Society (footnote 16).

[46] Dawid (2001: §18), emphasis original. This view is repeated in Dawid (2002: 76).

[47] Dawid (2001: Conclusion). It should be noted that Dawid's reference to 'murder' is mistaken and a more accurate category should have been used instead, such as 'causing the death'. 'Murder' is inaccurate because it assumes that all the material facts of the offence were proven beyond reasonable doubt and that no criminal defence was applicable. However, the SIDS statistics were brought to prove a specific material fact in the actus reus, namely, the fact of causation, and therefore, they should have been compared with the probability that it was the accused's conduct which caused the babies' deaths. Many cases which would not fit into the category of 'murder' would still fit into the category of 'causing the death' (e.g. cases in which the accused was insane or did not have the intent to cause the death).

To some extent, Dawid's conclusion already includes an objection to the use of the SIDS statistics. According to this objection, the absolute probability that the deaths occurred for innocent reasons (the first hypothesis) is meaningless on its own. It does not matter how likely or unlikely it is that the deaths occurred for innocent reasons. All that matters is how low (or high) this probability is *relative to the probability that the events occurred for culpable reasons* (the second hypothesis). Even if the probability of two SIDS deaths is strikingly small, all that matters is how it stands relative to the probability that a mother would murder both her babies, which was estimated by Dawid to be about 1 in 2 billion.[48] As this probability is much lower than the probability of two SIDS deaths, the SIDS statistics actually support Clark's *innocence*.[49] In addition to his criticism of Meadow's amateur calculation, Dawid's main point is that discussing the probability of two SIDS deaths in one family without referring to the alternative hypothesis is meaningless and misleading.[50]

In the first appeal, the court dismissed the exercise of comparing the probabilities of the two hypotheses as 'not realistic' and rejected any suggestion of estimating the probability of the second hypothesis (*Clark-I*: [176]). This dismissal was too quick. The probability of the first hypothesis (two SIDS deaths), as given by Meadow, was accepted by the court in the first appeal, after it had concluded unequivocally that this evidence was 'clearly relevant and admissible' (*Clark-I*: [166]). So why was it unrealistic to consider the probability of the second hypothesis (two murders)? The difference between the two pieces of evidence cannot lie in a lack of information, because Dawid's expert report offered preliminary statistical evidence for the second hypothesis.[51] Nor can the difference lie in a lack of statistical expertise, because the court in the first appeal was equipped with the expert opinions of two experienced statisticians, Professor Dawid and Dr Evett. Lastly, the difference

---

[48] Dawid, in his expert opinion, states the figure of 2,152,224,291 (Dawid 2001: §16), though he cautions that this is merely illustrative figure and 'its realistic estimation would be subject to all the caveats and cautions that have already been sounded above for the case of estimating the probability of two deaths from SIDS' (Dawid 2001: §17).

[49] Dawid (2001: §21). However, Dawid's preliminary calculation does not take into account at least two important factors. Since not all perpetrators are caught, indicted, and convicted, the recorded number of murders, on which Dawid's preliminary calculation is based, might be significantly smaller than its actual number. As a result, the actual probability of murder might be significantly higher than what Dawid's preliminary calculation shows. However, there is another neglected factor in his calculation, one which pushes the probability in the opposite direction. The prosecution is required to prove a specific unnatural cause of death (e.g. smothering, shaking, knifing). In contrast, Dawid's tentative suggestion that the probability of a mother murdering her two babies is about 1 in 2 billion refers to the *generic* unnatural cause of murder (i.e. it lumps together cases of different unnatural causes). If the court were to compare probabilities, the SIDS probability should be compared with the probability of a mother murdering her two babies *by smothering them*. This probability is probably much lower than the probability of murder to which Dawid refers.

[50] See also the warning given by the Royal Statistical Society, according to which '[a]side from its invalidity, figures such as the 1 in 73 million are very easily misinterpreted' (RSS 2001).

[51] Dawid (2001: §16), but see the reservations at footnotes 47 and 49.

cannot lie in a general antagonism to statistics.[52] Such an antagonism would apply equally to the SIDS statistics, which the court readily admitted. The approach of the court in the first appeal is therefore hard to understand or defend.

In the second appeal, the court reached a different conclusion, according to which the SIDS statistics probably should not have been admitted.[53] However, the court did not offer any explanation of why the first appeal's ruling regarding the admissibility of the SIDS statistics should be reversed. Nor did the court in the second appeal give its reasons for concluding that the SIDS statistics should not have been admitted. No guidance was provided for distinguishing this piece of statistical evidence from other kinds of statistical evidence which are regularly used in court (e.g. DNA evidence). The inconsistency between the two decisions and the lack of judicial reasoning in the second appeal demonstrate the need for a principled approach to the use of statistical evidence in court. Developing such a general approach requires a separate and extensive research project,[54] and thus it is beyond the scope of this chapter. However, the following explanation for why it was wrong in principle to use the SIDS statistics in *Clark* can be applied to other similar cases, and thus this case study of *Clark* is concluded with a more general recommendation.

The starting point of the proposed explanation is the issue of competing hypotheses, to which the expert statisticians drew attention. Competing hypotheses are central to the theory of legal fact-finding.[55] One context in which competing hypotheses are particularly important is that of determining the role of causal explanations in legal fact-finding. The importance of explanatory aspects of legal fact-finding has recently been highlighted by Allen and Pardo in their discussion of the theory of inference to the best explanation and its application to evidence law (Allen and Pardo 2008). A related theory, one which can shed light on the way the SIDS statistics were used to prove the material fact of causation, is the theory of *contrastive explanation* (van Fraassen 1980: 97–157; Lipton 1990).

The theory of contrastive explanation can be described as follows. The idea, in outline, is that most, if not all, requests for explanation ('why' questions) contain a contrast: instead of understanding the request as 'why P', the theory of contrastive explanation suggests understanding such questions as 'why P *and not Q*'. To borrow Lipton's terminology, 'why' questions contrast between facts and foils.[56] Sometimes the contrast is explicit: 'why did you order cheese quiche rather than

---

[52] See also Posner's criticism of the legal profession for its 'prevalent (and disgraceful) math-block' (Posner 1987: 778).

[53] 'If there had been a challenge to the admissibility of the evidence we would have thought that the wisest course would have been to exclude it altogether' (*Clark-II*: [177]).

[54] I began outlining such a general approach in Pundik (2009), and I intend to develop it further as part of my current research project, titled 'Generalizations in the Law'.

[55] See, in general, Kaye (1992), Robertson and Vignaux (1993) and Allen (1986). The issue of competing hypotheses also arises in the context of the story model. See Pennington and Hastie (1992) and Twining (2006).

[56] Lipton (1990: 249–252). For a more elaborated version of his fact/foil distinction, see Lipton (2004: 30–37).

beef lasagne?' Here the foil (beef lasagne) is stated explicitly as part of the question. However, the theory of contrastive explanation argues that often (if not always)[57] the contrast is implicit. For example, when someone asks 'why did the mercury in the barometer go up before the storm?', the implicit contrast is 'why did it go up *rather than stay where it is*', and not 'why did it go up rather than break the glass'.[58] If someone answered the question with a detailed explanation of the rigidity of the glass,[59] we would consider this explanation to be irrelevant and inadequate.[60]

Exploring the full application of the theory of contrastive explanation to legal fact-finding in general, and to the proof of causation in particular,[61] would probably require yet another separate research project. Nonetheless, in the limited context of analysing the use of the SIDS statistics in *Clark*, this theory can be employed to substantiate the expert statisticians' assertion that the SIDS statistics make sense

---

[57] For the issue of whether all why questions are contrastive, see Lipton (1990: 252–254).

[58] This example is taken from Lipton (1990: 252).

[59] The theory of contrastive explanation thus highlights the importance of the *context* in which the explanation is sought. Whether something counts as a *good* explanation depends on the context in which the question is asked (*ibid.*). If the question about the mercury rising is asked in a chemistry class about the qualities of glass, then the rigidity of the glass might be a good explanation. Thus to determine whether the answer constitutes a *good* explanation, we first need to know the context in which the question was put.

[60] Van Fraassen further suggests that a why question, a request for explanation, has three elements (van Fraassen 1980: 141–142). Firstly, it has a *topic*, which is the subject of the why question, the element that requires an explanation. For example, the topic of the question 'why did the mercury in the barometer go up' is the fact that the mercury went up. This is what the question assumes to be true. Secondly, the question has a *contrast class*, a group of propositions about the topic. For example, 'if the question is "why does this material burn yellow" the contrast-class could be the set of propositions: this material burned (with a flame of) colour *x*' (van Fraassen 1980: 142). The third element is *explanatory relevance*, which is determined by what is already known and what further information is required. For example, if it is already known that mercury in barometers goes up before storms (for instance, in the context of a discussion between weather forecasting experts), then reiterating what is already known will be irrelevant. In such a context, only answers that add new information will bear explanatory relevance (for instance, answers about the cause of the storm). Van Fraassen also suggests that an answer to a why question takes the form of *the preferred contrast* and not *the other contrasts* because of *the answer* (van Fraassen 1980: 144–145). For example, the mercury in the barometer went up (the preferred contrast) and did not stay where it was (the other contrast) because of the low air pressure that precedes storms (the answer). The answer includes what van Fraassen terms *the central presupposition*, which is that only the preferred contrast is true and the other contrasts are false. The question arises only when the background knowledge implies this central presupposition.

[61] Another related version of the theory of contrastive explanation which may yield interesting applications in the legal context is Schaffer's theory of *contrastive causation* (Schaffer 2005). According to Schaffer, it is misleading to construct questions of causation in terms of 'was it C which caused E'. Instead, the causal questions should be understood as having *four* elements: 'was it C rather than C* which caused E rather than E*'. Schaffer's work also includes an application of his theory to the law (Schaffer 2010). At this stage, it suffices merely to note the issue, as engaging with the metaphysics of causation will distract this chapter from its central question.

only if they are compared with the probability that a mother would smother her two babies. The fact-finder in *Clark* sought to answer the question of why the babies died. The contrast class of this why question was constructed from possible causes of death. The prosecution needed to establish that the preferred contrast was unnatural (smothering in this case)[62] rather than being any other contrast of natural causes of death such as SIDS. On its own, the very low probability of SIDS does not provide support for preferring one specific contrast to another. The low probability of SIDS supports the prosecution's preferred contrast only if this probability is low*er* than the probability of the prosecution's preferred contrast (smothering). But this comparative claim can be established only with evidence about the probability of the prosecution's preferred contrast. To support the prosecution's answer to the question of why the two babies died, the SIDS statistics must be accompanied by evidence detailing the rate of mothers smothering both their babies in the population of mothers who are similar to Clark.

The probability of smothering may be referred to either explicitly or implicitly. According to the expert statisticians, this reference should be made explicit: one should use empirical data to calculate the rate of mothers who smother both their babies in the wider population of non-smoking professional mothers aged over 26.[63] One might reject this idea and hold that the fact-finder should not be provided with any evidence of that sort. Yet ample empirical research shows that fact-finders consider explanations of innocence by contrasting them with explanations of guilt, and vice versa, *as a matter of course*.[64] In the absence of empirical data, the fact-finder might resort to general knowledge and common sense at best, or to prejudice and arbitrary guesswork at worst. Therefore, as supported by empirical research, emphasised by the expert statisticians and substantiated by the theory of contrastive explanation, using the SIDS statistics requires the fact-finder to compare, either explicitly or implicitly, the probability of SIDS with the probability that a professional non-smoking mother aged over 26 would smother both her babies on two separate occasions.

Once the need for this comparison is recognised, the reason why using the SIDS statistics in *Clark* was wrong in principle becomes clear. Developing a comprehensive and general account to justify why courts should not use statistical evidence about the rate of similar misconduct in a population similar to the accused is outside the scope of this chapter. Yet it is difficult to underplay the fact that justice systems around the world hardly ever, if at all, use such statistical evidence to convict.[65] While explaining why this is the case is a challenging theoretical question, the

---

[62] Interestingly, it was claimed that the prosecution had changed the allegation from shaking to smothering just before the trial commenced. See Batt (2004: 140).

[63] These three variables (professional, non-smoking and age over 26) were used by Meadow to extract the number of 1 in 73 million. See *Clark-I*: [118], and the empirical data in [121].

[64] See the various empirical studies surveyed in Heller (2006: 261–262).

[65] For descriptive research on the use of statistical evidence in United States courts, together with an attempt to identify patterns of when statistical evidence is used or rejected, see Koehler (2002).

probability of smothering seems a paradigmatic example of statistical evidence of a kind which should *not* be used in court.

Bearing in mind the scope of this chapter, a few preliminary remarks can nevertheless be made as to why evidence about the probability of smothering seems so intuitively objectionable. Using evidence about the rate of smothering among other similar mothers seems objectionable because it is inconsistent with regarding Clark as unique and morally autonomous individual. Using such evidence assumes that she would exhibit the typical behaviour of her peers (professional non-smoker mothers aged over 26). It also presupposes that these characteristics determine, either fully or partly, the individual's behaviour. Without presupposing that such a common determining property is shared between these mothers, it is unclear why this is the relevant group from which an inference to Clark's individual case should be made. Why not refer to mothers in general, parents of both genders, people whose last name starts with C and so on? The choice of this particular group as relevant to Clark's individual case thus implies that the members of this group share a property which affects their behaviour.[66] The guilt of an individual should be proved based on the particular facts of her case rather than on the rate of similar misconduct among other people with similar characteristics to hers.[67] These remarks are necessarily preliminary. But the main point is that evidence regarding the probability of smothering is clearly objectionable, even if it is difficult to account for why this is so.

5   Conclusion

This chapter has questioned whether it was wrong to use the SIDS statistics in *Clark*, and if so, why. Four common explanations were discussed and rejected. The first explanation refers to the flaws in Meadow's calculation of the 1 in 73 million figure. Yet, however serious these flaws are, it is difficult to accept that they can explain why it was wrong to use the SIDS statistics in *Clark*. The second explanation raises the suspicion that the SIDS statistics had an overwhelming psychological

---

[66] This point is linked to the problem of the reference class. Some legal scholars argue that relying on reference classes in legal fact-finding is problematic (e.g. Colyvan et al. 2001; Allen and Pardo 2007). However, these objections are unpersuasive, mainly because the use of *any* generalisation requires reliance on a reference class, so if there were something inherently wrong with relying on reference classes, the entire enterprise of legal fact-finding would become impossible. The point made in the text above is based on a different type of reference class argument: it assumes that the *choice* of one reference class over other alternative reference classes must be made for a reason. In the context of determining the individual's behaviour, it suggests that this reason is related to *causation*, namely, that the individual members of the reference class share something that causes them to behave in a similar way.

[67] It could be argued that this objection applies to any evidence rather than to statistical evidence alone because such generalisations are used in inferences from any type of evidence. This is an important objection, which is discussed and rejected in Pundik (2008: 312–315).

effect, which overshadowed other evidence more favourable to Clark. However, if there is a concern about the weight given to the SIDS statistics, it is more likely to be a concern of underweighting rather than overweighting. The third explanation focuses on the 'prosecutor's fallacy', yet it is hard to substantiate the concern that the court fell prey to this fallacy, especially given it was specifically warned about it by the expert statisticians. The last explanation considers the courts' refusal to use Bayes' Theorem. However, the difficulties with quantifying the complex medical evidence and applying this statistical method in court make explanations which hinge on it difficult to sustain.

A more general difficulty with all four explanations is that the connection between the SIDS statistics and the wrongful convictions is hard to sustain. The role of this evidence in *Clark* is much overrated, since the prosecution case was strong without the SIDS statistics. Furthermore, even the defence experts agreed that the deaths should not be categorised as SIDS, making the SIDS statistics inessential for the prosecution case. It is therefore difficult to accept that the wrongful convictions could have been prevented had the SIDS statistics been used correctly, or even had they not been used at all.

However, the question still remains whether it was wrong in principle to use the SIDS statistics in *Clark*, and if so, why. This chapter has argued that even if the issues identified by the existing explanations were properly addressed, it would still have been wrong *in principle* to use the SIDS statistics in *Clark*. This position is based on the theory of contrastive explanation. Its application to *Clark* begins with a similar point to that of the expert statisticians, namely, that the SIDS probability makes sense only when it is compared with the smothering probability. However, unlike the expert statisticians' approach, the theory of contrastive explanation does not require any commitment to Bayesian methods in order to reach this point. This is an advantage because Bayesian methods were explicitly rejected by the English Court of Appeals for '[plunging] the jury into inappropriate and unnecessary realms of theory and complexity deflecting them from their proper tasks' (*Adams-I*: 482).

Yet the main difference between the approach of this chapter and that of the expert statisticians lies in the conclusion. The expert statisticians' approach would require the application of Bayes' Theorem in order to make sense of the SIDS statistics, because using this method is 'the only logically sound and consistent approach to considering situations such as this'.[68] Their position thus implies that in order to make sense of the SIDS statistics, it would be necessary to use Bayes' Theorem and thus also necessary to adduce further statistical evidence to assess the probability that a mother similar to Clark would smother both her babies.

This chapter, by contrast, has reached a different conclusion. The problem with the use of statistical evidence in *Clark* was more fundamental than merely a flaw in the statistical analysis. The SIDS statistics should not have been used, for

---

[68] The phrase is taken from Professor Donnelly's response in *Adams*, after he was asked whether both the statistical and nonstatistical evidence could be evaluated in 'statistical terms' (namely, using Bayes' Theorem) (*Adams-I*: 471).

they would have required the use of another piece of evidence which is clearly objectionable: statistical evidence on the rate of smothering. If one piece of evidence cannot be used without another piece of objectionable evidence, then neither of them should be used. Regardless of whether the exercise of comparing probabilities of SIDS and smothering is 'realistic' or not, it should not be conducted as part of a criminal proceeding.

This chapter has focused on only a single case study, and hence any attempt to generalise from *Clark* to the wider issue of the use of statistical evidence in court should be made with caution. However, perhaps there is one lesson from *Clark* that can be phrased in more general terms. It is sometimes tempting to ask how likely it is that a given unusual event (e.g. two baby deaths in one family) will happen randomly, by accident, naturally, or for any other non-culpatory cause. If the event in question happens so rarely in the course of nature, this fact alone seems to provide evidential support for the hypothesis that the event must have happened as a result of deliberate human intervention, namely, the accused's misconduct. However, *Clark* alerts us to the fact that this type of inference is problematic, because the natural/random/non-culpatory causal explanation must be contrasted with a culpatory one. Using statistical evidence on the rate of a certain non-culpatory cause would thus require also using statistical evidence on the rate of the type of criminal behaviour attributed to the accused among other people similar to him or her.[69]

There may be contexts in which it would be appropriate to refer to the probability of an unusual event happening naturally and to use statistical evidence and methods to calculate this probability. For example, in the decision whether to equip parents with an apnoea monitor which detects pauses in breathing in young babies,[70] it may be wise to consider the probability of SIDS among families with similar characteristics. However, when the same question arises in the context of determining whether an individual is guilty of an alleged crime, using this kind of evidence becomes problematic. Since statistical evidence regarding the rate of misconduct among other people similar to the accused should not be used to determine the accused's guilt, the same goes for statistical evidence regarding the probability of non-culpatory causes. No doubt the use of statistical evidence in court is a complex issue, and the same logic would not necessarily apply

---

[69] Another case which illustrates the temptation to prove the fact of causation with statistical evidence is *Veysey*, in which the defendant was charged with arson and insurance fraud after his house was burnt down for the fourth time. See *United States v Veysey* 334F 3d 600 (7th Cir 2003). The conviction was based in part on an actuary's testimony according to which 'the probability of four residential fires occurring by chance during the 106 months between April 1989 (when Veysey bought the first house that he is known to have set fire to) and January 1998 (when he set fire to his last house) was only one in 1.773 trillion' (*ibid.*: [8]). It seems that the same objection against the use of the SIDS statistics in *Clark* would apply to the use of statistical evidence in *Veysey*.

[70] After the death of Christopher, the Care of Next Infant programme provided the Clarks with an apnoea monitor (*Clark-I*: [43]).

to statistical evidence used to prove other facts (such as identification proven with DNA evidence) or to statistical evidence used in noncriminal proceedings. However, this case study of the use of statistics in *Clark* exemplifies the following general point. Statistical evidence on the probability of non-culpatory causes should not be used in criminal courts to prove the material fact of causation. Before delving into the technical complexities of how to gather, analyse and present statistical evidence which shows the exact value of such probabilities, one should first ensure that raising the question of probabilities (and using statistical evidence to answer it) is appropriate in the given context. At least when determining an individual's guilt, it seems rather that it is not.

References

Allen, R. J. (1986). A reconceptualization of civil trials. *Boston University Law Review, 66*, 401–437.

Allen, R. J., & Pardo, M. S. (2007). The problematic value of mathematical models of evidence. *The Journal of Legal Studies, 36*(1), 107–140.

Allen, R. J., & Pardo, M. S. (2008). Juridical proof and the best explanation. *Law and Philosophy, 27*(3), 223–268.

Balding, D., & Donnelly, P. (1994). The prosecutor's fallacy and DNA evidence. *The Criminal Law Review, 10*, 711–721.

Barraclough, K. (2004). Stolen innocence: A mother's fight for justice—The story of Sally Clark (book review). *British Medical Journal, 329*, 177.

Batt, J. (2004). *Stolen innocence*. London: Random House.

BBC. (2005). *Cot death expert defends evidence*. http://news.bbc.co.uk/1/hi/health/4641587.stm. Accessed 22 June 2012.

BBC. (2007). *Alcohol killed mother Sally Clark*. http://news.bbc.co.uk/2/hi/uk_news/england/essex/7082411.stm. Accessed 22 June 2012.

Blom-Cooper, L. (2006). *Disciplining expert witnesses by regulatory bodies. Public Law, Spring*, 3–5.

Cohen, L. J. (1977). *The probable and the provable* (Clarendon library of logic and philosophy). Oxford: Clarendon.

Colyvan, M., Regan, H. M., & Ferson, S. (2001). Is it a crime to belong to a reference class? *The Journal of Political Philosophy, 9*(2), 168–181.

Dashash, M., Pravica, V., Hutchinson, I., Barson, A., & Drucker, D. (2006). Association of sudden infant death syndrome with VEGF and IL-6 gene polymorphisms. *Human Immunology, 67*(8), 627–633.

Dawid, A. P. (2001). *Expert report for Sally Clark appeal*. http://www.statslab.cam.ac.uk/~apd/SallyClark_report.doc. Accessed 16 June 2012.

Dawid, A. P. (2002). Bayes's theorem and the weighing evidence by juries. *Proceedings of the British Academy, 113*, 71–90.

Donnelly, P. (2005). *How juries are fooled by statistics*. http://www.ted.com/index.php/talks/view/id/67. Accessed 22 June 2012.

Dwyer, D. (2003). The duties of expert witnesses of fact and opinion: *R v Clark (Sally)* (Case Note). *International Journal of Evidence and Proof, 7*, 264–269.

Editorial. (2000). Conviction by mathematical error? Doctors and lawyers should get probability theory right. *British Medical Journal, 320*, 2–3.

Fairley, W. B., & Finkelstein, M. O. (1970). A Bayesian approach to identification evidence. *Harvard Law Review, 83*(3), 489–517.

Fairley, W. B., & Finkelstein, M. O. (1971). The continuing debate over mathematics in the law of evidence: A comment on "trial by mathematics". *Harvard Law Review, 84*(8), 1801–1809.

Good, I. J. (1950). *Probability and the weighing of evidence*. London: C Griffin.

Heller, K. J. (2006). The cognitive psychology of circumstantial evidence. *Michigan Law Review, 105*, 241–305.

Hill, R. (2004). Multiple sudden infant deaths – Coincidence or beyond coincidence? *Paediatric and Perinatal Epidemiology, 18*(5), 320–326.

Kahneman, D., & Tversky, A. (1980). Causal schemas in judgment under uncertainty. In M. Fishbein (Ed.), *Progress in social psychology* (Vol. 1, pp. 49–72). Hillsdale: Erlbaum.

Kahneman, D., & Tversky, A. (1982). Evidential impact of base rates. In D. Kahneman, P. Slovic, & A. Tversky (Eds.), *Judgment under uncertainty: Heuristic and biases* (pp. 153–160). Cambridge: Cambridge University Press.

Kaye, D. H. (1992). Proof in law and science. *Jurimetrics Journal, 32*, 313–322.

Koehler, J. J. (1992). The probity/policy distinction in the statistical evidence debate. *Tulane Law Review, 66*, 141–150.

Koehler, J. J. (2002). When do courts think base rate statistics are relevant? *Jurimetrics Journal, 42*, 373–402.

Lipton, P. (1990). Contrastive explanation. In D. Knowles (Ed.), *Explanation and its limits* (pp. 247–266). Cambridge: Cambridge University Press.

Lipton, P. (2004). *Inference to the best explanation* (International library of philosophy 2nd edn.). London: Routledge.

Nesson, C. (1985). The evidence or the event? On judicial proof and the acceptability of verdicts. *Harvard Law Review, 98*(7), 1357–1392.

Nobles, R., & Schiff, D. (2005). Misleading statistics within criminal trials – The Sally Clark case. *Significance, 2*(1), 17–19.

Pennington, N., & Hastie, R. (1992). A cognitive theory of juror decision making: The story model. *Cardozo Law Review, 13*, 519–557.

Pollock, J. L., & Cruz, J. (1999). *Contemporary theories of knowledge* (2nd edn.). Oxford: Rowman & Littlefield.

Posner, R. A. (1987). The decline of law as an autonomous discipline: 1962–1987. *Harvard Law Review, 100*(4), 761–780.

Pundik, A. (2008). Statistical evidence and individual litigants: A reconsideration of Wasserman's argument from autonomy. *International Journal of Evidence and Proof, 12*, 303–324.

Pundik, A. (2009). *Statistical evidence: In a search of a principle*. DPhil thesis, University of Oxford.

R v Adams (No 1) [1996] 2 Cr App R 467.

R v Clark (No 1) [2000] EWCA Crim 54.

R v Clark (Crown Court Chester 9 November 1999).

R v Clark (No 2) [2003] EWCA Crim 1020.

R v Doheny and Adams [1997] 1 Cr App R 369.

Roberts, P., & Zuckerman, A. A. S. (2010). *Criminal evidence* (2nd edn.). Oxford: Oxford University Press.

Robertson, B., & Vignaux, G. A. (1993). Probability—The logic of the law. *Oxford Journal of Legal Studies, 13*, 457–478.

RSS. (2001). *Press release on the Sally Clark case, Oct 2001*. http://www.rss.org.uk/uploadedfiles/documentlibrary/348.doc. Accessed 22 June 2012.

Schaffer, J. (2005). Contrastive causation. *Philosophical Review, 114*(3), 297–328.

Schaffer, J. (2010). Contrastive causation in the law. *Legal Theory, 16*, 259–297.

Schoeman, F. (1987). Statistical vs. direct evidence. *Nous, 21*(2), 179–198.

Shaikh, T. (2007). *Sally Clark, mother wrongly convicted of killing her sons, found dead at home*. http://www.guardian.co.uk/society/2007/mar/17/childrensservices.uknews. Accessed 22 June 2012.

Shaviro, D. (1989). Statistical-probability evidence and the appearance of justice. *Harvard Law Review, 103*(2), 530–554.

Summers, A. M., Summers, C. W., Drucker, D. B., Hajeer, A. H., Barson, A., & Hutchinson, I. V. (2000). Association of IL-10 genotype with sudden infant death syndrome. *Human Immunology, 61*(12), 1270–1273.

Sweeney, J., & Law, B. (2001). *Gene find casts doubt on double "cot death" murders.* http://www.guardian.co.uk/uk/2001/jul/15/johnsweeney.theobserver. Accessed 22 June 2012.

Telegraph. (2007). *Obituary: Sally Clark.* http://www.telegraph.co.uk/news/obituaries/1545933/Sally-Clark.html. Accessed 22 June 2012.

Tribe, L. H. (1971a). A further critique of mathematical proof. *Harvard Law Review, 84*(8), 1810–1820.

Tribe, L. H. (1971b). Trial by mathematics: Precision and ritual in the legal process. *Harvard Law Review, 84*(6), 1329–1393.

Twining, W. (2006). Narrative and generalizations in argumentation about questions of fact. In *Rethinking evidence: Exploratory essays* (2nd edn.). Cambridge: Cambridge University Press.

United States v Veysey 334F 3d 600 (7th Cir 2003).

van Fraassen, B. C. (1980). *The scientific image* (Clarendon library of logic and philosophy). Oxford: Clarendon.

Wansell, G. (2007, 18 March). Whatever the coroner may say, Sally Clark died of a broken heart. *The Independent.*

Wilson, A. (2005). Expert testimony in the dock. *Journal of Criminal Law, 69*(4), 330–348.

Part III
Modeling Rational Agents

A Bayesian Simulation Model of Group Deliberation and Polarization

Erik J. Olsson

Abstract This chapter describes a simulation environment for epistemic interaction based on a Bayesian model called Laputa. An interpretation of the model is proposed under which the exchanges taking place between inquirers are argumentative. The model, under this interpretation, is seen to survive the polarization test: If initially disposed to judge along the same lines, inquirers in Laputa will adopt a more extreme position in the same direction as the effect of group deliberation, just like members of real argumentative bodies. Our model allows us to study what happens to mutual trust in the polarization process. We observe that inquirers become increasingly trusting which creates a snowball effect. We also study conditions under which inquirers will diverge and adopt contrary positions. To the extent that Bayesian reasoning is normatively correct, the bottom line is that polarization and divergence are not necessarily the result of mere irrational "group think" but that even ideally rational inquirers will predictably polarize or diverge under realistic conditions. The concluding section comments on the relation between the present model and the influential and empirically robust Persuasive Argument Theory (PAT), and it is argued that the former is essentially subsumable under the latter.

1 Introduction

There has been a lot of experimental work in social psychology of group deliberation and some striking results as well (for an overview of early work, see Isenberg 1986). However, there does not seem to be much work focusing on computer

E.J. Olsson (✉)
Department of Philosophy, Lund University, Lund, Sweden
e-mail: Erik_J.Olsson@fil.lu.se

F. Zenker (ed.), *Bayesian Argumentation: The practical side of probability*,
Synthese Library 362, DOI 10.1007/978-94-007-5357-0_6,
© Springer Science+Business Media Dordrecht 2013

simulation of deliberative processes taking the role of argumentation seriously.[1] This is unlike many other areas studying complex systems, including economics, where simulation models abound. It is easy to understand why they are found to be so useful: The speed at which a computer simulation can be carried out should be compared with the sometimes many months required for meticulously planning and executing a controlled experiment, and, moreover, computer simulations allow for precise control for parameters that can be extremely difficult to control for in real experiments. This increased speed and control is gained, obviously, at the expense of realism because simulation models need to be idealized in order to be computationally workable. Laboratory experimentation and computer simulation are therefore complementary activities.

This chapter contributes to the study of simulation models of group deliberation with the aim of expanding the methodological toolkit available to researchers studying argumentation in a social setting. The model, called Laputa, allows for studying not only the dynamics of belief but also of trust, including mutual trust among inquirers. Laputa was developed by Staffan Angere and the author, with Angere being the main originator and also the programmer behind the simulation environment with the same name. The plan of this chapter is as follows: In Sect. 2, I describe Laputa as a simulation framework of epistemic interaction, postponing the description of the underlying Bayesian model until Sect. 3. In Sect. 4, an interpretation is proposed according to which inquirers in Laputa exchange novel arguments on a common issue. I proceed, in Sect. 5, to test whether this model of deliberation exhibits polarization effects. Conditions under which inquirers diverge are also studied. In the concluding section, I comment on the relation between the present model and the influential Persuasive Argument Theory (PAT).

2   The Laputa Simulation Framework

I will choose to introduce Laputa as a simulation framework, leaving the details of the underlying model for the next section. Social networks are represented and depicted in the program as directed graphs in which the nodes represent inquirers and the links represent communication channels (Fig. 1).

A number of parameters can be set for each inquirer. The *initial degree of belief* is the inquirer's initial credence in proposition *p*. *Inquiry accuracy* is the reliability of the inquirer's own inquiries. The *inquiry chance* is the probability that the inquirer will conduct an inquiry. The *inquiry trust* is the inquirer's degree of trust in her own inquiries. Likewise, there are a number of parameters for each link. The *listen trust* is the recipients trust in the sender. The *threshold of assertion* is the degree of confidence in a proposition ("*p*" or "not-*p*") required for the sender to submit a corresponding message to the recipient(s). Whether a message will then be submitted depends on the *listen chance*. For instances, if the threshold is set at 0.90,

---

[1] For an overview of exact models of opinion dynamics, see Hegselmann and Krause (2006). See also Zollman (2007).

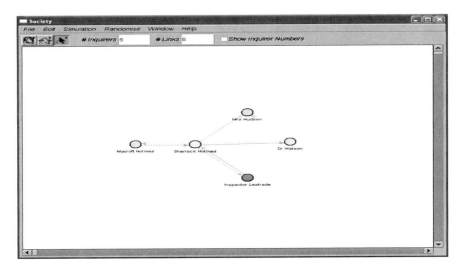

Fig. 1 The social network of Sherlock Holmes as represented in Laputa

this means that the sender needs to believe p (not-p) to a degree 0.90 in order for her to send a positive (negative) message in the network.

Running Laputa can mean to construct a network, such as that in Fig. 1; assign initial values to the inquirer and link parameters; and then click on a "run" button. What happens then is that Laputa runs through a series of steps, each step representing a chance for an inquirer to conduct an inquiry, to communicate (send, listen) to the other inquirers to which she is "hooked up," or to do both. After each step, Laputa will update the whole network according to the information received by the inquirers in accordance with the Bayesian model with which we shall soon become acquainted. Thus, a new degree of belief is computed for each inquirer based on the old degree of belief and the new information received through inquiry and/or listening to other inquirers. Laputa also updates the inquiry trust and listen trust parameters in accordance with Bayesian principles.

Laputa not just outputs what happens to the individual inquirers during simulation but also collects some statistical data. Thus, *error delta* is the difference between the initial and final average degrees of belief in the proposition p, which is assumed true by convention. Given error delta, we can compute the veritistic value (V-value) in the sense of Goldman (1999) for a network evolution according to the following simple rule: V-value $=$ −error delta. This means that an error delta of −0.076 equals a V-value of 0.076. Angere (forthcoming), Olsson (2011), and Olsson and Vallinder (in press) discuss various applications of Laputa relating to Goldman's veritistic social epistemology. See Vallinder and Olsson (in press b) for a further philosophical application of Laputa.

Laputa also allows its user to specify various features or "desiderata" of networks at an abstract level. The program can then randomly generate a large number of networks of different sizes having those features, letting them evolve while collecting various statistics. This is done in Laputa's "batch window" (Fig. 2), the perhaps most powerful feature of the program.

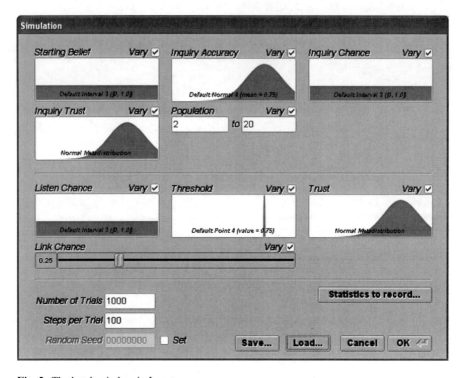

Fig. 2 The batch window in Laputa

In the batch window, various probability distributions can be selected for the several inquirer and link parameters. For instance, the flat distribution for "starting belief" indicates that Laputa, when selecting the initial credences in p for a generated network, will treat all possible credences as being equally likely to be realized. The selection of a normal distribution for "inquiry accuracy" centered around 0.75 means that Laputa, when selecting the inquiry accuracy for the inquirers in the generated networks, will have a preference for assigning an accuracy of 0.75 and surrounding values. The population feature allows the specification of the lower and upper sizes of the networks to be examined. In this case, Laputa is instructed to generate and study networks having 2–20 inquirers. "Link chance" specifies the "density" of the networks to be studied. A link chance of 0.25 indicates a 25 % chance that two inquirers will be connected by a directed communication link. In Fig. 2, the number of trials has been set to 1,000, meaning that Laputa will generate and study 1,000 networks in accordance with the statistical criteria specified in the batch window. Finally, the number of steps per trial has been set to 100, indicating that the focus is inquirer interaction over a longer period of time.

3 The Underlying Bayesian Model

It is time to elucidate the model underlying the simulation environment. This section follows the exposition in Angere (forthcoming), except in one main respect: Unlike Angere, I will describe the model in a way that does not presuppose any more specific interpretation of the exchanges taking place between inquirers. Formally, we can take a *social network S* to be a set Γ of *inquirers*, together with a binary relation R on Γ, which we call the *network structure*. This means that, abstractly speaking, a social network is a directed graph.

Following Bayesian tradition, the epistemic state of a person α at time t is assumed to be given by a *credence function* $C_\alpha^t : L \rightarrow [0, 1]$. L can be taken to be a classical propositional language, and C_α^t is assumed to fulfill the standard axioms of a probability measure. For the purposes of this chapter, let us confine ourselves to the case where inquiry is aimed at discovering whether a single proposition p is true or false. Every inquirer will then have a credence $C_\alpha^t(p)$ in p, which is a real number between 0 and 1, for every moment t.

In our model, there are two fundamentally different ways for the inquirers to receive new information: inquiry and communication. Inquiry can here be taken to include any kind of method of altering a credence function which does not base itself on information given by others in the network. Paradigmatic cases of inquiry include observation, experiment, and taking advice from persons outside the social network.

Not all participants' approaches to inquiry are the same, and they tend to vary in both their degree of activity and their effectiveness. We say that a result of inquiry is *positive* if it supports p, and *negative* if it supports not-p. Let $S_{i\alpha}^{t+}$ be the proposition "α's inquiry gives a positive result at time t," $S_{i\alpha}^{t-}$ be the proposition "α's inquiry gives a negative at t," and $S_{i\alpha}^t = S_{i\alpha}^{t+} \vee S_{i\alpha}^{t-}$ the proposition that "α's inquiry gives *some* result at t, positive or negative." We represent the participants' properties *qua* inquirers by two probabilities: The chance $P(S_{i\alpha}^t)$ that, at any moment t, α receives a result from her inquiries, and the chance $P(S_{i\alpha}^{t+}|S_{i\alpha}^t \wedge p)$ that when such a result is obtained, it is the right one. To simplify matters, we assume that the chance that inquiry gives an appropriate result does not depend on whether p is true or false.

$P(S_{i\alpha}^t)$ will be referred to as α's *activity* and $P(S_{i\alpha}^{t+}|S_{i\alpha}^t \wedge p)$ as her *aptitude*. An inquirer without interest in p would generally have a low activity value, while one very interested in p but engaging in inquiry using faulty methods would have a high activity value but an aptitude close to 0.5 or even below that. In the latter case, the results of her inquiry would actually be negatively correlated with the truth. As a simplification, we will assume α's activity and aptitude to be constant over time, so we will generally write them without the time index t.

Just as inquiry represents the flow of information into the network, communication deals with how this information is disseminated. Analogously to the inquiry notation, we define

$S_{\beta\alpha}^{t+} =_{df} \beta$ sends a positive message to α at t

$S_{\beta\alpha}^{t-} =_{df} \beta$ sends a negative message to α at t

$S_{\beta\alpha}^t =_{df} \beta$ sends a positive or a negative message to α at t

This strength of a link $\beta\alpha$ is then representable as a probability $P(S_{\beta\alpha})$ being the chance that β sends some message, whether positive or negative, to α.

Given that β communicates with α, what does she say? And what makes her say it? We will leave the first question for the next section. The second question can be answered by referring to a property of the link $\beta\alpha$ that we will call its *threshold of assertion*: a value $T_{\beta\alpha}$ between 0 and 1, such that

If $T_{\beta\alpha}>0.5$, β sends a positive message to α only if $C_\beta(p) \geq T_{\beta\alpha}$, and a negative message only if $C_\beta(p) \leq 1 - T_{\beta\alpha}$.

If $T_{\beta\alpha}<0.5$, β sends a positive message to α only if $C_\beta(p) \leq T_{\beta\alpha}$, and a negative message only if $C_\beta(p) \geq 1 - T_{\beta\alpha}$.

If $T_{\beta\alpha} = 0.5$ β sends a positive or a negative message to α independently of what she believes, which is modeled by letting her pick what to say randomly.

So far, we have described how the inquirers in a social network engage in inquiry and communication, but we have said nothing about how they react to the results of these practices. The purpose of the following considerations is to provide enlightenment in this regard.

We define the *reliability* of α's source σ as

$$R_{\sigma\alpha} =_{df} P(S_{\sigma\alpha}^+|S_{\sigma\alpha} \wedge p) = P(S_{\sigma\alpha}^-|S_{\sigma\alpha} \wedge \neg p)$$

This definition presupposes that the probability that any source sends a positive message, if p is the case, is equal to the probability that it sends a negative message, if not-p is the case. This *source symmetry* simplifies our calculations, although it can be relaxed if we encounter cases where it does not provide a reasonable approximation. For a discussion, see Olsson (2011).

It follows at once that the reliability of α's inquiry is identical to her aptitude. For other sources, it is an abstraction based on those sources' performances as indications of truth. In general, an inquirer has no direct access to this value, but this does not stop her from forming beliefs about it. Since the number of possible values for the chance $R_{\sigma\alpha}$ is infinite, we need to represent α's credence as a density function instead of a regular probability distribution. Thus, for each inquirer α, each source σ, and each time t, we define a function $\tau_{\sigma\alpha}^t : [0, 1] \to [0, 1]$, called α's *trust function for σ at t*, such that

$$C_\alpha^t(a \leq R_{\sigma\alpha} \leq b) = \int_a^b \tau_{\sigma\alpha}^t(\rho)d\rho$$

for a, b in [0,1]. $\tau_{\sigma\alpha}(\rho)$ then gives the credence density at ρ, and we can obtain the actual credence that α has in propositions about the reliability of her sources by integrating this function. We will also have use for the expression $1 - \tau_{\sigma\alpha}^t$, representing α's credence density for propositions about σ *not* being reliable, which we will refer to as $\bar{\tau}_{\sigma\alpha}^t$.

It is reasonable to think that an inquirer's credences about chances should influence her credences about the outcomes of these chances. The way this should be done is generally known as the *principal principle* (Lewis 1980). It says that if α knows that the chance that an event e will happen is ρ, then her credence in e should be exactly ρ. Applied to our case, this means that the following principle (PP) must hold:

$$C_\alpha^t\left(S_{\sigma\alpha}^{t+}|S_{\sigma\alpha}^t \wedge R_{\sigma\alpha} = \rho \wedge p\right) = \rho$$

$$C_\alpha^t\left(S_{\sigma\alpha}^{t-}|S_{\sigma\alpha}^t \wedge R_{\sigma\alpha} = \rho \wedge \neg p\right) = \rho$$

for all t, that is, α's credence in σ giving a positive report, given that the source gives any report at all, that σ's reliability is ρ, and that p actually is the case, should be ρ.

We also have use for an independence postulate. While not strictly necessary, such a postulate will simplify calculations and modeling considerably. The independence assumption we use here will be referred to as *communication independence* (CI):

$$C_\alpha^t\left(p \wedge S_{\sigma\alpha}^t \wedge R_{\sigma\alpha} = \rho\right) = C_\alpha^t(p)C_\alpha^t(S_{\sigma\alpha}^t)R_{\sigma\alpha}^t(\rho)$$

Communication independence implies that whether σ says anything is independent of whether p is actually true as well as of σ's reliability.

Given (PP) and (CI), we can now define the following expression for α's credence in σ's reliability (see Angere forthcoming, for the derivation):

$$C_\alpha^t\left(S_{\sigma\alpha}^{t+}|p\right) = C_\alpha^t\left(S_{\sigma\alpha}^t\right) \int_0^1 \rho\tau_{\sigma\alpha}^t(\rho)d\rho$$

The integral in this expression is the expected value $\langle \tau_{\sigma\alpha}^t \rangle$ of the trust function $\tau_{\sigma\alpha}^t$ whence

$$(*)\ C_\alpha^t\left(S_{\sigma\alpha}^{t+}|p\right) = C_\alpha^t(S_{\sigma\alpha}^t)\langle \tau_{\sigma\alpha}^t \rangle$$

Similarly,

$$(**)\ C_\alpha^t\left(S_{\sigma\alpha}^{t+}|\neg p\right) = C_\alpha^t(S_{\sigma\alpha}^t)\langle \overline{\tau}_{\sigma\alpha}^t \rangle$$

We can now derive the crucial expressions $C_\alpha^t(p|S_{\sigma\alpha}^{t+})$ and $C_\alpha^t(p|S_{\sigma\alpha}^{t-})$, the credence an inquirer should place in p at t given that she receives a positive or a negative message, respectively, from a single source σ:

$$C_\alpha^t\left(p|S_{\sigma\alpha}^{t+}\right) = \frac{C_\alpha^t(p)\langle \tau_{\sigma\alpha}^t \rangle}{C_\alpha^t(p)\langle \tau_{\sigma\alpha}^t \rangle + C_\alpha^t(\neg p)\langle \overline{\tau}_{\sigma\alpha}^t \rangle}$$

Table 1 Single message updating in Laputa (for credences strictly between 0 and 1)

	Message expected	Neither nor	Message surprising
Source trusted	(+, +) (a)	(+, 0) (b)	(, −) (c)
Neither nor	(0, +) (d)	(0, 0) (e)	(0, −) (f)
Source distrusted	(−, +) (g)	(−, 0) (h)	(+, −) (i)

$$C_\alpha^t\left(p|S_{\sigma\alpha}^{t-}\right) = \frac{C_\alpha^t(p)\langle\bar{\tau}_{\sigma\alpha}^t\rangle}{C_\alpha^t(p)\langle\bar{\tau}_{\sigma\alpha}^t\rangle + C_\alpha^t(\neg p)\langle\tau_{\sigma\alpha}^t\rangle}$$

where $\langle\tau_{\sigma\alpha}^t\rangle$ is the expected value of the trust function $\tau_{\sigma\alpha}^t$. By the Bayesian requirement of conditionalization, we must have $C_\alpha^{t+1} = C_\alpha^t(p|S_{\sigma\alpha}^{t+})$, whenever σ is the only source giving information to α at t. This means that these formulae completely determine how α should update her credence in such a case.

Not only α's credence in p should be updated, however. Equally important is for α to keep track of how much to trust her sources. A source that generally gives very unlikely reports is unlikely to be veridical, and an inquirer should adjust her trust function in light of this. It turns out that our model already determines how to do this, but we will not go into the details here. A full account can be found in Angere (forthcoming). Suffice it to mention the following consequence of our model: Even if an inquirer happens to be a perfect inquirer insofar as her inquiry always gives the right result, a fairly low stability of her faith in inquiry, together with her prior judgment that p is unlikely, may conspire to make her distrust her own inquiry. This, in turn, may give rise to a vicious circle in which she becomes more and more convinced that p is false and that her inquiry is negatively correlated with the truth.

The present model gives rise to a number of qualitative updating rules in the case of one message received. We say an inquirer *trusts* a given source if the inquirer's credence in the reliability of the source is greater than 0.5, *distrusts* the source if it is less than 0.5, and *neither trusts nor distrusts* the source otherwise. We say that a message that p (not-p) was surprising to an inquirer if, prior to receiving the message, the inquirer's credence in p (not-p) was less than 0.5, *expected* if it was greater than 0.5, and *neither surprising nor expected* otherwise. In Table 1, a "+" sign in the left component of a pair (_, _) means that the inquirer's current belief is reinforced (i.e., her credence in the conclusion is strengthened if above 0.5 and weakened if below 0.5). A "−" sign means that the inquirer's current belief is weakened (i.e., her credence in the conclusion is weakened if above 0.5 and strengthened if below 0.5), whereas 0 means that the inquirer's credence in the conclusion is left unchanged. A "+" sign in the right component of a pair (_, _) signifies that the juror's trust in the source (i.e., credence in its reliability) is strengthened, a "−" sign that it is weakened, and 0 that it is left unchanged. Table 1 shows how updating on the information from one source affects an inquirer under various circumstances.

Suppose, for example, that inquirer α's prior credence in p is 0.7. Now α receives a positive message, that is, a message in support of p, from β, who we assume to be trusted by α. Since the message is expected and the source is trusted, we have the situation described in cell (a) in Table 1. Accordingly, α will react by raising both her degree of belief in p and her degree of trust in β. If, by contrast, the message sent by β is negative, we have the situation depicted in cell (c), so that α will respond by lowering both her degree of belief in p and her trust in β.[2]

Let be the set of all sources from which α receives information at t. Our Bayesian framework requires that credences be updated by means of conditionalization:

$$\text{(Cond)} \; C_\alpha^{t+1}(p) = C_\alpha^t(p|\Lambda S_{\sigma\alpha}^{t*}),$$

where the conjunction runs over all σ in Δ_α^t. $S_{\sigma\alpha}^{t*}$ is the message that α receives from σ at t, that is, either $S_{\sigma\alpha}^{t+}$ or $S_{\sigma\alpha}^{t-}$. The right-hand side of (Cond) can be very hard to assess in the absence of further assumptions. We can simplify the situation considerably by assuming *source independence* (SI):

$$C_\alpha^t(\Lambda S_{\sigma\alpha}^{t*}|p) = \prod C_\alpha^t(S_{\sigma\alpha}^{t*}|p)$$

$$C_\alpha^t(\Lambda S_{\sigma\alpha}^{t*}|\neg p) = \prod C_\alpha^t(S_{\sigma\alpha}^{t*}|\neg p)$$

Source independence states that the information coming from the sources is independent conditional on the truth as well as on the falsity of p. This is the standard Bayesian way of capturing the idea that there is no direct influence between the sources, for example, that they have not conspired to give a certain message (see, for instance, Chap. 2 in Olsson 2005). Given source independence, we can relatively easily compute the left-hand side of (Cond) by relying on Bayes' theorem together with the theorem of total probability. See the Appendix to this chapter for an example of how the machinery works and of the important role played by the assumption of source independence in the updating of credences.

The bottom line is that, given the complexity of the subject matter, Laputa is a simple and workable model once we assume source independence. But that, of course, is a technical motivation and not a philosophical one. The question is whether an interpretation of Laputa can be found under which source independence is true or at least highly plausible. This is the issue to which we now turn.

4 Interpreting Laputa

In order to be informative, an interpretation of Laputa should say something more precise about what kind of messages inquirers receive from inquiry and from the other inquirers. On what I will call the *opinion disclosure* interpretation of the

---

[2] For proofs of the results summarized in Table 1 see Vallinder and Olsson (in press a), which is a detailed study of the dynamics of trust in the Laputa model.

model, the positive messages are simply messages to the effect that p is the case and the negative messages that not-p is the case. We let $S_{i\alpha}^{t+}$ be the proposition "α's inquiry signaled that p is the case at time t," $S_{i\alpha}^{t-}$ be the proposition "α's inquiry signaled that not-p is the case at t," and $S_{i\alpha}^t = S_{i\alpha}^{t+} \vee S_{i\alpha}^{t-}$ the proposition that "α's inquiry signaled either that p or that not-p is the case at t." Similarly,

$S_{\beta\alpha}^{t+} =_{df} \beta$ disclosed her opinion that p to α at t

$S_{\beta\alpha}^{t-} =_{df} \beta$ disclosed her opinion that not-p to α at t

$S_{\beta\alpha}^t =_{df} \beta$ disclosed her opinion that p or that not-p to α at t

Thus, what happens, at a given point in a social network evolution, is that one or more inquirers receive messages to the effect that p (not-p) is the case from their own inquiries and/or from the other inquirers. Social network interaction on this interpretation consists largely in repeated disclosure of opinions. The opinions are disclosed only to those other inquirers with whom the inquirer can communicate. The inquirers then update their credence in p at each round by conditionalization in the manner described above.

This was the original interpretation of Laputa as laid out in Angere (forthcoming) and Olsson (2011). Under it, Laputa can be used, at least in principle, for studying the *mere exposure effect* in social psychology, the claim being that mere exposure to other group members' positions on some issue can move a given member's credence in similar directions (for an overview, see Isenberg 1986, pp. 1142-1144). However, there is a problem with this interpretation which needs to be mentioned. Suppose an inquirer is repeatedly exposing other inquirers to her opinion without her receiving any new information from inquiry in the meantime. Suppose, for example, that she repeatedly informs the others that her opinion is that p is true in consecutive steps of the deliberation. As Laputa is built, this will typically lead the other inquirers to repeatedly update their credence in p in a positive direction and to adopt an ever increasing trust in the discloser. While this effect may be of little statistical significance in the end, it is certainly counterintuitive.

There is another interpretation which does not have this problem. On this interpretation, what are exchanged among the inquirers are not opinions but *arguments*. More precisely, inquirers exchange arguments for or against the proposition p. Since Laputa does not represent the structure of arguments, this interpretation is in some need of justification.

Our starting point will be the assumption that deliberation, as studied here, is *cooperative*, much in the sense of Grice's maxims for cooperative communication (Grice 1975). Thus, we assume that inquirers adhere to the maxims of quality and of relation. The former states that one should not convey what is believed to be false or unjustified. According to the latter, one should make contributions that are relevant. Giving an invalid argument or an argument with false premises would be in violation of the maxim of quality. Cooperative communication requires that all arguments be sound, that is, valid and based on true premises at least in the eyes of the proponent. In this chapter, we will take the inquirers' competence in this regard for granted.

The internal structure of arguments is important if the arguments presented can fail to be sound. The receiver can then determine whether the argument is valid and based on true premises by identifying the argument structure, including the premises and the mode of inference (deductive, inductive, etc.). But if all arguments presented are sound, as we have assumed them to be, then it is less obvious that argument structure is of statistical importance. The assumption of soundness can therefore be used to motivate viewing arguments as "black boxes" without any internal structure. What is important in an argument, from this perspective, is whether it is a pro or a con argument vis-à-vis the issue at stake. From this perspective, the Laputa model makes sense as a simplified and idealized model of argumentation.

We have yet to explain why the problem of repetition does not arise under this interpretation. The key idea is to think of the arguments that are put forward by inquirers in Laputa as *novel* arguments, that is, arguments that have not been advanced earlier in the deliberation process. Hence, if an inquirer repeatedly argues that p, this should not be interpreted as the inquirer repeating the same argument for p but as her advancing a series of novel arguments to that conclusion. If so, the fact that the inquirers on the receiving side will repeatedly update their credence in the conclusion and their trust in the proponent is not unreasonable. On the contrary, it is what one would expect should happen.

The assumption of novelty can be justified as follows: Kaplan (1977) found that if arguments are presented that the individual group member is already aware of, a shift in his or her position will not occur as a result of the discussion. The stating of the argument will be seen as an irrelevant deliberative contribution. Vinokur and Burnstein (1978) report similar findings. In other words, giving an argument which has already been taken into account violates the maxim of relation, which we have assumed that the inquirers adhere to. If the network is fully connected so that every argument is presented to everyone, there will be common knowledge about which arguments have already been presented. Hence, only novel arguments will be advanced. (If the network is not fully connected, we adopt the same assumption – that all arguments presented are novel – as a useful idealization.)

We say that an argument is *positive* if its conclusion is p and that it is *negative* if its conclusion is not-p. Putting together what was said above, the proposal is that we take $S_{i\alpha}^{t+}$ to mean "α's inquiry produced a novel positive argument at time t," $S_{i\alpha}^{t-}$ to mean "α's inquiry produced a novel negative argument at t," and $S_{i\alpha}^{t} = S_{i\alpha}^{t+} \vee S_{i\alpha}^{t-}$ to mean that "α's inquiry produced some novel argument, whether positive or negative, at t." Similarly,

$S_{\beta\alpha}^{t+} =_{df} \beta$ presented a novel positive argument to α at t

$S_{\beta\alpha}^{t-} =_{df} \beta$ presented a novel negative argument to α at t

$S_{\beta\alpha}^{t} =_{df} \beta$ presented a novel negative or a novel positive argument to α at t

The following is a consequence of Laputa under the argumentation interpretation:

If $T_{\beta\alpha}>0.5$, β presents a positive argument to α only if $C_\beta(p) \geq T_{\beta\alpha}$, and a negative argument only if $C_\beta(p) \leq 1 - T_{\beta\alpha}$.

Thus, if the threshold of assertion exceeds 0.5, then the inquirer will present an argument, whether it be positive or negative, only if her confidence in the conclusion exceeds the threshold. A threshold of assertion exceeding 0.5 captures a sense in which deliberating agents are *sincere*. While this is surely the normal case, the model is general enough to allow for inquirers to be insincere, in the following sense:

If $T_{\beta\alpha}<0.5$, β utters a positive argument to α only if $C_\beta(p) \leq T_{\beta\alpha}$ and negative argument only if $C_\beta(p) \geq 1 - T_{\beta\alpha}$.

In other words, a threshold of assertion below 0.5 is interpreted as a "liar threshold": The inquirer will give an argument for p only if her degree of belief in p is sufficiently low and an argument for not-p only if her degree of belief in not-p is sufficiently low. Setting the threshold of assertion to a number below 0.5 can be used to model a kind of strategic communication, for example, lying or acting as the "devil's advocate," in the sense of giving an argument for p (not-p) while personally believing p (not-p) to be false. Finally, if $T_{\beta\alpha} = 0.5$, β can utter a positive or a negative argument to α independently of what she believes, which is modeled by letting her pick what to say randomly.[3]

The source independence assumption states that inquirers treat other inquirers as giving independent information. Whether or not we choose the opinion disclosure or the argumentation interpretation of Laputa, assuming source independence has the effect of disconnecting inquirers from reality after a few deliberative rounds. The reason is that inquirers, when updating their credences in p, will take into account not only the result of their own inquiries but also the information coming from other inquirers, whether that information is interpreted as disclosed opinions or novel arguments. This will lead to the credences of inquirers becoming, with time, increasingly dependent. After a while, positive (negative) reports coming from other inquirers cannot be taken anymore as independent indications that p (not-p) is true, and yet the listening inquirers in Laputa will treat them as such. No reason has been presented, however, indicating that source independence systematically distorts simulation results in any particular direction. And arguably, source independence is psychologically realistic as a default strategy: Real inquirers have a tendency to assume source independence in the absence of concrete reasons to think that sources are not independent. Keeping in mind the considerable simplifying effects source independence has on the entire model, we are therefore justified in accepting it as a highly useful idealization.

---

[3] The original idea behind Laputa was to simulate communication based on inquiry. A possible drawback with the argumentation interpretation is that it decouples inquiry from communication. The existence of arguments is not brought in relation to the result of inquiry, and whether or not an inquirer possesses an argument is not represented in the model. We have been experimenting with a version of the program in which communication is possible only if new inquiry has taken place. Preliminary simulations suggest that this modification does not have any significant statistical effect on simulation outcome.

5 Do Bayesian Inquirers Polarize?

In early work in social psychology, it was observed that group decisions are sometimes riskier than the previous private decisions of the group's members.[4] This observation paved the way for numerous studies showing that *risky shift* is a pervasive phenomenon but also that on certain decisions groups are actually more cautious than their members. Both risky and cautious shifts are special cases of a group-induced attitude *polarization* (e.g., Moscovici and Zavalloni 1969). Group polarization is said to occur when "an initial tendency of individual group members toward a given direction is enhanced following group discussion" (Isenberg 1986, p. 1141) so that "members of a deliberating group predictably move toward a more extreme point in the direction indicated by the members' predeliberation tendencies" (Sunstein 2002, p. 176, italics removed). Thus, a group of moderately profeminist women will be more strongly profeminist following group discussion (Myers 1975).

Given that "[g]roup polarization is among the most robust patterns found in deliberating bodies" (Sunstein 2002, p. 177), we can use polarization as a test of empirical adequacy that any reasonably realistic model of group deliberation should satisfy. In this section, we test whether inquirers in Laputa polarize under what would appear to be normal circumstances characterized by (i) some prior trust in the reliability of the others, (ii) an inclination to give arguments only if the conclusion is perceived to be more likely to be true than false, and (iii) an admission to talk in the absence of a high degree of credence in the conclusion. Figure 3 shows the exact parameter settings in the batch window of Laputa.

It was assumed that the inquirers engage in a "closed room" debate without undertaking any inquiry while deliberating. Hence, the inquiry chance parameter was set to 0 and the link chance to 1, making every announcement public within the group. The threshold of assertion was taken to be normally distributed around 0.75. The social trust parameter (credence in the reliability of others) was assumed to be normally distributed in the area above 0.5. Finally, the initial degree of belief (credence) in p was taken to be positive and normally distributed just above 0.5. Laputa was then instructed to generate 1,000 networks ("trials") satisfying these constraints, allowing each network to evolve ten steps. The result is depicted in Fig. 4.

The lower diagram of Fig. 4 shows the evolution of the average credence in p over time. As we see, after a few steps, the average credence in p converged to a value slightly below 1. The upper diagram of Fig. 4 shows the number of inquirers per final credence in p after ten deliberative rounds. Virtually all inquirers ended up assigning p a credence close to 1. These observations confirm our prediction: Inquirers in Laputa polarize in the sense that if every inquirer is initially inclined to believe p, however cautiously, they will still believe p after deliberation, only much more strongly. The effect is the same *mutatis mutandis*, if the inquirers

---

[4] Isenberg (1986) credits an unpublished master thesis by James Stoner with this discovery (Stoner 1961).

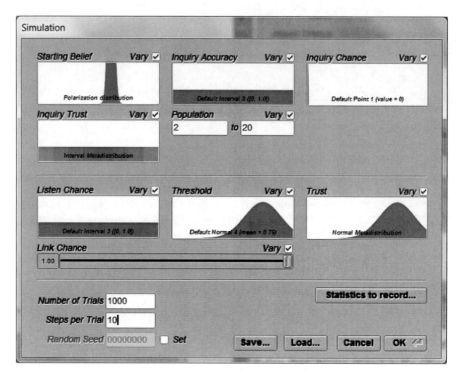

Fig. 3 Representation of a closed room debate in Laputa with starting beliefs biased towards p

initially favor not-p rather than p, in which case they will end up believing not-p more strongly.

We recall that inquirers in Laputa update their degree of trust in the other inquirers dynamically, although we have not detailed the mechanisms behind trust in this chapter (see Angere forthcoming). Intuitively, we would expect polarization with regard to the proposition at stake to be accompanied by increased mutual trust among the inquiring agents. This is indeed what happens in Laputa. This effect was studied for a small network of only two inquirers under circumstances similar to those in Fig. 3. More precisely, communication chances for inquirer 1 and inquirer 2 were set to 0.94 and 0.88, respectively, and the threshold for the links outgoing from inquirer 1 and outgoing from inquirer 2 was set to 0.66 and 0.67, respectively. Figure 5 shows the result.

The horizontal axis shows time. The vertical axis displays the relevant credences. We see that as the inquirers polarize with regard to their credence, or degree of belief (DB), in p, they become increasingly more trusting vis-à-vis each other.

These results are easily explained given what we know about the underlying Bayesian model. If the inquirers are initially inclined toward p and some have a threshold of assertion allowing them to communicate, the latter will give novel arguments in favor of p. These arguments will be taken into account by the listening inquirers in the manner previously described, leading them to adjust their credence

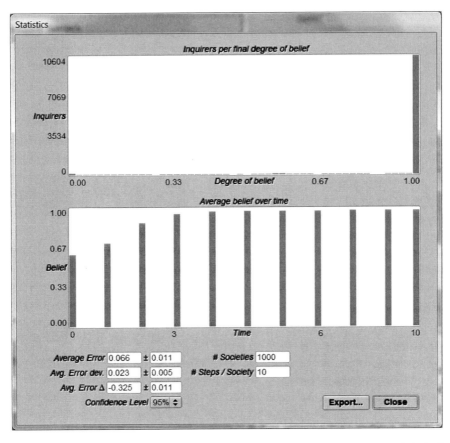

Fig. 4 Inquirers become increasingly certain that *p* is the case (lower diagram) and their final degree of belief is 1 (upper diagram)

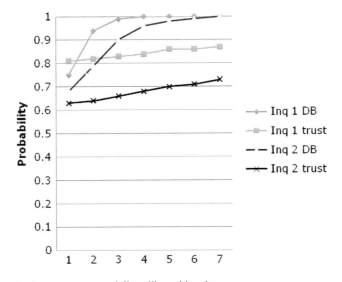

Fig. 5 Polarization among two socially calibrated inquirers

Table 2 Polarization and social calibration

	Trust	Distrust
Truth-telling	Polarization	Divergence
Lying	Divergence	Polarization

in p, as well as their trust in the source, upward (see cell (a) in Table 1). With time, an increasing number of inquirers will find their credence in p exceeds their threshold of assertion, encouraging them to give further arguments for p. This will push credences in p still further in the positive direction, and so on. At the same time, the growing sense of being confirmed by the others will lead to increased mutual trust among the inquirers, adding further momentum to their polarization. Moreover, this also shows that, in normal cases, polarization on the belief level is accompanied, in a sense, by polarization on the trust level: The initially shared attitude of trust is reinforced as the effect of deliberation.

Our study raises further the question of what happens in more unusual cases, for example, when people do not trust each other or they "lie" in the slightly technical sense of giving arguments for a conclusion they do not believe in. There are three cases to consider: people trust but lie, people distrust but tell the truth, and people distrust and lie. Using our simulation program, we tested these three cases while keeping all the other assumptions intact. The results are summarized in Table 2.

As we see, there are two situations that lead to polarization, as always in the sense that like-minded people are strengthened in their initial convictions as the effect of deliberation. One is the normal situation which we studied in the previous section, that is, when people trust other people and do so for good reasons because the others are in fact trustworthy. The other is when people distrust others, again for good reasons because the others are in fact untrustworthy. These two cases exemplify what we might call situations of *social calibration*: People's attitudes toward other people adequately reflect the actual trustworthiness of the latter. In the two remaining cases, in which there is lack of social calibration, we typically get a divided society: one camp believing the truth and the other camp believing the falsehood with the members of one camp distrusting the members of the other.[5]

We will close this section by studying an example of how a society consisting of serious (truth-telling) inquirers initially inclined to believe the same thing can still end up divided on the issue as the effect of a lack of social calibration. We will study a simple society consisting of only two inquirers: inquirer 1 (Inq 1) and inquirer 2 (Inq 2). We set *listen chance* for inquirer 1–0.94 and for inquirer 2–0.88

---

[5] At the end of a batch simulation, Laputa outputs the distribution of average final degrees of belief for all inquirers in all societies that were considered. For an example, see the upper diagram of Fig. 4. Laputa, as it stands, does not output the distribution of final degrees of belief for particular societies. Hence, we cannot conclude that societies that are not socially calibrated will divide from the data that we get from Laputa while in batch mode. However, during a batch simulation, Laputa randomly selects societies for visual representation on the computer screen. That visual information was used as additional data when concluding that a divided society results under the conditions given in Table 2.

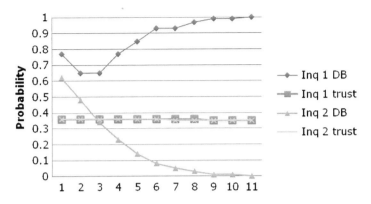

Fig. 6 Divergence among two inquirers lacking in social calibration

and the threshold for both inquirers to 0.58. We choose a normally distributed trust function for both inquirers with expected value 0.38. Figure 6 shows how the inquirer's degree of belief (DB) in p, and the expected value of their trust functions, changes with time.

We see that after some fluctuations, the general trend is that one inquirer will start believing p, while the other will start believing not-p.

Laputa allows us to inspect the relevant parameters in a stepwise fashion to see what causes this result. This reveals that the following transpires:

1. Both inquirers initially give arguments for p because their DB in p is above the threshold of assertion.
2. Since they distrust each other, they will take each other's arguments as evidence for not-p and lower their DB in p (see cell (g) in Table 1).
3. Inquirer 1 still has a DB in p which is above the threshold, and so she gives an argument for p.
4. Given her distrust in inquirer 1, inquirer 2 becomes rather confident that not-p, so she gives an argument for not-p (cell (g) in Table 1).
5. Given her distrust in inquirer 2, this is taken by inquirer 1 to be an evidence for the opposite, namely, p (cell (i) in Table 1).
6. By the same token, inquirer 1 will continue to argue for p, while inquirer 2 will continue to argue for not-p, and they will become ever more confident in the conclusions of their arguments.
7. Eventually, inquirer 1 will become certain of p and inquirer 2 certain of not-p.
8. Meanwhile, they will continuously downgrade their degree of trust still further because, as they see it, they repeatedly receive surprising messages from a distrusted source (see cell (i) in Table 1).

We note that while divergence occurs with respect to credence in p, polarization occurs with respect to trust: The inquirers initially distrusted each other, and this initial tendency is reinforced as the effect of deliberation.

6   Conclusion and Discussion

I have argued that the original interpretation of Laputa as a model of opinion disclosure is somewhat problematic due to a problem of repetition. Instead, I proposed an interpretation according to which inquirers are exchanging novel arguments for or against a target proposition. I went on to show that the model exhibits polarization much like real argumentative bodies. Inquirers in Laputa, if initially disposed to believe in a given proposition, will see their credences in that proposition increase as a result of group deliberation. This lends additional credibility to the model as a reasonably realistic representation of the phenomena in question. We also studied conditions under which inquirers diverge in their opinions. To the extent that Bayesian reasoning is normatively correct, the perhaps most surprising, and disturbing, results of this study are that polarization and divergence are not necessarily the result of mere irrational "group thinking" but that even ideally rational inquirers will predictably polarize or diverge under realistic conditions. It remains to compare the present theory with the influential Persuasive Argument Theory (PAT) which also predicts polarization.[6]

According to PAT an individual's position on an issue is a function of the number and persuasiveness of pro and con arguments that the person recalls from memory when formulating his or her own position. Thus, in assessing the guilt or innocence of an accused in trial, jurors come to predeliberation decisions on the basis of the relative number and persuasiveness of arguments favoring guilt or innocence. Group deliberation will cause an individual to shift in a given direction to the extent that the discussion exposes that individual to persuasive arguments favoring that direction rather than to arguments favoring the opposite direction. How persuasive an argument is to a given individual is determined by the validity and novelty of the argument. One factor, among several, affecting perceived validity is the extent to which the argument fits into the person's previous views. Novelty has to do with how new and unusual the argument is to the person in question. Everything else equal, a novel argument has a greater persuasive force than a commonplace argument.

Laputa, as I have proposed to interpret it, is clearly in the spirit of PAT. Thus, Laputa is also based on the assumption that the persuasive effect of an argument depends essentially on two factors: its perceived validity (including the trustworthiness of the presenter) and novelty. There are also differences. For instance, Laputa is more specific than PAT in assuming that individual inquirers update their degrees of belief in a particular way, namely, that dictated by Bayesianism. PAT as such does not postulate any more specific updating mechanism, let alone a Bayesian one. Laputa assumes, in addition, that individuals' degrees of trust are dynamically updated in a Bayesian fashion.

Furthermore, inquirers in Laputa engaging in group deliberation update their credences in a piecemeal or sequential fashion. The presentation of a novel

---

[6] The following account is based on the overview in Isenberg (1986), pp. 1145-1148.

argument, or collection of arguments, will normally affect the receiving inquirer's credence in the conclusion. As PAT is normally formulated, inquirers are supposed to collect in memory all the arguments they are presented with during group deliberation, postponing their own verdict on the matter until deliberation has come to an end. When the deliberation has ended, the inquirer takes a stand on the basis of a holistic assessment of the number and merits of the pro and con arguments retained in memory. This "holistic" aspect of PAT is not unproblematic in the light of experiments indicating that the order in which arguments are presented will affect the conclusion reached. Thus, Kaplan and Miller (1977) found that subjects tend to recall persuasive arguments that they had been exposed to most recently rather than the ones they had been exposed to first.

While there may be doubts about some of the details of PAT, there are many experimental studies pointing to its broad empirical adequacy. It is reasonable to suppose that a fair number of these studies will give (indirect) support for Laputa under the argumentation interpretation considering the fact that the latter is, by and large, subsumable under the former. A more careful assessment of this claim which has the status of a reasonable conjecture is, however, outside the scope of the present article.

Acknowledgement I am grateful to Staffan Angere and Stephan Hartmann for their comments on previous versions of this chapter.

Appendix

To illustrate the role played by the condition of source independence, we consider the case of one inquirer α receiving, at time t, positive messages from two sources, σ_1 and σ_2. By (Cond),

$$C_\alpha^{t+1}(p)$$

$$= C_\alpha^t\left(p \mid S_{\sigma_1\alpha}^{t+} \wedge S_{\sigma_2\alpha}^{t+}\right)$$

$$= \frac{C_\alpha^t(p)C_\alpha^t\left(S_{\sigma_1\alpha}^{t+} \wedge S_{\sigma_2\alpha}^{t+} \mid p\right)}{C_\alpha^t\left(S_{\sigma_1\alpha}^{t+} \wedge S_{\sigma_2\alpha}^{t+}\right)} \qquad \text{(Bayes' theorem)}$$

$$= \frac{C_\alpha^t(p)C_\alpha^t\left(S_{\sigma_1\alpha}^{t+} \wedge S_{\sigma_2\alpha}^{t+} \mid p\right)}{C_\alpha^t\left(S_{\sigma_1\alpha}^{t+} \wedge S_{\sigma_2\alpha}^{t+} \mid p\right)C_\alpha^t(p) + C_\alpha^t\left(S_{\sigma_1\alpha}^{t+} \wedge S_{\sigma_2\alpha}^{t+} \mid \neg p\right)C_\alpha^t(\neg p)} \qquad \text{(Total probability)}$$

$$= \frac{C_\alpha^t(p)C_\alpha^t\left(S_{\sigma_1\alpha}^{t+} \mid p\right)C_\alpha^t S\left(S_{\sigma_2\alpha}^{t+} \mid p\right)}{C_\alpha^t\left(S_{\sigma_1\alpha}^{t+} \mid p\right)C_\alpha^t(p) + C_\alpha^t\left(S_{\sigma_1\alpha}^{t+} \mid \neg p\right)C_\alpha^t\left(S_{\sigma_2\alpha}^{t+} \mid \neg p\right)C_\alpha^t(\neg p)} \qquad \text{(Source independence)}$$

$$= \frac{C_\alpha^t(p)\left\langle\tau_{\sigma_1\alpha}^t\right\rangle\left\langle\tau_{\sigma_2\alpha}^t\right\rangle}{C_\alpha^t(p)\left\langle\tau_{\sigma_1\alpha}^t\right\rangle\left\langle\tau_{\sigma_2\alpha}^t\right\rangle + C_\alpha^t(\neg p)\left\langle\bar\tau_{\sigma_1\alpha}^t\right\rangle\left\langle\bar\tau_{\sigma_2\alpha}^t\right\rangle} \qquad \text{(By (\,$*$\,) and (\,$**$\,))}$$

This means that we only need three pieces of information in order to compute α's posterior credence in p: α's prior credence in p, the expected value of α's trust function for σ_1 and for σ_2. Supposing these values to be 0.8, 0.7, and 0.9, respectively, we get a 0.99 posterior credence in p.

The example can be generalized as follows:

Theorem 1: *Suppose that α at t receives messages from exactly n sources $\sigma_1, \ldots, \sigma_n$ and that all messages are positive. Then*

$$C_\alpha^{t+1}(p) = \frac{C_\alpha^t(p)\prod_{i=1}^n\left\langle\tau_{\sigma_i\alpha}^t\right\rangle}{C_\alpha^t(p)\prod_{i=1}^n\left\langle\tau_{\sigma_i\alpha}^t\right\rangle + C_\alpha^t(\neg p)\prod_{i=1}^n\left\langle\bar\tau_{\sigma_i\alpha}^t\right\rangle}$$

Proof: Left to the reader.

We can generalize this still further.

Theorem 2: *Suppose that α at t receives messages from exactly n sources $\sigma_1, \ldots, \sigma_n$. Let Pos_α^t be the set of all indices of sources giving positive messages and $Negs_\alpha^t$ be the set of all indices of sources giving negative messages. Then*

$$C_\alpha^{t+1}(p) = C_\alpha^t(p) \prod_{i\in Pos_\alpha^t}^n \left\langle\tau_{\sigma_i\alpha}^t\right\rangle \prod_{i\in Neg_\alpha^t}^n \left\langle\bar\tau_{\sigma_i\alpha}^t\right\rangle + C_\alpha^t(\neg p) \prod_{i\in Pos_\alpha^t}^n$$

Proof: Left to the reader.

Corollary 1: *Suppose that α at t receives messages from exactly n sources $\sigma_1, \ldots, \sigma_n$, for an even $n > 0$, that $\left\langle\tau_{\sigma_i\alpha}^t\right\rangle = \tau_{\sigma_j\alpha}^t$, and that there is an equal number of positive and negative messages. Then $C_\alpha^{t+1}(p) = C_\alpha^t(p)..$*

Proof: Follows from theorem 2.

References

Angere, S. (forthcoming). Knowledge in a social network (submitted paper).

Goldman, A. I. (1999). *Knowledge in a social world.* Oxford: Clarendon.

Grice, P. (1975). Logic and conversation. In P. Cole & J. Morgan (Eds.), *Syntax and semantics, 3: Speech acts* (pp. 41–58). New York: Academic.

Hegselmann, R., & Krause, U. (2006). Truth and cognitive division of labour: First steps towards a computer-aided social epistemology. *Journal of Artificial Societies and Social Simulation, 9*(3).

Isenberg, D. (1986). Group polarization: A critical review and meta-analysis. *Journal of Personality and Social Psychology, 50*(6), 1141–1151.

Kaplan, M. F. (1977). Discussion polarization effects in a modified jury decision paradigm: Informational influences. *Sociometry, 40*, 262–271.

Kaplan, M. F., & Miller, C. E. (1977). Judgments and group discussion: Effect of presentation and memory factors on polarization. *Sociometry, 40*, 337–343.

Lewis, D. (1980). A subjectivist's guide to objective chance. In R. C. Jeffreys (Ed.), Studies in inductive logic and probability, vol. 2. University of California Press.

Moscovici, S., & Zavalloni, M. (1969). The group as a polarizer of attitudes. *Journal of Personality and Social Psychology, 12*, 125–1135.

Myers, D. G. (1975). Discussion-induced attitude polarization. *Human Relations, 28*, 699–714.

Olsson, E. J. (2005). *Against coherence: Truth, probability, and justification*. Oxford/New York: Oxford University Press.

Olsson, E. J. (2011). A simulation approach to veritistic social epistemology. *Episteme, 8*(2), 127–143.

Stoner, J. A. F. (1961). *A comparison of individual and group decisions involving risk*. Unpublished master's thesis, Massachusetts Institute of Technology, Cambridge, MA.

Sunstein, C. R. (2002). The law of group polarization. *The Journal of Political Philosophy, 10*(2), 175–195.

Vallinder, A., & Olsson, E. J. (in press a). Trust and the value of overconfidence: A Bayesian perspective on social network communication. Synthese.

Vallinder, A., & Olsson, E. J. (in press b). Does computer simulation support the argument from disagreement? Synthese.

Vinokur, A., & Burnstein, E. (1978). Novel argumentation and attitude change: The case of polarization following group discussion. *European Journal of Social Psychology, 8*, 335–348.

Zollman, K. J. (2007). The communication structure of epistemic communities. *Philosophy of Science, 74*(5), 574–587.

Degrees of Justification, Bayes' Rule, and Rationality

Gregor Betz

Abstract Based on the theory of dialectical structures, I review the concept of degree of justification of a partial position a proponent may hold in a controversial debate. The formal concept of degree of justification dovetails with our pre-theoretic intuitions about a thesis' strength of justification. The central claim I am going to defend in this chapter maintains that degrees of justification, as defined within the theory of dialectical structures, correlate with a proponent position's verisimilitude. I vindicate this thesis with the results of simulations of controversial argumentation.

1 Introduction

Justification comes in degrees. In a controversy, some theses are typically better justified than others, and we use to make intuitive judgements by comparing the different statements' strength of justification. Inasmuch as debates hardly lead to clear-cut and irrevocable refutations of contested claims, such comparative judgements regarding the strength of justification appear to represent a core cognitive capacity for evaluating argumentation.

It is anything but clear what exactly is referred to by the pre-theoretic notion of strength of justification. But it is even less clear, why strength of justification should guide our convictions and beliefs as rational beings. Logical relations between sentences, fair enough, ought to guide our beliefs for we would be trapped in plain contradictions if we ignored them. But refusing to assent to a statement that is strongly justified does not necessarily lead to a contradiction: hence the question in which way it is rational to approve of claims with high degree of justification.

Building on previous work in argumentation theory, primarily the so-called theory of dialectical structures, this chapter introduces a formal explication of the

G. Betz (✉)
Karlsruhe Institute of Technology, Karlsruhe, Germany
e-mail: gregor.betz@kit.edu

F. Zenker (ed.), *Bayesian Argumentation: The practical side of probability*,
Synthese Library 362, DOI 10.1007/978-94-007-5357-0_7,
© Springer Science+Business Media Dordrecht 2013

pre-theoretic notion of strength of justification that does justice to our argumentative intuitions (Sects. 2, 3, 4). It is then shown, by means of computer simulation, that acquiring beliefs with high degree of justification fosters the fundamental epistemic aim of acquiring true beliefs (Sect. 5). In this final step, this chapter goes substantially beyond the current literature and presents a surprising result obtained by innovative, formal methods.

2 The General Framework: Theory of Dialectical Structures

A *dialectical structure* $\tau = \langle T, A, U \rangle$ is a set of deductive arguments (premiss-conclusion structure), T, on which an attack relation, A, and a support relation, U, are defined as follows ($a, b \in T$):

- $A(a, b)$: a's conclusion is contradictory to one of b's premisses.
- $U(a, b)$: a's conclusion is equivalent to one of b's premisses.

Complex debates can be reconstructed as dialectical structures. Figure 1 depicts the dialectical structures of different philosophical classics. Obviously, these reconstructions represent interpretations and hence face the same hermeneutic challenges as any other interpretative analysis. In particular, reconstructions are typically underdetermined by the textual basis so that there is no single dialectical structure that captures best the texts' argumentation. Dialectical structures represent a powerful tool to sort out the diverse inferential relations in a complex debate and help proponents to navigate in an otherwise intransparent controversy.

The following example (A) depicts a purely formal dialectical structure composed of ten arguments and two theses. Positive integers stand for sentences, and a negative integer represents the negation of the sentence which is referred to by the corresponding positive number. Dashed arrows indicate attack; solid arrows mark support relationships between arguments and theses.

Example (A).

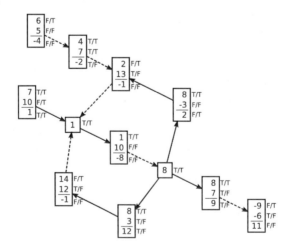

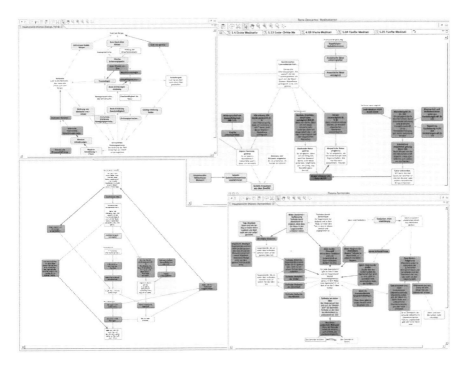

Fig. 1 Four screenshots that depict dialectical structures of different classical philosophical texts. Clockwise, starting in the *upper right corner*: Descartes' Second Meditation, Plato's Parmenides, Descartes' Third Meditation, and Hume's Dialogues Concerning Natural Religion. Dialectical structures have been reconstructed with the argument-mapping software Argunet (See http://www. argunet.org for more examples)

In addition to generating transparency, dialectical structures may also help to evaluate a controversy in a structured way. This motivates the introduction of the concept of a (coherent) position proponents can adopt on a dialectical structure.

A *complete position* $\mathcal{Q}$ (a proponent can adopt) on τ is a truth-value assignment to all sentences which figure in arguments in T, that is, $\mathcal{Q} : S \rightarrow \{t,f\}$, where S is the set of all sentences in τ.

A *partial position* $\mathcal{P}$ (a proponent can adopt) on τ is a truth-value assignment to some sentences which figure in arguments in T, that is, $\mathcal{P} : S' \rightarrow \{t,f\}$, where $S' \subset S$.

Example (A) displays, besides the dialectical structure, two complete positions. According to the left-hand side complete position, sentence 6 is false, sentence 5 is false, etc. According to the right-hand side complete position, however, sentence 6 is true, 5 is false, and so on.

The following example (B) depicts a partial position that is defined on the very same dialectical structure as the two complete positions in example A. This partial position assigns 2 the value 'false' and 8 the value 'true', for instance, whereas 3 and 4 are assigned no truth value whatsoever.

Example (B).

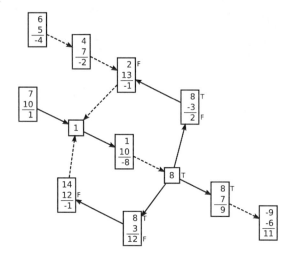

Obviously, the logico-inferential relations encoded in a dialectical structure imply that not any complete or partial position can be reasonably, that is, in a noncontradictory way, adopted by a proponent. Thus, we introduce the following: A complete position Q on τ is *coherent* if and only if:

(1) Equivalent sentences are assigned the same truth value.
(2) Contradictory sentences are assigned complementary truth values.
(3) If every premiss p of some argument $a \in T$ is assigned the value 'true', then a's conclusion is assigned the value 'true', too.

A partial position $\mathcal{P} : S' \to \{t,f\}$ on τ is *coherent* if and only if it can be extended to a complete position Q on $\tau(\mathcal{P} = Q|s')$ which is coherent.

Example A (continued).
- *The left-hand-side complete position in example A is coherent.*
- *The right-hand-side complete position in example A is not coherent. It violates constraint (1)—cf. sentence 10—, constraint (2)—cf. sentences 3/-3—, and constraint (3)—cf. argument (4,7;−2).*

Example B (continued).
- *The partial position in example B is not coherent since it cannot be extended to a complete, coherent position—cf. arguments (8,−3;2) and (8,3;12): −3 has to be false; otherwise constraint (3) would be violated; for analogous reasons, 3 has to be false, but then constraint (2) is not satisfied.*

3   Degrees of Partial Entailment

This section introduces the formal concepts of degree of justification and degree of partial entailment and argues that these theoretic notions suit our pre-theoretic intuitions regarding strength of justification (Betz 2011).

Following Wittgenstein's basic idea[1] and identifying 'cases' in the following general formula with complete and coherent positions on τ, the *degree of partial entailment* of a partial position $\mathcal{P}_1$ by a partial position $\mathcal{P}_2$ can be defined as:

$$\text{DOJ}(\mathcal{P}_1|\mathcal{P}_2) = \frac{\text{number of cases with } \mathcal{P}_1 \& \mathcal{P}_2}{\text{number of cases with } \mathcal{P}_2} \tag{1}$$

$$= \frac{\text{positions that extend } \mathcal{P}_1 \& \mathcal{P}_2}{\text{number of complete \& coherent positions that extend } \mathcal{P}_2} \tag{2}$$

Degrees of partial entailment satisfy, under certain conditions which we shall assume to hold, the *axioms of probability theory* [cf. Betz 2011].

The *degree of justification* of a partial position $\mathcal{P}$ can be defined as its degree of partial entailment from the empty set:

$$\text{DOJ}(\mathcal{P}) = \text{DOJ}(\mathcal{P}|\emptyset) \tag{3}$$

$$= \frac{\text{number of complete \& coherent positions that extend } \mathcal{P}}{\text{number of complete \& coherent positions}} \tag{4}$$

Formally defined degrees of justification dovetail with our pre-theoretic intuitions. To see this, note that the degree of justification of some partial position crucially depends on the respective dialectical structure, that is, the state of a debate. As new arguments are introduced, the dialectical structure changes, some previously coherent complete positions become incoherent, and degrees of justification are altered, as a result. The effects on formally defined degrees of justification of introducing specific arguments into a debate correspond closely to our intuitive judgements and match our everyday argumentative practice. Thus, in particular, DOJ $(\mathcal{P})$—with $\mathcal{P}$ but assigning the thesis t the value 'true'—is increased by:

- Supporting t with a new, independent argument
- Supporting a supporting argument of t
- Attacking an argument that attacks t
- Incorporating premises of supportive arguments into the body of background knowledge
- Incorporating the negations of premises of opposing arguments into the body of background knowledge
- Increasing the degree of justification of premises of supportive arguments[2]
- Decreasing the degree of justification of premises of opposing arguments[3]

---

[1] See Wittgenstein (1984, 5.15) and Carnap (1950), who seized on this idea.

[2] Proof sketch: Consider a supportive argument $(p_1 \ldots p_n; t)$. This argument increases DOJ $(\mathcal{P})$ by rendering all positions incoherent according to which $p_1 \ldots p_n$ are true and t is false. The more such positions are rendered incoherent, the more DOJ $(\mathcal{P})$ is, ceteris paribus, increased. And the greater the degree of justification of some premiss pi, the more positions assign, ceteris paribus, $p_1 \ldots p_n$ the truth value 'true' and t the value 'false'.

[3] To be shown in analogy to sketch in footnote 2.

Likewise, DOJ($\mathcal{P}$) is decreased by:

- Attacking t with a new, independent argument
- Supporting an attacking argument of t
- Attacking an argument that supports t
- Incorporating premises of opposing arguments into the body of background knowledge
- Incorporating the negations of premises of supportive arguments into the body of background knowledge
- Decreasing the degree of justification of premises of supportive arguments[4]
- Increasing the degree of justification of premises of opposing arguments[5]

Moreover, degrees of justification are invariant to introducing entirely unrelated arguments into a debate. All these properties of formal degrees of justification corroborate the claim that we have successfully explicated our pre-theoretic notion of strength of justification.

4   Bayes' Rule

The entailment relation is, in dialectical structures, typically not symmetric. If p entails, against the background of B, q, this does not imply that q entails p (given B).

Example (C).

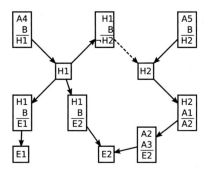

In this illustrative dialectical structure, thesis H_1 entails, based on the arguments uncovered so far, both sentence E_1 and sentence E_2, provided the background knowledge B is given. Likewise, H_2 entails E_2 relative to A_1 and A_3. The reverse, however, is not true. Neither E_1 nor E_2 implies H_1. And E_2 does not entail H_2, either.

But we have noted above that degrees of justification satisfy the probability axioms (Sect. 3). As a consequence, *Bayes' rule* holds, and we have, in particular,

$$\text{DOJ}(\mathcal{P}|\mathcal{Q}) \cdot \text{DOJ}(\mathcal{Q}) = \text{DOJ}(\mathcal{Q}|\mathcal{P}) \cdot \text{DOJ}(\mathcal{P}), \tag{5}$$

---

[4] To be shown in analogy to sketch in footnote 2.
[5] To be shown in analogy to sketch in footnote 2.

for two arbitrary partial positions $\mathcal{P}, \mathcal{Q}$. Hence, the more $\mathcal{P}$ entails $\mathcal{Q}$, the more $\mathcal{Q}$ entails—*ceteris paribus*—$\mathcal{P}$. The relation of partial entailment is, apparently, *symmetric*.

Example C (continued). Let us define partial positions on the dialectical structure depicted above as follows:

- $\mathcal{H}_1 := H_1$ *is true;* H_2 *is false.*
- $\mathcal{H}_2 := H_1$ *is false;* H_2 *is true.*
- $\varepsilon := E_1$ *and* E_2 *are true.*

  Then:

	$\mathrm{DOJ}(\varepsilon\|\mathcal{H}_i)$	$\mathrm{DOJ}(\mathcal{H}_i\|\varepsilon)$
$i = 1$	1	0.44
$i = 2$	0.3	0.33

In other words, $\mathcal{H}_1$ entails ε more strongly than $\mathcal{H}_2$. And, symmetrically, ε entails $\mathcal{H}_1$ to greater extent than it entails $\mathcal{H}_2$.

The symmetry of the partial entailment relation, which we have briefly exposed in this section, paves the way for justifying inference to the best explanation (Betz 2010b) and for revamping the hypothetico-deductive account of confirmation (Betz 2010a).

5   Rationality, Robustness, and Verisimilitude

Why, and in which sense, is it rational to strive, as a proponent in a debate, to hold a partial position with a high degree of justification? Why should degrees of justification guide our beliefs? As indicated in the introductory section, an answer to the similar question in the case of logical entailment is straightforward: We better take account of deductive arguments and logical entailment when assessing our convictions, for otherwise we will be trapped in plain contradictions. Yet denying a sentence which possesses a high degree of justification given the current state of the debate does not lead to any contradiction whatsoever: hence the question why strength of justification should matter to the assessment of our beliefs at all.

This section unfolds two lines of reasoning which address the aforementioned issue. A first answer (a) stresses that partial positions with high degree of justification are robust vis-à-vis different future evolutions of a controversy, no matter how the background knowledge will change; such partial positions can be coherently retained, that is. A second answer (b) relates degrees of justification to verisimilitude and the fundamental epistemic aim of acquiring true beliefs. Partial positions with a high degree of justification are, in the terminology of Goldman (Goldman 1999), veritistically valuable. This result is obtained by computer simulations and statistical assessment of debate dynamics.

(a) Degrees of justification are an indicator of the *robustness* of a proponent's core position. A partial position $\mathcal{P}$ which is said to be robust:

- Can be extended in very different ways to a complete, coherent position
- Hardly determines the truth values of sentences outside $\mathcal{P}$
- Is therefore immune to falsification by fixing truth values outside $\mathcal{P}$

A position $\mathcal{P}$ which is not robust:

- Can be extended in very few ways to a complete, coherent position
- More or less fully determines the truth values of sentences outside $\mathcal{P}$
- Is therefore prone to falsification by fixing truth values outside $\mathcal{P}$

In sum, we obtain a Lakatosian picture of proponent positions and the import of degrees of justification [Lakatos 1999]. Inasmuch as a proponent aims at adopting a partial position, as a core position, which can be retained come what may, she should maximise the degree of justification of her core position. For this ensures (to some degree) that she may coherently hold on to her position no matter how truth values are altered outside her core position.

(b) Degrees of justification are an indicator of the likelihood that a thesis is true. This bold claim can be substantiated with computer simulations of formal debate dynamics, as the remainder of this section will explain.

To probe the relationship between degrees of justification and truth, we have conducted simulations of formal debate dynamics. These simulations, which employ the ArDys framework,[6] mimic the evolution of controversies, where each state of a debate is represented by a purely formal dialectical structure as depicted, for instance, in examples A and B; that is, sentences are represented by integers, their negations are referred to by the corresponding negative numbers. The simulation of a debate evolution starts with a pool sentences (typically 20 sentences plus their negations). Note that the internal semantic structure of these sentences is not represented in the model. Initially, an arbitrarily chosen truth-value assignment is designated as the truth. Next, arguments, which are presumed to be deductively valid, are successively introduced into the debate. These arguments are constructed randomly, that is, two premises and a conclusion are chosen randomly from the sentence pool. The sole condition a new argument has to satisfy is that it leaves the truth coherent. The simulation stops when there is but one coherent position left (which is, given the design of the simulation, necessarily identical with the truth).

Figure 2 depicts four different states of a simulated formal controversy, with 5, 10, 15, and 20 arguments introduced, respectively. We have carried out this kind of debate simulation not only once but 1.000 times in order to obtain an ensemble of individual debate evolutions. As the argument construction mechanisms are indeterministic, the debates in the ensemble differ substantially.

---

[6] See http://ardys.sourceforge.net/

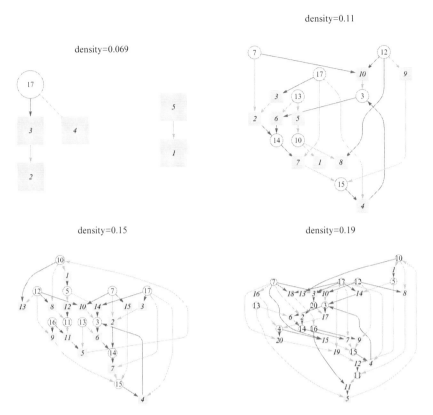

Fig. 2 Four different states of a single member of the debate ensemble. The inferential densities of the dialectical structures with 5, 10, 15, and 20 arguments are shown on *top* of each argument map. *Yellow boxes* represent (numbered) arguments. Sentences which occur in several arguments are introduced as theses (circle) into the map (Color figure online)

As the four argument maps in Fig. 2 illustrate, the number of dialectic relations increases and the argumentation becomes ever more interconnected as more and more arguments are introduced. The extent to which sentences are interrelated via arguments in a debate can be precisely gauged by the *inferential density* of a dialectical structure, a concept which is formally defined in Appendix A. In the absence of any arguments, the inferential density of a debate equals 0. Introducing arguments increases the inferential density. And an inferential density of 1 signifies that there is but one single coherent position left. Figure 2 displays the corresponding inferential densities on top of each dialectical structure. The inferential density of the dialectical structure in example A equals 0.30.

Now, consider the following question: How many sentences that possess a given degree of justification are actually true? It is clear how to answer this question given the ensemble simulation. One simply has to calculate degrees of justification of every sentence, at every time step, in every debate of the ensemble (where the degree of justification of a sentence is, more precisely, the degree of justification of

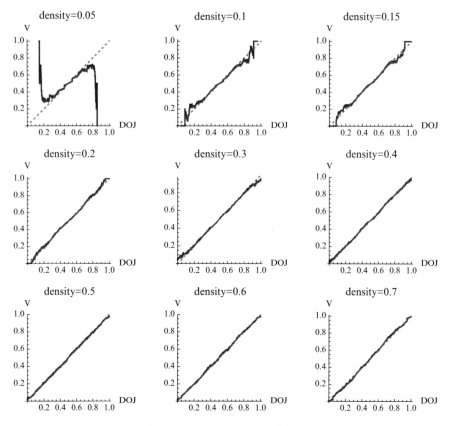

Fig. 3 Results from the ensemble simulation. The plots depict the ratio V of true sentences in a class of sentences with a certain degree of justification DOJ. Each plot but considers dialectical structures that possess (approximately) the indicated density

the partial position which considers but the corresponding sentence true[7]). Next, simply pick those sentences that possess the specified degree of justification and check which of these are true (according to the position initially designated as true in the corresponding simulation).

To account for debate progression, we shall differentiate the previous question as follows: How many sentences that possess a given degree of justification are actually true in dialectical structures with a certain inferential density? Addressing this more specific question allows us to see, in particular, whether degrees of justification have anything to do with truth at low densities, that is, densities we may hope to reach in real debates. The results that provide an answer to the above question are shown in Fig. 3.

---

[7] Carrying out these calculations, complete positions are defined on the entire sentence pool, and not merely on the sentences which occur in arguments already introduced.

The ratio of true sentences, V, is not only strongly correlated with the sentences' degree of justification: Both values are more or less identical. Degrees of justification show directly the ratio of true sentences. Of all sentences with a degree of justification of 0.8, for example, 80 % are true (in the ensemble). This astonishing relationship holds even for very low inferential densities.

Degrees of justification, the simulations of debate dynamics hence demonstrate, are a reliable indicator of the likelihood that some sentence is in fact true. Partial positions with a high degree of justification are therefore veritistically valuable (Goldman 1999). Adopting positions with a high degree of justification fosters the achievement of a basic epistemic aim, and that's why degrees of justification should guide the belief-formation process of rational beings.

6 Conclusion

We have introduced, within the framework of the theory of dialectical structures, the concept of degree of justification. We saw that the concept of degree of justification, as formally defined, agrees with our argumentative practice and may hence be considered an appropriate explication of our pre-theoric (comparative) notion of strength of justification. Moreover, we saw how Bayes' rule, which applies to degrees of justification, fits into this framework: It reflects the symmetry of the relation of partial entailment, which paves the way, or so this chapter claimed, for justifying inference to the best explanation and for revamping the hypothetico-deductive account of confirmation.

Going beyond the current literature, we have addressed the fundamental question why degrees of justification should guide the belief formation of rational agents. In the final section, we offered two alternative answers. (a) Proponents in a controversy should seek to adopt core positions with a high degree of justification inasmuch as they strive to hold robust core positions, that is, core positions which can (to a large degree) be retained come what may. (b) Proponents should take account of degrees of justification when assessing their position in regard of acquiring beliefs that are likely to be true. Specifically, degrees of justification have been shown to reliably indicate a sentence's likelihood to be correct The latter finding, linking degrees of justification to veritistic aims, has been vindicated by novel simulations of formal debate dynamics.

Appendix A: Inferential Density

A pivotal characteristic of a dialectical structure is its inferential density. Intuitively, it can be understood as measure of the inferential constraints encoded in τ. Roughly, the more arguments a dialectical structure hosts, the higher its inferential density. However, not every additional argument changes the inferential relations encoded in τ—some arguments are redundant and do not render any previously coherent position dialectically incoherent. It is thus appropriate to explicate the notion of a dialectical structure's inferential density in terms its coherent positions rather than in terms of the argument map itself. The smaller the number of coherent positions (left) on some τ, the greater its inferential density. More precisely, we define the inferential density of some τ with a pool of $2n$ sentences as,

$$D(\tau) = \frac{n - \lg(\sigma_\tau)}{n}, \tag{6}$$

where σ_τ refers to the number of coherent and complete positions on τ. The inferential density, thus defined, relates the number of binary choices that one has to make when adopting a position in τ to the number of (initial) binary choices which determine a position in the absence of any arguments. Whatever the arguments contained in τ, n binary choices (one true/false choice for every pair of contradictory sentences) are necessary to specify a complete position. Yet, it requires but $\lg(\sigma_\tau)$ binary choices to pick one of the σ_τ coherent positions. Obviously, $D(\tau)$ is strictly monotonic in σ_τ: The fewer coherent positions, the higher the inferential density. Moreover, since $\sigma_\tau \leq 2^n$, we have

$$D(\tau) = \frac{n - \lg(\sigma_\tau)}{n} \geq \frac{n - \lg(2^n)}{n} = 0.$$

Let us consider some extreme cases. If there is no coherent position on τ at all, $\sigma_\tau = 0$, we have $D(\tau) = \infty$. In this case, the reconstruction logic (the inference rules underlying the individual arguments) is inconsistent. If exactly one complete position is coherent, $\sigma_\tau = 1$, then $D(\tau) = 1$. Finally, if every combinatorially possible position is coherent, $\sigma_\tau = 2^n$, then $D(\tau) = 0$ and the dialectical structure imposes no inferential constraints whatsoever.

References

Betz, G. (2010a). *Revamping hypothetico-deductivism: A dialectic account of confirmation* (Unpublished manuscript, available from the author).

Betz, G. (2010b). *Justifying inference to the best explanation as a practical metasyllogism on dialectical structures* (Unpublished manuscript, available from the author).

Betz, G. (2011). On degrees of justification. *Erkenntnis*, forthcoming.

Carnap, R. (1950). *Logical foundations of probability*. Chicago: University of Chicago Press.

Goldman, A. I. (1999). *Knowledge in a social world*. Oxford/New York: Clarendon Press; Oxford University Press.

Lakatos, I. (1999). Falsification and the methodology of scientific research programs. In I. Lakatos & A. Musgrave (Eds.), *Criticism and the growth of knowledge* (pp. 91–196). Cambridge: Cambridge University Press.

Wittgenstein, L. (1984). *Tractatus logico-philosophicus*. Frankfurt a. M: Suhrkamp.

Argumentation with (Bounded) Rational Agents

Robert van Rooij and Kris de Jaegher

Abstract A major reason for our communication is to influence our conversational partners. This is so both if our preferences are aligned, and when they are not. In the latter case, our communicative acts are meant to manipulate our partners. We all know that attempts to manipulate are nothing out of the ordinary. Unfortunately, the standard theory of rational communicative behavior predicts that any such attempt will be seen through and is thus useless. The main aim of this chapter is to investigate which assumptions of the standard theory we have to give up to account for our communicative behavior, when preferences between partners are not aligned.

1 Introduction: Communicate to Influence Others

Why do we talk? What is the purpose of our use of language? It is obvious that language is used for more than one purpose. Sometimes we use language with an *expressive* purpose: guess what our roommate just did when his computer crashed again. Sometimes language is being used to *strengthen relationships* between people: Our colleagues gossip a lot during lunch. We have to admit, however, that we normally use language just to *influence* the *behavior* of others. And to be honest, we think you are exactly like us. Indeed, although language is a multipurpose instrument, the purpose to influence other's behavior seems to be basic.

We would like to thank Frank Zenker for valuable comments and corrections and the participants of the Bayesian argumentation workshop for useful discussion.

R. van Rooij (✉)
Institute for Logic, Language and Computation, University of Amsterdam,
Amsterdam, The Netherlands
e-mail: R.A.M.vanRooij@uva.nl

K. de Jaegher
Utrecht School of Economics, Utrecht University, Utrecht, The Netherlands

F. Zenker (ed.), *Bayesian Argumentation: The practical side of probability*,
Synthese Library 362, DOI 10.1007/978-94-007-5357-0_8,
© Springer Science+Business Media Dordrecht 2013

Table 1

	a_1	a_2
t_1	1,−2	0,0
t_2	1,3	0,0
t_3	1,−2	0,0

Now, why do we want to influence each others behavior, and how are we going to analyze this? Well, let us again speak for ourselves: We want to influence your behavior by our use of language because we believe that your changing behavior would be profitable for *us*. So we consider one communicative act better than another, when we expect the former to have a more profitable effect than the latter. This suggests that language use is very much like other kinds of economic behavior and that it can be studied profitably by means of *decision* and *game theory*.

According to decision theory, an agent should choose that action which has the highest expected utility. Consider now the following decision problem with an agent wondering which of $\{a_1, a_2\}$ she should perform:

	a_1	a_2
t_1	−2	0
t_2	3	0
t_3	−2	0

On the assumption that the three states are equally likely, it is clear that the agent will choose action a_2 because that has, on average, a higher utility than action a_1, 0 versus −1/3. If an agent receives new information, and the agent believes it, this will turn the old decision problem into a new one. Suppose, for instance, that the agent receives the information that the actual state is in $\{t_1, t_2\}$. As a reaction, the agent will adapt her probability function such that the posterior function gives a probability 0 to state t_3. Maximizing expected utility with respect to this new probability function now results in action a_1 because that has now, on average, the highest utility: 1/2 versus 0. But now suppose that the actual state is actually t_1. Although on the basis of this new information it was *rational* for the agent to choose for a_1, it still was *actually* the *wrong decision*.

Until now we assumed that our agent simply received truthful information. We haven't considered how she received it. Suppose that she received it from another agent. This other agent might also care about which action our agent is going to perform. For instance, he might prefer our agent to perform a_1 instead of a_2, independent of which state actually holds. In such a case, the combined utility table of the answerer (first entry) and our agent can be pictured as follows (Table 1).

For a situation that can be modeled by the above multiagent decision table, it makes a lot of sense for the informer to provide our agent with information $\{t_1, t_2\}$ in case the actual state is t_1: If the agent just accepts what she is informed of, she will perform action a_1, which is exactly what the informer hoped for. Thus, if our agent takes the new information at face value, she can be *manipulated* by the informer and will act in accordance with his, but not her own, preferences.

Table 2

	t_1	t_2		m_1	m_2		ρ_1	ρ_2	ρ_3	ρ_4
σ_1	m_1	m_1	ρ_1	a_1	a_1	σ_1	x, x	x, x	y, y	y, y
σ_2	m_1	m_2	ρ_2	a_1	a_2	σ_2	x, x	$1, 1$	$0, 0$	y, y
σ_3	m_2	m_1	ρ_3	a_2	a_1	σ_3	x, x	$0, 0$	$1, 1$	y, y
σ_4	m_2	m_2	ρ_4	a_2	a_2	σ_4	x, x	y, y	x, x	y, y

But now suppose that our agent knows the preferences of the informer as well and that this, in fact, is common knowledge. If she is also rational, our agent will see through the attempt of manipulation of the informer and will not take the new information at face value. If the informer is rational as well, she will see trough this in turn and will realize that it doesn't make sense to provide information $\{t_1, t_2\}$, because the acting agent won't take this information to be credible. A new question comes up: How much can an agent credibly communicate in a situation like that above? This type of question is studied by economists making use of signaling games.

2   Signaling Games and Nonaligned Preferences

In his classic work on conventions, Lewis (1969) proposed to study communication by means of so-called signaling games. In this section, we will only consider cheap talk games: games where the messages are not directly payoff relevant. A signaling game with payoff irrelevant messages is a sequential game of incomplete information with two players involved, player 1, the sender, and player 2, the receiver. Both players are in a particular state, an element of some set T. Player 1 can observe the true state, but player 2 cannot. The latter has, however, beliefs about what the true state is, and it is common knowledge between the players that this belief is represented by probability function P over T. Then, player 1 observes the true state t and chooses a message m from some set M. After player 2 observes m (but not t), he chooses some action a from a set A, which ends the game. The utilities of both players are given by $U_1(t, a)$ and $U_2(t, a)$. The (pure) strategies of the player 1 and player 2 are elements of $[T \rightarrow M]$ and $[M \rightarrow A]$, respectively. In simple communication games, we call these functions sending and receiving strategies, that is, σ and ρ.

What strategy combinations are *equilibria* of the game depends on the probability distribution. With distribution P, the strategy pair $\langle S, R \rangle$ is an equilibrium if, as usual, neither player can do any better in terms of expected utility by unilateral deviation. As a small example, consider the signaling game with only two states t_1 and t_2, two messages m_1 and m_2, and two actions a_1 and a_2, and utility functions $U(t_i, a_j) = 1$, if $i = j$, o otherwise. Obviously, both players have four (pure) strategies each. Furthermore, let $x = P(t_1) > P(t_2) = y$. Then, we have the payoff matrix in Table 2.

It is easy to see that the signaling game described above has four Nash equilibria: $\langle \sigma_1, \rho_1 \rangle, \langle \sigma_2, \rho_2 \rangle, \langle \sigma_3, \rho_3 \rangle$, and $\langle \sigma_4, \rho_1 \rangle$. But what we are interested in here are the cases where communication takes place, meaning that in different states, different messages are sent. It is easy to see that this is the case only in the equilibria $\langle \sigma_2, \rho_2 \rangle$ and $\langle \sigma_3, \rho_3 \rangle$. In cheap talk games, the messages are not directly payoff relevant: The utility functions do not mention the messages being used. Thus, the only effect that a message can have in these games is through its information content: by changing the receiver's belief about the situation the sender (and receiver) is in. If a message can change the receiver's beliefs about the actual situation, it might also change the receiver's optimal action and thus indirectly affect both players' payoffs.

In an important article, Crawford and Sobel (1982) show that cheap talk can have real strategic impact in that it might change the receiver's optimal action but also that the amount of possible communication in cheap talk games depends on how far the preferences of the participants are aligned. They show that when the preferences are more aligned, more communication can occur through costless signaling. To put it more negatively, they show that in Lewisean cheap talk games communication is possible only if the preferences of speaker and hearer are aligned. In a zero-sum two-person game, for instance, it is predicted that communication with cheap messages is impossible: Whatever is said by the sender will be ignored by the receiver. One might think of this result as a motivation of Grice's cooperative principle, which assumes that the participants are cooperative—thus have aligned preferences—in a conversation (Grice 1967).

To establish the fact proved by Crawford and Sobel, no mention was made of any externally given meaning associated with the messages. What happens if we assume that these messages *do* have an externally given meaning, taken to be sets of situations? Thus, what happens when we adopt an externally given interpretation function "[[·]]" that assigns to every $m \in M$ a subset of T? The interesting question is now not whether the game has equilibria in which we can associate meanings with the messages, but rather whether there exist equilibria where the messages are sent in a *credible* way. That is, are there equilibria where a speaker sends a message with meaning $\{t_i\}$ if and only if she is in state t_i? As it turns out, the old question concerning informative equilibria in signaling games without preexisting meaning and the new one concerning credible equilibria in signaling games with messages that have a preexisting meaning are closely related. Farrell (1988, 1993), Rabin (1990), Matthews et al. (1991), and Stalnaker (2006) show that costless messages with a preexisting meaning can be used to credibly transmit information only if it is known by the receiver that it is in the sender's interest to speak the truth. Communication is predicted to be possible only if the preferences are aligned. But this immediately gives rise to a *problem*. It seems that agents—human or animal—also send messages to each other, even if the preferences are less harmonically aligned. Why would they do that? In particular, how could it be that natural language is used for communication even in these unfavorable circumstances?

Reputation effects of lying in repeated games have been proposed (e.g., Axelrod and Hamilton 1981) to explain reliable communication. But experiments show that communication takes place even in one-shot games. To account for these cases, it is standardly assumed both in *economics* (starting with Spence 1973) and in *biology* (Zahavi 1975; Grafen 1990; Hurd 1995) that reliable communication is possible, if we assume that signals can be too *costly* to fake. The utility function of the sender

Table 3

u_s, u_r		t_1	t_2	t_3	t_4
Utility	t_1	1, 0	2, −1	3, −4	4, −9
	t_2	1, −1	2, 0	3, −1	4, −4
	t_3	1, −4	2, −1	3, 0	4, −1
	t_4	1, −9	2, −4	3, −1	4, 0

takes no longer only the benefit of the receiver's action for a particular type of sender into account but also the cost of sending the message. But assuming that messages of natural languages can be costly seems counterintuitive.[1] Until now, we have not assumed that speakers are required to speak truly. Perhaps by adding this constraint, we can explain communication in more general settings. This issue is discussed in persuasion games, to which we will turn now.

2.1 Persuasion Games

Persuasion games are very similar to signaling games, but where the messages do have preexisting meaning, and it is assumed that signallers can only send true messages.

In general, we can think of a persuasion game as a game between an interested party (the sender) and a decision maker (the receiver). Let T be a finite set of *states of the world* and P a full support probability on T. The decision maker is interested in predicting the value of a *payoff relevant state* or $t_i \in T$ by choosing a state $t_j \in T$ as close as possible to the actual state t_i. The interested party's utility function u_S is strictly increasing in T. Thus, for all $t_i \in T$, $u_s(t_i, t_j) > u_s(t_i, t_k)$ just in case $j > k$. This, of course, is common knowledge, which means that the decision maker knows the ordinal preferences of the interested party. As usual, the decision maker doesn't know the actual state, but the interested party tries to persuade the decision maker that the true state is high by revealing some information. A sender strategy σ is a function from states to messages, such that for any $t \in T : t \in [\![\sigma(t)]\!]$. Thus, the set of available messages for each type, $\Omega(t)$, is a subset of $\{m \in M: t \in [m]\}$. What is important is that when the actual state is t, the sender has available a report m that rules out lower quality types. In symbols, $\forall t \in T : \exists m \in \Omega(t) : \forall t' < t : m \notin \Omega(t')$. This assumption would be satisfied, for example, if the sender could always prove the precise quality of its products or if it can prove a tight lower bound on the quality of its product. A decision maker's utility function consistent with the above assumptions can be given by $u_r(t_i, t_j) = -(j - i)^2$. This gives rise to the following type of payoff table, where the rows represent the actual states, while the columns represent the choice of the decision maker (Table 3).

We will assume that a receiver strategy is a function from messages to a probabilistic function over T, such that $\forall m \in M : \sum_t \rho(m)(t) = 1$. The identity of

---

[1] Though see de Jaegher (2003) for more discussion.

$\rho(m)$ will depend on what the decision maker believes, represented by probability function μ. This function μ specifies what the receiver, or decision maker, believes when the sender makes a report. Let us call a pair $\langle \rho, \mu \rangle$ a "posture" for the decision maker. Every posture requires that the decision maker forms beliefs consistent with his information and maximizes accordingly. A *naively credulous* posture is one in which the decision maker takes the sender's report at face value and simply puts $\mu(t|m) = \dfrac{P(t)}{P(\llbracket m \rrbracket)}$ for $t \in \llbracket m \rrbracket$. A *skeptical* posture $\langle \bar{\rho}, \bar{\mu} \rangle$ is one such that, for every report m, $\bar{\mu}(t_j|m) = 1$ for the *minimal* t as far as the sender is concerned, that is, $t \in \llbracket m \rrbracket$ and $\forall t' \in \llbracket m \rrbracket : u_s(\cdot, t') \geqslant u_s(\cdot, t_i)$. A skeptical posture minimizes (over all postures) the state he is going to guess. In terms of seller and buyer, a skeptical posture minimizes the quantity the buyer will purchase. Equilibria of this game are defined in terms of triples like $\langle \sigma, \rho, \mu \rangle$, where σ is a sender strategy and $\langle \rho, \mu \rangle$ is a receiver posture. The triple $\langle \sigma, \rho, \mu \rangle$ is a *sequential equilibrium* if (i) σ is the sender's best response to ρ for whatever type he is; (ii) for all m, $\rho(m)$ is the best guess of the receiver given his beliefs, and (iii) $\mu(t|m) = \dfrac{P(t)}{P(\sigma^{-1}(m))}$ for $t \in \sigma^{-1}(m)$ and is zero otherwise.

Milgrom and Roberts demonstrate that in such persuasion games, it is best for the decision maker to "assume the worst" about what the seller reports and that they have omitted information that would be useful (Milgrom and Roberts 1986). Their optimal equilibrium strategy will always be the *skeptical posture*. What is more, sellers will know that this is the decision maker's optimal strategy. Given this, sellers could as well reveal all they know.[2] In terms of our topic, this means that sellers/informed speakers might try to manipulate the beliefs of the decision maker by being less precise than they could be; this won't help because the decision maker will see through this attempt of manipulation. So, again, the conclusion is that standard economic theory predicts that manipulation by communication is impossible, a result that is very much in conflict with what we perceive daily.[3]

Glazer and Rubinstein have recently studied a somewhat different type of persuasion games. For them, a persuasion problem is a quadruple $\langle \{S, H\}, S, A, p, \sigma \rangle$, with speaker S, hearer H, hearer's goal A, and where p is H's probability function over S. The idea is that S wants H to do a, but H only wants to do it if the actual state s_0 is in A, $s_o \in A \subseteq S$. As in other persuasion games, also Glazer and Rubinstein assume that S can only use true messages. A crucial role in their games is the

---

[2] The argument used to prove the result is normally called the *unraveling argument*. See Jager et al. (to appear) for a slightly different version.

[3] As noted by Shin (1994), the unraveling argument is extremely sensitive to any uncertainty concerning what the informed parties *actually know*. To give a very simple example, suppose that $T = \{t_1, t_2\}$, but that the decision maker is not sure whether the sender knows the true state. Then, if the sender announces that the true state is either t_1 or t_2, the decision maker *cannot* appeal to the unraveling argument to conclude that t_1 is the true state. There is now a positive probability that the seller is genuinely uninformed and is in fact telling the whole truth. Still, one can prove a generalization of the result of Milgrom and Roberts that there always exists a sequential equilibrium $\langle \sigma, \rho, \mu \rangle$ of the persuasion game in which the disclosure strategy σ is perfectly revealing in the sense that the sender will say exactly what he knows.

persuasion function f. It is a function from messages to a number in $[0, 1]$, where this number measures the probability that H is persuaded to do a. Assuming that both players are rational, S wants to choose m that maximizes f, while H wants to minimize the error probability: $\mu_{w_0}(f) = 1 - max_{m \in \sigma(s_0)} f(s)$, if $s_0 \in A$, and $max_{m \in \sigma(s_0)} f(s)$ otherwise.

For illustration, look at the following coin toss example. This is a game about the result of five coin tosses. It is easy to see that this gives rise to 32 possible outcomes. S knows the actual outcome, but H does not. It is common knowledge that S wants H to perform a whatever the outcome is, but H wants to do a only if she is persuaded that the coin landed heads at least three times. Unfortunately, S can only inform H about the outcomes of two coin tosses. What is the optimal way for S and H to proceed? Well suppose that H's rule is to do a iff S demonstrates that the coin came up heads two times. In that case, there are 10 of the 32 possible outcomes where H will make the wrong choice: Do a although the coin came up heads only two times. Thus, the error probability is 10/32. But H can do better: He can perform a only if S demonstrates that the coin came up heads at two *consecutive* tosses. In this case, the error possibility is only 5/32. Glazer and Rubinstein prove that this is also the *optimal* strategy for H to choose. From our point of view we are interested in something else: Can this persuasion game perhaps explain how we try and can manipulate others? But the straightforward answer is again "no." The unique best strategy used by the hearer will always be a *skeptical* one: Always assume the worst. For instance, if the speaker would have said that the coin came up heads on the 1*st* toss and the 3*rd*, the hearer will conclude that the coin didn't come up heads in the 2*nd* trial. Manipulation can't succeed.

3   Giving Up Some Standard Assumptions

We communicate more than standard game theory predicts. This strongly suggests that standard game theory is based on some unrealistic assumptions. In this section, we will discuss three of such assumptions and indicate what might result if we give these up. First, we will discuss the assumption that what game is being played is common knowledge. Second, we will see the implications of giving up the unrealistic hypothesis that everybody is completely rational and this is common knowledge. Finally, we will discuss the assumption that our assessment of probabilities and our decisions is independent of the way the alternatives and decision problems are stated. Giving up either of these assumptions will make more room for communication and will thus be more realistic.

3.1   No Common Knowledge of the Game Being Played

In standard game theory, it is assumed that players model the game in the same way: It is common knowledge what game is played. But this seems like a highly idealized assumption. Is it not the case that players might model the game

Table 4

		b_1	b_2	b_3
Game 1. Actual game	a_1	0,2	3,3	0,2
	a_2	[2,2]	2,1	2,1
	a_3	1,0	4,0	0,1

Table 5

		b_1	b_2	b_3
Game 2. A thinks that B thinks	a_1	0,2	[3,3]	0,2
	a_2	2,2	2,1	2,1

differently or at least view others as modeling it as differently? In recent work, Feinberg (2008) demonstrates that if this possibility is taken into account, a new rationale for communication shows up. Instead of giving his theory, we will just motivate his approach by discussing one of his examples. Consider the following strategic game between row player Alice and column player Bob (Table 4).

This game has obviously exactly one Nash equilibrium: $\langle a_2, b_1 \rangle$. Standard game theory predicts that this equilibrium will be played, if it is assumed that it is common knowledge between the players that the above is indeed the game that is being played. Suppose, however, that Alice believes that Bob thinks that the only actions between which Alice can choose are a_1 and a_2, that is, Alice believes that Bob is unaware of action a_3 and thinks that the following game will be played:

In fact, however, Bob believes that it is the actual game in Fig. 1 that is being played, although he recognizes that Alice is unaware that he is considering a_3 (Table 5).

Bob also thinks that Alice thinks that Bob is considering game 2 as the actual game. Notice that although game 1 has $\langle a_2, b_1 \rangle$ as its unique Nash equilibrium, game 2 has $\langle a_2, b_2 \rangle$ as its unique equilibrium. As a result, Alice thinks it is likely that Bob will play action b_2. Alice's actual best response (i.e., in game 1) to b_2, however, is not a_2, but a_3. But because of Bob's knowledge (he is aware that Alice thinks that Bob is unaware of action a_3), he can figure out that Alice would play a_3, and his best response to this in game 1—the actual game and the game that he thinks he is playing—is action b_3. Thus, this reasoning of Alice and Bob would result in play $\langle a_3, b_3 \rangle$, which is strictly worse for both agents than the Nash equilibria play in either game.

Suppose that before the agents make their choice, agents are allowed to send a message. We have seen that in standard game theory, pre-play communication can normally be ignored (the messages are not credible) if the preferences of the agents are not well aligned. On the other hand, if it were common knowledge that the game was game 1, for example, pre-play communication would be ignored as well because that game has only one Nash equilibrium. We will see that in our case, however, pre-play communication makes perfect sense. Bob can send a message ("I know you can also play a_3") which makes clear to Alice that he is aware of action a_3. It is immediately clear that this message is credible: There is no reason for Alice to think she is being manipulated. As a result, it becomes common knowledge that it is actually game 1 that is being played and that Alice should thus choose a_1 instead of a_3. Together with Bob's best response, we end up with the Nash equilibrium $\langle a_2, b_1 \rangle$ which gives rise to a higher utility for Alice and for Bob. Thus, it was indeed rational for Bob to communicate as he did. Feinberg (2008) discusses more cases like this.

Thus, we can explain more cases of rational communication than we could before if we don't make the ideal, but unrealistic assumption that it is always common knowledge which game is being played.

3.2   No Common Knowledge of Rationality

A Nash equilibrium is the solution concept in game theory, but it is not always easy to reach it. In quite a number of games, however, a simple procedure will do: (iterated) elimination of strategies that violate the canons of rationality, that is, that are strongly dominated. In case we end up with exactly one (rationalizable) strategy for each player, this strategy combination must be a Nash equilibrium. This procedure crucially depends, however, on a very strong epistemic assumption: *common knowledge of rationality*; not only must every agent be ideally rational, everybody must also know of each other that they are rational, and they must know that they know it and so on ad infinitum. It is harder to justify Nash equilibria in general, but also such a justification leans heavily on this strong assumption. Unfortunately, there exists a large body of evidence that the assumption of common knowledge of rationality is highly unrealistic.

The p-beauty contest game (Moulin 1986) is based on a similar game by Keynes (1936) and was introduced to highlight how unrealistic this assumption is. In this game, each of $n > 2$ players chooses a whole number between 0 and 100. Let us say that k is the average of these n numbers. The winners of the game are those players who choose their numbers closest to $2k/3$, and they share the prize equally. Obviously, you shouldn't choose any number greater than $\frac{2}{3} \times 100 \approx 67$, because such a strategy has payoff 0, whereas the mixed strategy playing 0–67 with equal probability has a strictly positive payoff. Thus, any of the former strategies is strongly dominated by the latter mixed strategy and should thus be eliminated after one round of eliminating strongly dominated strategies. A second round of eliminating strongly dominated strategies, however, eliminates choices above $\frac{2^2}{3} \times 100 \approx 44$ in a similar way. Continuing in this manner, we see that the only strategy that is not eliminated in any round is the strategy to choose is 0. Experimental evidence, however, shows that this would be a very poor choice. Working with various groups of size 14–16, Nagel (1995) found that the average number chosen was 35, which is between two and three rounds of iterated elimination of strongly dominated strategies. Thus, in this game, we cannot assume common knowledge of rationality: Agents "think ahead" only a very limited number of rounds.

In the previous sections, we have seen that deception and manipulation could not be explained within standard game theory. One reason for this is that it assumes common knowledge of rationality. If it is common knowledge that everybody is rational, any attempt of deception will be anticipated, and the anticipation thereof will be anticipated as well and so on *ad infinitum*. But we have seen above that it is not in accordance with experimental evidence to assume common knowledge of rationality. Is it possible to explain deception and manipulation if we give up this assumption?

Indeed, it can be argued that wherever we do see attempted deceit in real life, we are sure to find at least a belief of the deceiver (whether justified or not) that the agent to be deceived has some sort of limited reasoning power that makes the deception at least conceivably successful. Some agents are more sophisticated than others and think further ahead. To model this, one can distinguish different *strategic types* of players. A strategic type captures the level of strategic sophistication of a player and corresponds to the number of steps that the agent will compute in a sequence of iterated best responses. One can start with unstrategic level-0 players. An unstrategic level-0 hearer (a credulous hearer), for example, takes the semantic content of the message he receives literally, and doesn't think about why a speaker used this message. Obviously, such a level-0 receiver can sometimes be manipulated by a level-1 sender, as we have seen in Section 1. But such a sender can in turn be "seen through" by a level-2 receiver if she understood why the level-1 sender sent what he sent, etc. In general, a level-$k + 1$ player is one who plays a best response to the behavior of a level-k player. (A *best response* is a rationally best reaction to a given belief about the behavior of all other players.) A fully sophisticated agent is a level-inf player. In a very interesting article, Crawford (2003) shows that in case sender and/or receiver believes that there is a possibility that the other player is less sophisticated than he is himself, deception is possible. Moreover, even sophisticated players can be deceived if they are not sure that the opponent is fully rational or not. Crawford assumed that messages have a specific semantic content, but did not presuppose that speakers can only say something that is true. It is possible, however, to use the same kind of idea to show that manipulation is possible in such circumstances as well in persuasion games as discussed in Section 2.1 of this chapter.

We can conclude that (i) it is unnatural to assume common knowledge of rationality, and (ii) by giving up this assumption, we can explain much better why people communicate than standard game theory can: Sometimes we communicate to manipulate others on the assumption that the others don't "see it through," that is, that we are smarter than them (whether this is justified or not).

3.3   Framing and Reference-Point-Based Preferences

Although our standard of living increased a lot the last decades, psychological research on happiness finds that subjective measures of well-being are relatively stable over time. This suggests that one's well-being crucially depends on the value of one's own properties compared to that of others. In more abstract terms, *utility* is *reference-based*, which is in contrast with the additive utility function underlying standard game theory. The most natural reference point to compare one's welfare is the current *status quo* position. Now, psychologists have discovered that people value payoffs according to whether they are *gains* or *losses* compared to their current status quo position. Subjective well-being is associated not so much with the *level* of income, but more with *changes* of income. Moreover, agents are much more averse to lose X euros than that they are attracted to winning X euros. These phenomena can be illustrated by the following famous Asian disease experiment due to Tversky and Kahneman (1981).

In the two versions of this experiment, which takes the form of a questionnaire, a separate but similar population was confronted with the following hypothetical scenario: "Imagine that the USA is preparing for the outbreak of an unusual Asian disease, which is expected to kill 600 people. Two alternative programs to combat the disease have been proposed."

In version 1 of the experiment, subjects were offered the choice between programs A and B, which are described as follows: "If program A is adopted, 200 people will be saved. If program B is adopted, there is 1/3 probability that 600 people will be saved and 2/3 probability that no people will be saved."

In version 2 of the experiment, subjects were offered the choice between programs C and D: If program C is adopted, 400 people will die. If program D is adopted, there is 1/3 probability that nobody will die and 2/3 probability that 600 people will die.

When the choice is between A and B, 72% of the subjects choose A; when the choice is between C and D, 78% choose D. This is in spite of the fact that, from the perspective of expected utility maximization, the two examples are perfectly equivalent. Apparently, the experimenter, by framing the example in a different manner, can influence the reference point of the subject and can cause a preference reversal.

Let the US population have size X before the outbreak, and let us assume that the decision maker is an expected utility maximizer with an increasing, strictly concave Bernouilli utility function $u(\cdot)$ over the post-outbreak US population. Then it is easy to see that the decision maker should not make any difference between versions 1 and 2. The expected utility of programs A and C is equally $u(X - 400)$. The expected utility of programs B and D is $\frac{1}{3} \times u(X) + \frac{2}{3} \times u(X - 600)$. Note that the numbers are chosen such that if for any Y we have $u(Y) = U$, then $u(X - 400) = \frac{1}{3} \times u(X) + \frac{2}{3} u(X - 600)$. It follows that as soon as $u(\cdot)$ is strictly concave, then $u(X - 400) > \frac{1}{3} \times u(X) + \frac{2}{3} \times u(X\,600)$ so that programs A and C should be preferred. But this is contradicted by the results of Kahneman and Tversky's experiment.

In order to account for such choices counter to expected utility theory (in this and other experiments), Kahneman and Tversky construct *prospect theory*. The elements of this theory are that decision makers think in terms of gains and losses with respect to an exogenously given reference point. Decision makers are risk averse with respect to gains and risk loving with respect to losses (reflection effect). They are loss averse, in that, for example, they are hurt more by a 100 loss than they enjoy a 100 gain. Finally, they overweigh small probabilities.

We only need the reference point and the reflection effect to account for the choices in the Asian disease problem. Let r be the reference point of the decision maker, in this case, a reference post-outbreak US population. Consider a strictly concave valuation function $v(\cdot)$, which is defined both over gains and losses, and with $v(0) = 0$. In the loss region, for a post-outbreak population of Y, the consumer's utility then takes the form $v(Y - r)$ if $Y \geq r$ (gains region) and takes the form $- v(Y - r)$ if $Y < r$ (loss region). The consumer's utility is then indeed strictly convex in the loss region and strictly concave in the gains region. For the rest, all is the same as in expected utility theory.

Assume now that in version 1 of the experiment, the reference point is that nobody is saved so that any person saved is seen as a gain. It follows that $r = X - 600$ and that we are everywhere in the gains region. In this case, the decision maker prefers program A if and only if:

$$v(X - 400 - (X - 600)) > \frac{1}{3} v(X - (X - 600)) + \frac{2}{3} v((X - 600) - (X - 600)) \text{ if}$$

$$v(200) > \frac{1}{3} \times v(600) \text{ if and only if}$$

$$3 \times v(200) > v(600).$$

It is clear that this is valid as soon as we have a strictly concave $v(\cdot)$ so that the decision maker's utility is strictly concave in the gain region.

Assume that in version 2 of the experiment, the reference population is that nobody dies so that any person who dies is seen as a loss. It follows that $r = X$ and that we are everywhere in the loss region. The decision maker now prefers program C if and only if

$$- V(X - (X - 400)) < - \frac{1}{3} V(X - X) - \frac{2}{3} V(X - (X - 600)) \text{ if and only if}$$

$$V(400) > \frac{1}{3} V(600) \text{ if and only if}$$

$$V(600) < 1.5V(400).$$

Again, this is valid as soon as we have a strictly concave $v(\cdot)$ so that the decision maker's utility is strictly convex in the loss region.

But why would the reference points be different in version 1 and version 2? It seems that a reference point is induced merely by expressing the news as a gain ("are saved") or as a loss ("die") with respect to a reference population. In version 1, by expressing the news as a gain with respect to a reference population where 600 people are killed, the decision maker is induced to be risk averse. In version 2, by expressing the news as a loss with respect to a reference population the decision maker is induced to be risk averse.

Ducrot (1973) and Anscombre and Ducrot (1983) have argued that we have to look at language use from an *argumentative perspective* to be able to explain the appropriate use of certain adversarial connectives. Merin (1999) sought to provide a formal analysis of their insights, but failed (cf. van Rooij 2004). We believe that a more appropriate formalization is possible making use of prospect theory. The idea is that the argumentative function of an adversary connective used by a manipulative persuader is to suggest a reference point with respect to which the main body of information given should be compared. Consider the following modified statements for the two versions. In version 1*, the first sentence is now stated as a lack of a gain. Further, the adversarial connective "still" induces a contrast with this situation of no gain. By their nature, such adversarial connectives would seem to invite the listener to make comparisons and so to think in terms of gains and losses. For the rest, all the populations are stated as gains. In version 2*, the first sentence is clearly stated as a loss. The adversarial connective "however" contrasts this with situations where the losses are smaller. All further populations are expressed as losses. Further, the order in which programs C and D are expressed is reversed in comparison to the original experiment. The order in which the alternatives are expressed may also induce a reference point.

Thus, an empirical question here lies in the extent to which adversarial connectives and expressions suggesting gains and/or losses, and the order in which alternatives are presented, are successful in creating reference points with listeners.

Version 1*: Imagine that the USA is preparing for the outbreak of an unusual Asian disease. If no program is adopted, there will be no rescue for 600 people. Still, if program A is adopted, 200 people will be saved, and if program B is adopted, there is 1/3 probability that all 600 people will be saved and 2/3 probability that none of them is saved.

Version 2*: Imagine that the USA is preparing for the outbreak of an unusual Asian disease. If we fail to interfere, 600 people will lose their lives. However, if program B is adopted, there is 1/3 probability that none of these people will die and a 2/3 probability that all 600 of them will continue to die. If program A is adopted, 400 of these people will die.

It should be noted that applications of prospect theory are not confined to uncertainty. Another example (due to Anscombre and Ducrot 1983), which does not involve uncertainty and where both the order of the statements and adversarial connectives seem to play a role, is the following. Consider a restaurant critic who objectively observes a restaurant to be both more expensive than other good restaurants and better than other expensive restaurants.

Version 1** The restaurant is expensive, but good.
Version 2** The restaurant is good, but expensive.

Each time, the earliest statement may induce the reference point. Version 1** could induce a reference point with the decision maker of considering restaurants as expensive. Yet, among expensive restaurants, the restaurant is one of the good ones. Version 2** could induce as a reference point that restaurants serve good food. Yet, among restaurants serving good food, the restaurant at hand is expensive. If the decision maker reads the critics review of the restaurant, and considers eating home as a choice with a utility of zero, then in version 1[**], the decision maker would decide to go to the restaurant (as she perceives positive utility in going to the restaurant), and in version 2[**], she would prefer to stay at home (as she perceives a negative utility in going to the restaurant).

4   Conclusion

So, why do we talk so much? Perhaps because our preferences are much aligned and participants of a conversation all profit from a larger distribution of knowledge. This would be the ideal picture, but we doubt it is the true reason behind (all) our talking. We also talk if our preferences are not aligned. No, we talk so much, we argue, because, among others, (i) we think we know better in which situation we are than others (3.1), (ii) we think we are smarter than others (3.2), or (iii) we think we can influence the probabilities and utilities of others by the way we frame their decision problems. In short, we talk and argue so much because we believe others are *bounded rational agents*.

References

Anscombre, J. C., & Ducrot, O. (1983). *L'Argumentation dans la Langue*. Brussels: Mardaga.

Axelrod, R., & Hamilton, W. (1981). The evolution of cooperation. *Science, 411*, 1390–1396.

Crawford, V. (2003). Lying for strategic advantage: rational and boundedly rational misrepresentations of intentions. *American Economic Review, 93*, 133–149.

Crawford, V., & Sobel, J. (1982). Strategic information transmission. *Econometrica, 50*, 1431–1451.

de Jaegher, K. (2003). Error-proneness as a handicap signal. *Journal of Theoretical Biology, 224*, 139–152.

Ducrot, O. (1973). *La preuve et le dire*. Paris: Mame.

Farrell, J. (1988). Communication, coordination and Nash equilibrium. *Economic Letters, 27*, 209–214.

Farrell, J. (1993). Meaning and credibility in cheap-talk games. *Games and Economic Behavior, 5*, 514–531.

Feinberg, Y. (2008). Meaningful talk. In K. Apt & R. van Rooij (Eds.), *New perspectives on games and interaction* (pp. 105–120). Amsterdam: Amsterdam University Press.

Franke, M. (2009). *Signal to act. Game theory in pragmatics*. PhD thesis, University of Amsterdam.

Glazer, J., & Rubinstein, A. (2008). A study in the pragmatics of persuasion: A game theoretical approach. In K. Apt & R. van Rooij (Eds.), *New perspectives on games and interaction* (pp. 121–140). Amsterdam: Amsterdam University Press.

Grafen, A. (1990). Biological signals as handicaps. *Journal of Theoretical Biology, 144*, 517–546.

Grice, H. P. (1967). *Logic and conversation*. Typescript from the William James Lectures, Harvard University (Published in Grice, P. (1989), *Studies in the way of words*. Cambridge, MA: Harvard University Press, pp. 22–40).

Horn, L. (1989). *A natural history of negation*. Chicago: University of Chicago Press.

Hurd, P. (1995). Communication in discrete action-response games. *Journal of Theoretical Biology, 174*, 217–222.

Keynes, J. M. (1936). *The general theory of employment, interest and money*. New York: Harcourt Brace and Co.

Lewis, D. (1969). *Convention*. Cambridge, MA: Harvard University Press.

Matthews, S., Okuno-Fujiwara, M., & Postlewaite, A. (1991). Refining cheaptalk equilibra. *Journal of Economic Theory, 55*, 247–273.

Merin, A. (1999), *Die Relevanz der Relevanz: Fallstudie zur formalen Semantik der englishen Konjunktion 'but'* (Arbeitspapiere SFB 340, nr. 142), Stuttgart: Stuttgart University.

Milgrom, P., & Roberts, J. (1986). Relying on the information of interested parties. *Journal of Economics, 17*, 18–32.

Moulin, H. (1986). *Game theory for the social sciences* (2nd ed.). New York: NYU Press.

Nagel, R. (1995). Unraveling in guessing games: An experimental study. *American Economic Review, 85*, 1313–1326.

Rabin, M. (1990). Communication between rational agents. *Journal of Economic-Theory, 51*, 144–170.

Spence, M. (1973). Job market signalling. *Quarterly Journal of Economics, 87*, 355–374.

Stalnaker, R. (2006). Saying and meaning, cheap talk and credibility. In A. Benz, G. Jäger, & R. van Rooij (Eds.), *Game theory and pragmatics*. Basingstoke: Palgrave MacMillan.

Tversky, A., & Kahneman, D. (1979). Prospect theory: An analysis of decision under risk. *Econometrica, 47*, 263–291.

Tversky, A., & Kahneman, D. (1981). The framing of decisions and the psychology of choices. *Science, 211*, 453–458.

van Rooij, R. (2004). Cooperative versus argumentative communication. *Philosophia Scientia, 2*, 195–205.

Zahavi, A. (1975). Mate selection – A selection for a handicap. *Journal of Theoretical Biology, 53*, 205–214.

Part IV
Theoretical Issues

Reductio, Coherence, and the Myth of Epistemic Circularity

Tomoji Shogenji

Abstract In the argument by reductio ad absurdum, we prove the conclusion by showing that its negation is inconsistent with the premises. I extend this argument pattern to probabilistic support, viz., if the negation of the hypothesis is incoherent with the body of evidence (in the sense of mutual reduction of the probabilities), then the body of evidence confirms (raises the probability of) the hypothesis. The following comparative form of the principle also holds: If the body of evidence is more coherent with the hypothesis than it is with the negation of the hypothesis, then the body of evidence confirms the hypothesis. The principle reveals that the charge of circularity that is still common in epistemology is misguided—for example, it is perfectly legitimate to confirm the reliability of memory by memorial evidence and the reliability of sense perception by sense perceptual evidence.

1 Introduction

Despite occasional protests, the charge of circularity is still common in epistemology and often considered decisive.[1] For example, it is widely thought to be illegitimate to invoke sense perceptual evidence in support of the reliability of sense perception, memorial evidence in support of the reliability of memory, or testimonial evidence in support of the reliability of testimony. This is because we must avail ourselves of the hypothesis of reliability that is in question when we make use of the perceptual, memorial, or testimonial evidence. We are then arguing in a vicious circle—or so the charge goes. This is a myth and I am going to debunk it in this chapter. The myth of epistemic circularity is a relic of an era when many

---

[1] See Alston (1993) for a clear statement of the charge and Shogenji (2000, 2006) for two of the protests against the charge.

T. Shogenji (✉)
Philosophy Department, Rhode Island College, Providence, RI, USA
e-mail: tshogenji@ric.edu

F. Zenker (ed.), *Bayesian Argumentation: The practical side of probability*,
Synthese Library 362, DOI 10.1007/978-94-007-5357-0_9,
© Springer Science+Business Media Dordrecht 2013

epistemologists hoped to prove the truth of an empirical hypothesis with absolute certainty by deductive reasoning. Once we abandon the dream of absolute certainty and settle for probabilistic reasoning, as most contemporary epistemologists do, it is perfectly legitimate to argue for a hypothesis by the use of the very hypothesis.

I want to clarify the thesis I defend—and what I do not defend—with two examples. One of them concerns memory and the other sense perception.[2] For the first example, suppose you wish to confirm the reliability of your memory from its track record. It is not your goal (let us assume) to establish the perfect reliability of your memory with absolute certainty. So, a few errors in your memory do not wreck your project. Nor is it necessary to eliminate the remote possibility that the entire world, including yourself, sprang up five minutes ago with many years' worth of nonexistent events written in your memory. You are only hoping that the track record confirms (raises the probability of) the hypothesis that most of your memories are accurate. The evidence is promising—you recall that almost all your memories were corroborated by your sense perception later. There are some assumptions I am going to make. For the purpose of investigating your memory, I assume that your meta-beliefs about the contents of your own memory are true. I also assume that your sense perception is reliable and that corroborating evidence in general raises the probability of the hypothesis. So, the body of corroborating sense perceptual evidence does confirm the reliability of your memory, that is, it raises the probability that your memory is reliable. The problem, of course, is that you only *recall* almost all your memories were corroborated by your sense perception later. This is itself memorial evidence, and it is illegitimate—or so it is commonly thought—to invoke memorial evidence in support of the reliability of memory. This is a myth, and I am going to show that given the assumptions made, your memory of corroborating sense perception does confirm the reliability of your memory.

In the second example you wish to confirm the reliability of sense perception (*human* sense perception, hereafter this is assumed) by examining the physiological process of sense perception. As in the first example, it is not your goal to establish the perfect reliability of sense perception with absolute certainty. So, a few errors in sense perception do not wreck your project. Nor is it necessary to eliminate the remote possibility that all humans are brains in a vat manipulated by an evil scientist's supercomputer. You are only hoping that the examination of the physiological process of perception confirms (raises the probability of) the hypothesis that most of what we perceive by senses is accurate. The evidence is promising—you discover information-preserving paths in the physiological process of sense perception as one would expect if sense perception is reliable. There are again some assumptions that I am going to make. I assume for the purpose of investigating sense perception that your meta-beliefs about the content of your sense perception are true. I also assume that the existence of information-preserving paths in the physiological process of sense perception confirms (raises the probability of) the hypothesis that sense perception is reliable. The problem is again circularity. You

---

[2] See Shogenji (2006) for an extended discussion of epistemic circularity involving testimonial evidence.

examine the physiological process of sense perception by your sense perception (aided by various devices). So, the discovery of information-preserving paths is itself sense perceptual evidence, and it is illegitimate—or so it is commonly thought—to invoke sense perceptual evidence in support of the reliability of sense perception. This is again a myth, and I am going to show that given the assumptions made, your sense perception of information-preserving paths in the physiological process of sense perception does confirm the reliability of sense perception.

Note that in both examples, the charge of circularity is not that the hypothesis in question appears as one of those premises that describe the body of evidence. If it were part of the body of evidence, then circularity would be harmless though the probabilistic reasoning would become superfluous—the evidence would establish the truth of the hypothesis directly and trivially. The charge of circularity in the two examples is that the body of evidence confirms the hypothesis only if we assume the truth of the very hypothesis in the process of reasoning. This type of circularity is sometimes called *epistemic circularity* as distinguished from *logical circularity*, and it is the myth of *epistemic circularity* that I am going to debunk in this chapter.[3]

This chapter proceeds as follows. Section 2 reviews the argument by reductio ad absurdum in deductive logic where we make use of a hypothesis in the process of refuting it. Section 3 extends this reasoning pattern to probabilistic reasoning and proposes the principle of probabilistic support in two forms. The presentation in that section is informal and appeals to intuitive judgment, but the relevant concepts of confirmation and coherence are formulated in probabilistic terms in Sect. 4, and the principle of probabilistic support is formally validated in Sect. 5. With the principle of probabilistic support in hand, Sect. 6 returns to the two examples described in this section to debunk the myth of epistemic circularity. Section 7 addresses some objections.

2 Reductio Ad Absurdum

This section reviews the argument by reductio ad absurdum in deductive logic. The argument pattern of reductio ad absurdum resembles the supposedly circular reasoning in support of the reliability of memory and sense perception described in Sect. 1, viz., in reductio ad absurdum, we argue against a hypothesis by making use of the very hypothesis. More specifically, we disprove a hypothesis (and prove its negation) by adding the hypothesis to the set of the premises and deriving a contradiction. An analysis of reductio ad absurdum is in a sense an analysis of deductive validity in general since any valid argument in classical logic can be transformed in a familiar way into an argument by reductio ad absurdum:

$$\{\, p_1, \ldots, p_n \,\} \vdash c \text{ if and only if } \{ p_1, \ldots, p_n, \neg c \} \vdash \bot$$

---

[3] See Alston (1989, pp. 326–329, 1993, pp. 15–17) for the distinction between logical circularity and epistemic circularity.

So, whenever we wish to show that the argument from the premises $p_1, \ldots, p_n$ to the conclusion c is valid, we can add the negation of the conclusion $\neg c$ to the premises $p_1, \ldots, p_n$ and derive a contradiction. Making use of the negation of the conclusion does not make reductio ad absurdum circular because we are not making any *presupposition* or even a *presumption* that the conclusion c is false. We are using the negation of the conclusion only for a hypothetical reasoning to establish the conditional claim that if the negation of the conclusion is added to the set of the premises, we obtain a contradiction. When this conditional claim is established, we declare that the argument from the premises to the conclusion is valid.

Since my main concern in this chapter is epistemic circularity in probabilistic reasoning, I want to make a change in the formulation of reductio ad absurdum in anticipation of its extension to probabilistic reasoning. There are well-known degenerate cases in deductive reasoning where the validity of an argument has nothing to do with the conclusion; viz., an argument is valid regardless of the conclusion if the set of premises is inconsistent.[4] Of course, if the set of premises $\{p_1, \ldots, p_n\}$ is inconsistent, then its superset $\{p_1, \ldots, p_n, \neg c\}$ is also inconsistent. So, the account above is formally correct, but the premises do not deductively *support* the conclusion in these cases. There are two simple ways of excluding the degenerate cases. One is to introduce the requirement that $\{p_1, \ldots, p_n\}$ is consistent. If we adopt this amendment, the premises $p_1, \ldots, p_n$ prove (deductively *support*) the conclusion c and disprove its negation $\neg c$ if $\{p_1, \ldots, p_n\}$ is consistent, while $\{p_1, \ldots, p_n, \neg c\}$ is inconsistent.[5] The other way is to introduce the requirement that $\{p_1, \ldots, p_n, c\}$ is consistent. If we adopt this amendment, the premises $p_1, \ldots, p_n$ prove the conclusion c and disprove its negation $\neg c$ if $\{p_1, \ldots, p_n, c\}$ is consistent, while $\{p_1, \ldots, p_n, \neg c\}$ is inconsistent. The two ways of excluding the degenerate cases are equivalent, that is, under the condition that $\{p_1, \ldots, p_n, \neg c\}$ is inconsistent, $\{p_1, \ldots, p_n\}$ is consistent if and only if $\{p_1, \ldots, p_n, c\}$ is consistent.

Once we formulate reductio ad absurdum in these ways to exclude the degenerate cases, it becomes clear that what makes the premises deductively support the conclusion is the *pairwise* inconsistency between the conjunction of the premises $p_1 \wedge \ldots \wedge p_n$ and the negation of the conclusion $\neg c$.[6] Of course, when $p_1 \wedge \ldots \wedge p_n$ and $\neg c$ are pairwise inconsistent, the set $\{p_1, \ldots, p_n, \neg c\}$ is inconsistent, but stating the condition in the latter form is misleading because given the consistency of

---

[4] I ignore the other type of degenerate cases in which the conclusion is logically true, by assuming that the conclusion is contingent. The reason for the different treatment is that probabilistic support, to which I will extend the argument pattern of reductio ad absurdum, only concerns a hypothesis that is not certain. If the hypothesis is logically true, then the question does not arise whether a body of evidence confirms (raise the probability of) the hypothesis.

[5] The principle is not biconditional so as to allow for the possibility that an inconsistent set of premises may deductively *support* the conclusion, for example, when the conclusion is one of the premises.

[6] In case some people worry that we cannot form the conjunction $p_1 \wedge \ldots \wedge p_n$ if the set of premises is infinite, they may recall that by the compactness theorem if an infinite set of premises logically entails a conclusion, there is a finite subset of it that also logically entails the conclusion, so that we can form the conjunction of the premises. The issue is of little relevance anyway to our actual reasoning since our epistemic resource is finite.

$\{p_1, \ldots, p_n\}$ (or given the consistency of $\{p_1, \ldots, p_n, c\}$ if we choose the second way of excluding the degenerate cases), it is due to the pairwise inconsistency of $p_1 \wedge \ldots \wedge p_n$ and $\neg c$ that the premises deductively support the conclusion. In consideration of this, I state the two forms of the principle of deductive support as follows:

Principle of Deductive Support (First Form): The premises $p_1, \ldots, p_n$ prove (deductively *support*) the conclusion c and disprove its negation $\neg c$ if $p_1 \wedge \ldots \wedge p_n$ is consistent, while $p_1 \wedge \ldots \wedge p_n$ and $\neg c$ are inconsistent.

Principle of Deductive Support (Second Form): The premises $p_1, \ldots, p_n$ prove (deductively *support*) the conclusion c and disprove its negation $\neg c$ if $p_1 \wedge \ldots \wedge p_n$ and c are consistent, while $p_1 \wedge \ldots \wedge p_n$ and $\neg c$ are inconsistent.

3   The Principle of Probabilistic Support

The preceding section reviewed the argument by reductio ad absurdum and introduced the principle of deductive support in two forms. This section extends the principle to probabilistic reasoning to obtain the principle of probabilistic support. The presentation and reasoning in this section is informal and sometimes appeals to intuitive judgment, but the principle is formally validated in Sect. 5 below.

In order to convert the principle of deductive support into the principle of probabilistic support, it is necessary to replace the deductive concepts of proof, disproof, consistency, and inconsistency by their respective counterparts in probabilistic reasoning, which are confirmation, disconfirmation, coherence, and incoherence. Just as the deductive concepts are closely related among themselves, their probabilistic counterparts are also related among themselves. First, the evidence confirms (raises the probability of) the hypothesis if and only if it disconfirms (reduces the probability of) the negation of the hypothesis. Second, coherence is (taken here to be) mutual confirmation, while incoherence is (taken here to be) mutual disconfirmation. The basic idea in this section is to exploit these relations among probabilistic concepts in support of the principle of probabilistic support, which replaces the deductive concepts in the principle of deductive support by their probabilistic counterparts. In addition to the replacement, I make one adjustment in the setting that makes the resulting principle directly relevant to the suspected cases of epistemic circularity, viz., I draw a distinction between the pieces of evidence $e_1, \ldots, e_n$ and the background assumptions b, so that the "premises" that confirm or disconfirm the hypothesis are pieces of evidence $e_1, \ldots, e_n$ we have obtained, and the confirmation of the hypothesis requires that the pieces of evidence make the probability of the hypothesis higher than it is by the background assumptions alone.[7] Similarly, the disconfirmation of the hypothesis requires that the pieces of

---

[7] Section 7 addresses the role of the background assumptions in suspected cases of epistemic circularity.

evidence make the probability of the hypothesis lower than it is by the background assumptions alone. I will call the conjunction $e_1 \wedge \ldots \wedge e_n$ of the pieces of evidence "the body of evidence e." Since the body of evidence can confirm the hypothesis without establishing the truth of the hypothesis conclusively, I will avoid the term "conclusion." The hypothesis remains defeasible in most cases even after confirmation.

We are now ready to extend the principle of deductive support to probabilistic reasoning. If we replace the deductive concepts in the principle of deductive support (first form) by their probabilistic counterparts in a straightforward way, we obtain the following statement: The body of evidence e confirms the hypothesis h and disconfirms its negation $\neg h$ if the body of evidence e is coherent, while e and $\neg h$ are incoherent. The statement is defective, as it stands, because in many normal cases of confirmation, the pieces of evidence $e_1, \ldots, e_n$ that make up the body of evidence e are not coherent. Oftentimes the hypothesis is confirmed strongly when otherwise incoherent pieces of evidence are made coherent by the hypothesis. It is fine for the pieces of evidence $e_1, \ldots, e_n$ to be incoherent as long as they are *consistent*. So, I will keep the requirement of consistency in the principle of deductive support (first form) unchanged and propose the following principle of probabilistic support:

Principle of Probabilistic Support (Simple Form): The body of evidence e confirms the hypothesis h and disconfirms its negation $\neg h$ if e is consistent and e is incoherent with $\neg h$.

The resulting principle is intuitively plausible. In fact it must be true given the relationship among the concepts involved. For, if $\neg h$ and e are incoherent in the sense of disconfirming each other, then obviously e disconfirms $\neg h$, and if e disconfirms (reduces the probability of) $\neg h$, then e confirms (raises the probability of) h. So, the body of evidence e confirms the hypothesis h and disconfirms its negation $\neg h$ if e is incoherent with $\neg h$. The additional condition that e is consistent only excludes the degenerate cases where we cannot sensibly evaluate probabilistic support because the evidence is impossible to be true.

Let us now turn to the principle of deductive support in the second form. By replacing the deductive concepts in the principle by their probabilistic counterparts in a straightforward way, we obtain the following statement: The body of evidence e confirms the hypothesis h and disconfirms its negation $\neg h$ if e and h are coherent, while e and $\neg h$ are incoherent. The statement does not exclude the degenerate cases explicitly where e is inconsistent, but this is actually implied by the condition that e and h are coherent since a statement that is inconsistent by itself cannot be coherent (in the sense of mutual confirmation) with any other statement. Of course, the condition that e and h are coherent says more than the condition in the first form that e is consistent. So, it looks as though an extension of the principle of deductive support (second form) introduces a stronger requirement for probabilistic support than does the principle of probabilistic support (simple form), and that would be unnecessary if the latter is correct. As it turns out, however, the condition is not stronger because h and e confirm each other if and only if $\neg h$ and e disconfirm each other. If the condition in the principle of probabilistic support (simple form) is satisfied, then the condition in the extension of the principle of deductive support (second form) is also satisfied. This still makes the latter redundant—it seems the principle of deductive support (second form) has no interesting counterpart in probabilistic reasoning.

There is however a different way of looking at the second form of the principle of deductive support, viz., $p_1 \wedge \ldots \wedge p_n$ proves c and disproves $\neg c$ if pairing $p_1 \wedge \ldots \wedge p_n$ with $\neg c$ instead of paring it with c *turns* the consistent pair inconsistent. One natural translation of this idea into probabilistic reasoning is that pairing e with $\neg h$ instead of pairing it with h *reduces* the degree of coherence, which suggests the following principle:

Principle of Probabilistic Support (Comparative Form): The body of evidence e confirms the hypothesis h and disconfirms its negation $\neg h$ if e is more coherent with h than it is with $\neg h$.

The principle in this comparative form is more useful in application than the principle in the simple form since comparing degrees of coherence is often much easier than an absolute judgment of incoherence we need to make in the principle of probabilistic support (simple form).

But is the principle of probabilistic support (comparative form) true? It turns out the principle of probabilistic support (comparative form) is not only true, but it is equivalent to the principle of probabilistic support (simple form). The reason is that e is incoherent with $\neg h$ if and only if e is more coherent with h than it is with $\neg h$. I will provide its formal validation in Sect. 5, but we can reason informally as follows. One direction of the biconditional is uncomplicated; viz., if e is incoherent with $\neg h$, then e is more coherent with h than it is with $\neg h$. Suppose e is incoherent with $\neg h$. e is then coherent with h. It follows immediately that e is more coherent with h than it is with $\neg h$. The opposite direction requires more steps. Suppose e is more coherent with h than it is with $\neg h$. Assume, for reductio, that e is not incoherent with $\neg h$. We can then think of two possibilities, viz., (1) e is coherent with $\neg h$ or (2) e is neither coherent nor incoherent with $\neg h$. In the first case, e must be incoherent with h, but then e is not more coherent with h than it is with $\neg h$, contradicting the supposition. In the second case, e must be neither coherent nor incoherent with h, but then e is not more coherent with h than it is with $\neg h$, contradicting the supposition. Since both (1) and (2) lead to a contradiction, we conclude that if e is more coherent with h than it is with $\neg h$, then e is incoherent with $\neg h$, thereby proving the opposite direction of the biconditional.

4   Formal Measures of Confirmation and Coherence

The presentation of the two forms of the principle of probabilistic support in Sect. 3 was informal, and the reasoning for them appealed to intuitive judgments. This section begins the process of their formal validation by providing probabilistic formulations of the two key concepts, confirmation and coherence. Confirmation is a concept with degrees. In some cases the body of evidence strongly confirms the hypothesis, while in other cases it confirms the hypothesis only weakly. There are two ways of formalizing the degree of confirmation in probabilistic terms. One of them—the degree of *absolute* confirmation—is simply the conditional probability of the hypothesis h given the body of evidence e, or $P(h|e)$. The other—the degree of *incremental* confirmation—is the degree of increase in the probability of h that is brought on by the body of evidence e. Incremental confirmation is an increasing function of the conditional probability $P(h|e)$, that is, the higher the conditional probability is, the greater the amount of incremental confirmation (given the same prior probability). But it is also a decreasing function of the prior probability $P(h)$, that is, the lower the prior probability is, the greater the amount of incremental confirmation (given the same conditional probability). Of these two ways of formalizing the degree of confirmation—absolute and incremental—it is the latter that captures the sense of confirmation ("raising the probability") used in Sect. 3. So, "confirmation" hereafter means incremental confirmation.

There are, however, still many ways of measuring the degree of (incremental) confirmation. One of them—the difference measure—takes the difference between the conditional probability $P(h|e)$ and the prior probability $P(h)$ to be the degree of incremental confirmation:

$$\text{Con}_D(h, e) = P(h|e) - P(h)$$

Another measure—the ratio measure—takes the ratio of the conditional probability $P(h|e)$ to the prior probability $P(h)$ to be the degree of incremental confirmation:

$$\text{Con}_R(h, e) = \frac{P(h|e)}{P(h)}$$

There are many other measures proposed in the literature, but I will not go over them here.[8] Common to all measures of incremental confirmation are the following three features:

(1) Con(h, e) is an increasing function of $P(h|e)$.
(2) Con(h, e) is a decreasing function of $P(h)$.
(3) Con(h, e) is equi-neutral [constant regardless of $P(h)$] when $P(h|e) = P(h)$.

The neutral value for the difference measure is $P(h|e) - P(h) = 0$, while the neutral value for the ratio measure is $P(h|e)/P(h) = 1$.[9] The body of evidence e

---

[8] See Fitelson (1999, 2001) and Crupi et al. (2007) for lists of measures proposed in the literature.

[9] Those who like the neutral value 0 may prefer the log-ratio measure $\text{Con}_{LR}(h, e) = \log[P(h|e)/P(h)]$ to the ratio measure. They are ordinally equivalent, but the neutral value for the log-ratio measure is 0.

confirms (disconfirms) the hypothesis h if the degree of confirmation $\text{Con}(h, e)$ is above (below) the neutral value. It follows immediately from this formal characterization that the body of evidence e confirms the hypothesis h if and only if the body of evidence e disconfirms the negation $\neg h$ of the hypothesis, that is, $P(h|e) > P(h)$ iff $P(\neg h|e) < P(\neg h)$.

Coherence is also a concept with degrees. The body of evidence and the hypothesis may be strongly coherent in some cases, while in others they may be coherent only weakly. As in the case of confirmation, there have been many proposals in the literature to unpack the concept of coherence.[10] Fortunately, we need not consider all of the proposals here since many of them differ only with regard to the degree of n-member coherence $\text{Coh}(x_1, \ldots, x_n)$, while for our present purpose only the degree of pairwise coherence $\text{Coh}(x_1, x_2)$ is relevant. Once we narrow our focus on the degree of pairwise coherence, there remain only two types of measures. One of them regards coherence as mutual confirmation and incoherence as mutual disconfirmation. The other considers coherence to be a generalization of logical equivalence, that is, logical equivalence is the limiting case of coherence.

It may appear that these two characterizations of coherence are not different from each other because logical equivalence is the limiting case of mutual confirmation. Unfortunately, the two characterizations are not compatible. Those who regard coherence as mutual confirmation and incoherence as mutual disconfirmation accept that the measure of coherence should be equi-neutral in the sense that any pair of statements that are probabilistically independent of each other (the truth of one member does not affect the probability of the other, and vice versa) should have the same neutral degree of coherence (i.e., they are neither coherent nor incoherent) regardless of any other conditions. Meanwhile, those who consider coherence to be a generalization of logical equivalence accept that the measure of coherence should be equi-maximal in the sense that any pair of statements that are logically equivalent to each other should have the same maximal degree of coherence (i.e., the most coherent possible) regardless of any other conditions. Each of these requirements seems plausible when taken by itself, but in combination they lead to an unacceptable consequence. Suppose we obtain two statements (from different witnesses) and each of them is logically true. They are then both probabilistically independent of each other (truth of one testimony does not affect the probability of the other, and vice versa) and logically equivalent to each other. As a result, their degree of coherence is both neutral (neither coherent nor incoherent) and maximal (the most coherent possible). This is absurd.[11]

---

[10] For a variety of probabilistic measures of coherence, see Bovens and Hartmann (2003), Douven and Meijs (2007), Fitelson (2003), Glass (2002), Meijs (2005), Olsson (2002), Schupbach (2011), and Shogenji (1999).

[11] Fitelson's (2003) measure circumvents the problem by making an exception for the case of logically true members, but as Meijs (2006) points out, Fitelson's measure behaves strangely when the members are *almost* logically true. The reason is that almost logically true members should have an almost neutral degree of coherence and an almost maximal degree of coherence at the same time.

So, we must make up our mind between the two conceptions, and it is clear from the informal discussion in Sect. 3 that the relevant conception of coherence for our purpose is that of mutual confirmation. The measure of confirmation is then equi-neutral, that is, x_1 and x_2 are neither coherent nor incoherent with each other when both $P(x_1|x_2) = P(x_1)$ and $P(x_2|x_1) = P(x_2)$, regardless of any other conditions. However, it is redundant to say "when both $P(x_1|x_2) = P(x_1)$ and $P(x_2|x_1) = P(x_2)$" because the two conjuncts are equivalent, that is, $P(x_1|x_2) = P(x_1)$ if and only if $P(x_2|x_1) = P(x_2)$.[12] Each side, expressed in a symmetrical form, amounts to $P(x_1 \wedge x_2) = P(x_1) \times P(x_2)$. This point on redundancy also applies to the conditions of coherence and incoherence. The two statements x_1 and x_2 are coherent with each other when they confirm each other, that is, when both $P(x_1|x_2) > P(x_1)$ and $P(x_2|x_1) > P(x_2)$, but it is redundant to say "when both $P(x_1|x_2) > P(x_1)$ and $P(x_2|x_1) > P(x_2)$" because the two conjuncts are equivalent to each other, that is, $P(x_1|x_2) > P(x_1)$ if and only if $P(x_2|x_1) > P(x_2)$. Each side, expressed in a symmetrical form, amounts to $P(x_1 \wedge x_2) > P(x_1) \times P(x_2)$. The greater the inequality is, the greater the degree of coherence (the degree of mutual confirmation). Similarly, the two statements x_1 and x_2 are incoherent with each other when $P(x_1 \wedge x_2) < P(x_1) \times P(x_2)$. The greater the inequality is, the greater the degree of incoherence (the degree of mutual disconfirmation).

To summarize the nature of the probabilistic measure of coherence that is relevant to our present purpose, the degree of coherence $Coh(x_1, x_2)$ should have the following three features:

(4) $Coh(x_1, x_2)$ is an increasing function of $P(x_1 \wedge x_2)$.
(5) $Coh(x_1, x_2)$ is a decreasing function of $P(x_1) \times P(x_2)$.
(6) $Coh(x_1, x_2)$ is equi-neutral [neither coherent nor incoherent, regardless of $P(x_1)$ and $P(x_2)$] when $P(x_1 \wedge x_2) = P(x_1) \times P(x_2)$.

There are many ways of meeting these conditions. For example, we may measure the difference between $P(x_1 \wedge x_2)$ and $P(x_1) \times P(x_2)$, or alternatively we may measure their ratio:

$$\mathrm{Coh}_D(x_1, x_2) = P(x_1 \wedge x_2) - P(x_1) \times P(x_2)$$

$$\mathrm{Coh}_R(x_1, x_2) = \frac{P(x_1 \wedge x_2)}{P(x_1) \times P(x_2)}$$

The neutral value for the difference measure is $P(x_1 \wedge x_2) - P(x_1) \times P(x_2) = 0$, while the neutral value for the ratio measure is $P(x_1 \wedge x_2)/[P(x_1) \times P(x_2)] = 1$.[13]

---

[12] I am assuming here (and in what follows) that the conditional probabilities $P(x_2|x_1)$ and $P(x_1|x_2)$ are defined, that is, $P(x_1) \neq 0$ and $P(x_2) \neq 0$.

[13] $\mathrm{Coh}_R(x_1, x_2)$ is a restricted (to $n = 2$) version of the measure of coherence proposed in (Shogenji (1999). Those who dislike the neutral value 1 of the ratio measure may prefer its logarithmic variant $\mathrm{Coh}_{LR}(x_1, x_2) = \log [P(x_1 \wedge x_2)/P(x_1) \times P(x_2)]$. The logarithmic variant is ordinally equivalent to the ratio measure, but its neutral value is 0.

The two statements x_1 and x_2 are coherent (incoherent) with each other if the degree of coherence $\text{Coh}(x_1, x_2)$ is above (below) the neutral value. It does not matter for our present purpose whether we adopt the difference measure, the ratio measure, or any other measure—provided the measure satisfies the conditions (4), (5), and (6). It follows from these general conditions that the two statements x_1 and x_2 are coherent with each other (they confirm each other) if and only if x_1 and $\neg x_2$ are incoherent with each other (they disconfirm each other), that is, $P(x_1 \wedge x_2) > P(x_1) \times P(x_2)$ iff $P(x_1 \wedge \neg x_2) > P(x_1) \times P(\neg x_2)$.

5 Validation of the Principles of Probabilistic Support

Once we become clear about the formal characteristics of the measures of confirmation and coherence, the validation of the principle of probabilistic support (simple form) is straightforward:

Principle of Probabilistic Support (Simple Form): The body of evidence e confirms the hypothesis h and disconfirms its negation $\neg h$ if e is consistent and e is incoherent with $\neg h$.

Translation: $P(h|e) > P(h)$ and $P(\neg h|e) < P(\neg h)$ if $\{e\} \nvdash_b \perp$ and $P(\neg h \wedge e) < P(\neg h) \times P(e)$.

From the condition that e is incoherent with $\neg h$, that is, from $P(\neg h \wedge e) < P(\neg h) \times P(e)$, it follows immediately that $P(\neg h|e) < P(\neg h)$, which is equivalent to $P(h|e) > P(e)$. So, the body of evidence e confirms the hypothesis and disconfirms its negation $\neg h$ if e is incoherent with $\neg h$. The way the concept of incoherence is formalized makes the other condition that e is consistent redundant because $P(\neg h \wedge e) < P(\neg h) \times P(e)$ only if $P(e) \neq 0$ and $P(e) \neq 0$ only if e is consistent.

I now move to the principle of probabilistic support (comparative form) whose validation requires more steps of reasoning:

Principle of Probabilistic Support (Comparative Form): The body of evidence e confirms the hypothesis h and disconfirms its negation $\neg h$ if e is more coherent with h than it is with $\neg h$.

Translation: $P(h|e) > P(h)$ and $P(\neg h|e) < P(\neg h)$ if $\text{Coh}(h, e) > \text{Coh}(\neg h, e)$.

I show the truth of this form by proving its equivalence with the simple form above whose truth has been established. As in the informal reasoning in Sect. 3, the equivalence of the two forms is proven by establishing that $\neg h$ is incoherent with e if and only if e is more coherent with h than it is with $\neg h$, that is, $P(\neg h \wedge e) < P(\neg h) \times P(e)$ if and only if $\text{Coh}(h, e) > \text{Coh}(\neg h, e)$.

The proof from the left to the right is uncomplicated. It follows from $P(\neg h \wedge e) < P(\neg h) \times P(e)$ that $P(e) - P(h \wedge e) < (1 - P(h)) \times P(e)$, and hence $P(h \wedge e) > P(h) \times P(e)$. Further, $\text{Coh}(\neg h, e) < k$ from $P(\neg h \wedge e) < P(\neg h) \times P(e)$, and $\text{Coh}(h, e) > k$ from $P(h \wedge e) > P(h) \times P(e)$, where k is the neural value at which the pair is neither coherent nor incoherent. It follows from these that $Coh(\neg h, e) < Coh(h, e)$. Proof in the opposite direction is by reductio ad absurdum. Suppose $Coh(h, e) > Coh(\neg h, e)$, but assume, for reductio, that it is not the case that $P(\neg h \wedge e) < P(\neg h) \times P(e)$. The assumption leaves us with two possibilities, viz., either (1) $P(\neg h \wedge e) > P(\neg h) \times P(e)$ or (2) $P(\neg h \wedge e) = P(\neg h) \times P(e)$. Suppose (1) $P(\neg h \wedge e) > P(\neg h) \times P(e)$. It then follows that $P(e) - P(h \wedge e) > (1 - P(h)) \times P(e)$, and hence $P(h \wedge e) < P(h) \times P(e)$. Further, $Coh(\neg h, e) > k$ from $P(\neg h \wedge e) > P(\neg h) \times P(e)$, and $Coh(h, e) < k$ from $P(h \wedge e) < P(h) \times P(e)$. So, $Coh(\neg h, e) > Coh(h, e)$, which contradicts the supposition that $Coh(h, e) > Coh(\neg h, e)$. Suppose next (2) $P(\neg h \wedge e) = P(\neg h) \times P(e)$. It then follows that $P(e) - P(h \wedge e) = (1 - P(h)) \times P(e)$, and hence $P(h \wedge e) = P(h) \times P(e)$. It follows from $P(\neg h \wedge e) = P(\neg h) \times P(e)$ and $P(h \wedge e) = P(h) \times P(e)$ that $Coh(\neg h, e) = Coh(h, e) = k$, which contradicts the supposition that $Coh(h, e) > Coh(\neg h, e)$. So, we conclude by reductio ad absurdum that $P(\neg h \wedge e) < P(\neg h) \times P(e)$ if $Coh(h, e) > Coh(\neg h, e)$, thereby proving the opposite direction of the biconditional.

I want to stress that these proofs are *robust* in that the choice of specific measures of confirmation and coherence does not affect them. As long as we are measuring the degree of incremental confirmation (as distinguished from the degree of absolute confirmation) and thus the measure satisfies the conditions (1), (2), and (3) described in Sect. 4, no matter which specific measure of confirmation we adopt—the difference measure, the ratio measure, or some other measure—the proofs come through. Similarly, as long as we understand coherence to be mutual confirmation and incoherence to be mutual disconfirmation (as distinguished from coherence as a generalization of logical equivalence) and thus the measure satisfies the conditions (4), (5), and (6) described in Sect. 4, no matter which specific measure of coherence we adopt—the difference measure, the ratio measure, or some other measure—the proofs come through. The choice of measures does affect the *extent* to which the body of evidence confirms the hypothesis, but the qualitative claims of the principle of probabilistic support both in the simple form and in the comparative form hold regardless of the specific measures of confirmation and coherence.

I want to add one more remark before we return to the issue of epistemic circularity. The principle of probabilistic support (simple form) relates incoherence to confirmation, and the principle of probabilistic support (comparative form) relates difference in the degrees of coherence to confirmation. However, in most cases of their actual applications, the body of evidence e confirms the hypothesis h only against certain background assumptions b we tentatively accept as true at least in the context of the present inquiry. For example, in the context of inquiring into the reliability of memory, we may tentatively accept as true that sense perception is reliable. So, the degree of confirmation is not really the function $Con(h, e)$ with two arguments (the hypothesis and the body of evidence) but the function $Con(h, e|b)$ with three arguments (the hypothesis, the body of evidence, and the background assumptions). This is also true of the degree of coherence, that is, in most cases we measure the degree of coherence between the two statements x_1 and x_2 against certain background assumptions b. So, the degree of pairwise coherence is not really the function $Coh(x_1, x_2)$ with two arguments (the two statement) but the function Coh(x_1, $x_2|b$) with three arguments (the two statement and the background assumptions).

Fortunately, this does not change the substance of our discussion. All that is needed is adding b to the conditions in the formal measures of confirmation and coherence. For example, the difference measure Con$_D(h, e)$ and the ratio measure Con$_R(h, e)$ mentioned earlier are now written as follows:

$$\text{Con}_D(h, e|b) = P(h|e \wedge b) - P(h|b)$$

$$\text{Con}_R(h, e|b) = \frac{P(h|e \wedge b)}{P(h|b)}$$

More generally, the body of evidence e confirms the hypothesis h given b if and only if e raises the probability of h given b, that is, if and only if $P(h|e \wedge b) > P(h|b)$. The three conditions (1), (2), and (3) mentioned in Sect. 4 that any measure of incremental confirmation should satisfy are now written as follows:

(1*) Con(h, $e|b$) is an increasing function of $P(h|e \wedge b)$.
(2*) Con(h, $e|b$) is a decreasing function of $P(h|b)$.
(3*) Con(h, $e|b$) is equi-neutral [constant regardless of $P(h|b)$] when $P(h|e \wedge b) = P(h|b)$.

We can also incorporate the background assumptions b into the measure of coherence. For example, the difference measure Coh$_D(x_1, x_2)$ and the ratio measure Con$_R(x_1, x_2)$ mentioned earlier are now written as follows:

$$\text{Coh}_D(x_1, x_2|b) = P(x_1 \wedge x_2|b) - P(x_1|b) \times P(x_2|b)$$

$$\text{Coh}_R(x_1, x_2|b) = \frac{P(x_1 \wedge x_2|b)}{P(x_1|b) \times P(x_2|b)}$$

The three conditions (4), (5), and (6) mentioned in Sect. 4 that any measure of coherence as mutual confirmation should satisfy are now written as follows:

(4*) Coh(x_1, $x_2|b$) is an increasing function of $P(x_1 \wedge x_2|b)$.
(5*) Coh(x_1, $x_2|b$) is a decreasing function of $P(x_1|b) \times P(x_2|b)$.
(6*) Coh(x_1, $x_2|b$) is equi-neutral [neither coherent nor incoherent, regardless of $P(x_1|b)$ and $P(x_2|b)$] when $P(x_1 \wedge x_2|b) = P(x_1|b) \times P(x_2|b)$.

Nothing of substance changes because of the systematic addition of the background assumptions b. All formal reasoning presented above is still correct *mutatis mutandis*, viz., modulo b throughout. The simple and comparative forms of the principle of probabilistic confirmation are then generalized as follows:

Generalized Principle of Probabilistic Support (Simple Form): The body of evidence e confirms the hypothesis h and disconfirms its negation $\neg h$ given the background assumptions b if e is consistent given b and $\neg h$ is incoherent with e given b.

Translation: $P(h|e \wedge b) > P(h|b)$ and $P(\neg h|e \wedge b) < P(\neg h|b)$ if $\{e\} \not\Vdash_b \perp$ and $P(\neg h \wedge e|b) < P(\neg h|b) \times P(e|b)$.

Generalized Principle of Probabilistic Support (Comparative Form): The body of evidence e confirms the hypothesis h and disconfirms its negation $\neg h$ given the background assumptions b if e is more coherent with h than it is with $\neg h$ given b.
Translation: $P(h|e \wedge b) > P(h|b)$ and $P(\neg h|e \wedge b) < P(\neg h|b)$ if $\text{Coh}(h, e|b) > \text{Coh}(\neg h, e|b)$.

The two forms of the principle of probabilistic support described earlier are special cases where the background assumption b only contains logical truth.

6   The Myth of Epistemic Circularity

With the principle of probabilistic support in hand, I now return to the issue of epistemic circularity. Let us recall the two examples described in Sect. 1. In the first example, you wish to confirm the reliability of your memory from its track record. You have the seemingly strong body of evidence e for the hypothesis h that memory is reliable. Namely, you recall almost all your memories were corroborated by your sense perception later. Part of the background assumptions b in the context of this inquiry is that your sense perception is reliable and that the corroborating sense perceptual evidence confirms the reliability of memory. The charge of epistemic circularity arises because you only *recall* almost all your memories were corroborated by your sense perception later. If the hypothesis h is true and thus this recollection itself is reliable, then the memorial evidence e supports the claim e^* that almost all your memories were indeed corroborated by your sense perception later, which in turn will support the hypothesis h. But we cannot assume the truth of the very hypothesis at issue in support of the hypothesis, according to the charge of epistemic circularity.

This is a myth and we can now debunk it. One source of the confusion is an ambiguity of the term "assume." We may assume a hypothesis in the sense of presupposing its truth, which is inappropriate when we are investigating the hypothesis. However, we can also assume a hypothesis in the sense of envisioning its truth in order to see its consequence, as in reductio ad absurdum where we assume the negation of the conclusion to derive a contradiction. It is perfectly legitimate to assume the hypothesis at issue in this second sense. Indeed, the comparative form of the principle of probabilistic support, which I am going to use in this section, urges us to envision the truth of the hypothesis and then the truth of its negation to compare their respective degrees of coherence with the body of evidence. In our memory example, we envision the truth of the hypothesis h that your memory is reliable and then the truth of its negation $\neg h$ that your memory is not reliable, to compare their respective degrees of coherence with the body of memorial evidence e that you recall almost all your memories were corroborated by your sense perception later. We make this comparison given certain background assumptions b—in particular, it is assumed (presupposed) that your sense perception is reliable.

Once we see the situation in this way, it is clear that the memorial evidence e does confirm the hypothesis h that your memory is reliable. First, if your memory is reliable, as we are urged to envision, then we expect e^* that almost all your memories were corroborated by your sense perception later, given the background assumption that your sense perception is reliable. Further, since we are envisioning here that your memory is reliable, you should have the memorial evidence e of recalling these corroborations by sense perception. So, the body of memorial evidence e is highly coherent with the hypothesis h, given the background assumptions b. Meanwhile, if your memory is not reliable, as we are urged to envision next, then we have no expectation e^* that almost all your memories were corroborated by your sense perception later, even given the background assumption that your sense perception is reliable. Of course, if we envision that your memory is not reliable, we have no expectation that you recall failed corroborations. However, there is no reason, either, to expect that you have the specific (false) memorial evidence e that your memories were corroborated by sense perception later. So, your memorial evidence e is not coherent with the negation of the hypothesis $\neg h$, and certainly the memorial evidence e is much less coherent with $\neg h$ than it is with the hypothesis h. We can therefore conclude by the principle of probabilistic support (comparative form) that your memorial evidence e confirms the hypothesis h that your memory is reliable, given the background assumptions b. It is a perfectly legitimate case of confirmation with no epistemic circularity.

The situation is essentially the same in the second example where you wish to confirm the reliability of sense perception by examining the physiological process of sense perception. You discover information-preserving paths in the physiological process of sense perception, and given the relevant background assumptions, the existence of information-preserving paths will confirm the hypothesis h that sense perception is reliable. The charge of epistemic circularity arises because the evidence e is itself obtained by sense perception. As in the memory case, there is actually no circularity. We need to assume the hypothesis that sense perception is reliable only in the sense of envisioning its truth. The principle of probabilistic support (comparative form) urges us to envision the hypothesis h that sense perception is reliable and then the negation of the hypothesis $\neg h$ that sense perception is not reliable, to compare their respective degrees of coherence with the sense perceptual evidence e.

It is quite clear, given the background assumptions b, that the evidence e is more coherent with the hypothesis h than it is with the negation of the hypothesis $\neg h$. If sense perception is reliable, as the principle of probabilistic support (comparative form) urges us to envision, then we expect e^* that information-preserving paths exist in the physiological process of sense perception. Further, if sense perception is reliable, we expect that we observe information-preserving paths in the physiological process of sense perception. That is exactly the sense perceptual evidence e that is obtained in the example. On the other hand, if sense perception is not reliable, as the principle of probabilistic support (comparative form) urges us to envision next, then we have no reason to expect e^* that information-preserving paths exist in the physiological process of sense perception. Of course, if we envision that sense perception is not reliable, we do not expect to observe the absence of information-preserving paths in the physiological process of sense perception. However, there is no reason, either, to expect that you should have the (false) sense perceptual observation of information-preserving paths in the physiological process of sense perception. So, the sense perceptual evidence e that is obtained in the example is not coherent with the assumption that sense perception is not reliable, and certainly the sense perceptional evidence e is much less coherent with $\neg h$ than it is with the hypothesis h. We can therefore conclude by the principle of probabilistic support (comparative form) that the sense perceptual evidence e confirms the hypothesis h that sense perception is reliable, given the background assumptions b. This is again a perfectly legitimate case of confirmation with no circularity.

Here is a general procedure for avoiding epistemic circularity. Suppose the suspicion of epistemic circularity arises because the evidence that we hope to use for confirming the hypothesis is useful only if the truth of the hypothesis is assumed. To avoid epistemic circularity, assume the hypothesis only in the sense of envisioning its truth. This is no more problematic than assuming the truth of a hypothesis for reductio ad absurdum. Assume next the negation of the hypothesis—again in the sense of envisioning its truth. Then proceed to compare the degree of coherence between the evidence and the hypothesis and the degree of coherence between the evidence and the negation of the hypothesis, using the background assumptions when necessary. If the evidence is more coherent with the hypothesis than it is with the negation of the hypothesis, then the evidence confirms the hypothesis, given the background assumptions. The myth of epistemic circularity is hereby debunked.

7   Objections and Replies

I have proposed a general procedure for avoiding epistemic circularity. One worry is that the procedure may legitimize some obvious cases of bad reasoning. Suppose you suspect that your witness may be deliberately misleading people. It seems silly under the circumstance to ask her or him the question "Are you a reliable witness?" and use her or him answer "Yes, I am" to confirm the hypothesis that she or he is reliable. But if epistemic circularity is a myth, as I have argued, then we should be able to use her or him testimony that she or he is reliable to confirm the hypothesis that she or he is reliable. This cannot be right. The general procedure also makes it much too easy—it seems—to overcome philosophical skepticism. If we can use sense perceptual evidence to confirm the reliability of sense perception, then we should have no problem in disconfirming skeptical hypotheses, for example, the hypothesis that we are brains in a vat manipulated by an evil scientist's supercomputer. That does not seem right—it should be impossible for *empirical* evidence to epistemically differentiate hypotheses that are *empirically equivalent* to each other.

These worries stem from misconceptions of the principle of probabilistic support. We can avoid epistemic circularity without any difficulty by following the general procedure, but that does not mean that the body of evidence actually confirms the hypothesis. The principle of probabilistic support (comparative form) makes it clear that the body of evidence can fail to confirm the hypothesis when the body of evidence is no more coherent with the hypothesis than it is with the negation of the hypothesis. It is comparable to a failure of the reductio ad absurdum argument in the absence of a contradiction. Just as the reductio ad absurdum argument can fail for reasons that have nothing to do with epistemic circularity, an attempt at confirmation can fail for reasons that have nothing to do with epistemic circularity—viz., the evidence may be no more coherent with the hypothesis than it is with the negation of the hypothesis. In the case of the witness whom you suspect is deliberately misleading people, you are considering two possibilities, viz., either the witness is reliable or she or he is deliberately misleading people. It is silly under the circumstance to ask her or him the question "Are you a reliable witness?" because she or he will say she or he is reliable, no matter which of the two hypotheses is true. Her answer is therefore as coherent with one hypothesis as it is with the other. If the background assumptions make these two hypotheses the only possibilities, then her answer is no more coherent with the reliability hypothesis than it is with its negation. This is why the evidence fails to confirm the hypothesis. Epistemic circularity has nothing to do with it.

An empirical attempt to overcome the challenge of philosophical skepticism fails for the same reason. If the brain-in-a-vat hypothesis h_{BIV} is empirically equivalent to the favorite hypothesis h_{REL} that sense perception is reliable, then empirical evidence of any kind, including the observation of information-preserving paths in the physiological process of sense perception, is no more coherent with h_{REL} than it is with h_{BIV}. No empirical evidence can epistemically differentiate empirically equivalent hypotheses, but that has nothing to do with epistemic circularity. More importantly in this case, even though no empirical evidence can epistemically differentiate empirically equivalent hypotheses, it does not mean that empirical evidence cannot confirm the hypothesis h_{REL} that sense perception is reliable. This is because it is not necessary for the purpose of confirming h_{REL} to disconfirm h_{BIV}. All that is needed for confirming h_{REL} is that the empirical evidence is more coherent with h_{REL} than it is with its negation $\neg h_{REL}$. Of course, the truth of h_{BIV} makes h_{REL} false, but there are myriad other ways in which h_{REL} can be false. If the empirical evidence is incoherent with a significant portion of those myriad ways in which h_{REL} can be false, then the evidence could be much more coherent with h_{REL} than it is with $\neg h_{REL}$ and thus strongly confirms h_{REL} even if h_{BIV} remains intact. In fact, if the evidence is *no less coherent* with h_{REL} than it is with any of the myriad alternative hypotheses that make h_{REL} false, then all that is needed for confirming h_{REL} is that the evidence is more coherent with h_{REL} than it is with *some* of the alternative hypotheses.

Note that empirical evidence of any kind is no less coherent with h_{REL} than it is with any of its empirically equivalent rivals, such as h_{BIV}. So, empirical evidence that is strongly coherent with h_{REL} confirms h_{REL} unless there is some surprising hypothesis with which the evidence is *more* coherent than it is with h_{REL} since such evidence is certainly more coherent with h_{REL} than it is with *some* alternative hypotheses. Recall the discovery of information-preserving paths in the process of sense perception in our first example. This evidence is certainly more coherent with h_{REL} than it is with *some* alternative hypotheses, for example, the hypothesis that sense perception is produced randomly with no systematic correlation with any part of reality. Some people may point out that the empirical evidence that confirms h_{REL} also confirms h_{BIV} for exactly the same reason; viz., the evidence that confirms h_{REL} is no less coherent with h_{BIV} than it is with any of its empirically equivalent rivals, such as h_{REL}, and the evidence that confirms h_{REL} is certainly more coherent with h_{BIV} than it is with *some* alternative hypotheses, for example, the hypothesis that sense perception is produced randomly with no systematic correlation with any part of reality. So, unless there is some surprising hypothesis with which the evidence is more coherent than it is with h_{BIV}, the evidence confirms h_{BIV}. This reasoning is correct. Any empirical evidence that confirms h_{REL} also confirms any hypothesis that is empirically equivalent to h_{REL}. This is not surprising because no empirical evidence can epistemically differentiate empirically equivalent hypotheses. This means that empirical evidence can confirm any hypothesis only *up to empirical equivalence*. This may be disappointing to some people, but it has nothing to do with epistemic circularity. What I have shown in this chapter is that we can confirm the reliability of memory by memorial evidence and the reliability of sense perception by sense perceptual evidence without epistemic circularity.

There is one more objection that I want to address. Some people may suspect that the myth of epistemic circularity is not really debunked by the principle of probabilistic support but is only swept under the rug of the background assumptions. We can see the reason for the suspicion in the two examples I have used. It is shown in the second example that sense perceptual evidence can confirm the reliability of sense perception, where one of the background assumptions is that the existence of information-preserving paths in the physiological process of sense perception confirms the hypothesis that sense perception is reliable. This is an assumption in the sense of *presupposition*—we are not merely envisioning its truth but accepting it as true at least in the context of this investigation. The question arises at this point whether this presupposition may itself be based on some observations made in the past. If that is the case, as it seems to be, then we are making the *presupposition* that our memory of the past observation is reliable. Of course, it is not epistemically circular to confirm the reliability of sense perception given the presupposition that our memory is reliable. However, in the first example about memory, where we confirmed the reliability of memory by memorial evidence, one of the background assumptions I made was that sense perception is reliable. It now looks as though we needed the presupposition of reliable memory to confirm the reliability of sense perception, and then we needed the presupposition of reliable sense perception to confirm the reliability of memory. Is it not epistemically circular?

The challenge provides an excellent opportunity to test the general procedure for avoiding epistemic circularity. We have the suspicion of epistemic circularity because the evidence that we hope to use for confirming the hypothesis is useful only if the truth of the hypothesis is assumed, where the hypothesis is that *both* memory and sense perception are reliable. It looks as though we need to assume the reliability of memory to confirm the reliability of sense perception, but we need to assume the reliability of sense perception to confirm the reliability of memory. The solution is, again, to assume the hypothesis and its negation in the sense of envisioning their truth and compare their respective degrees of coherence with the evidence. Let us use the evidence from the first example, viz., you recall that almost all your memories were corroborated by your sense perception later. If we assume that the hypothesis is true, that is, if we assume that *both* sense perception and memory are reliable, then we expect this recollection because almost all your (reliably produced) memories should be corroborated by your (reliable) sense perception later, and you should be able to recall these corroborations by your reliable memory. So, the evidence is highly coherent with the hypothesis. On the other hand, if we assume that the negation of the hypothesis is true, that is, if we assume that either sense perception or memory is not reliable, then we do not expect to obtain this memorial evidence. First, if either sense perception or memory is not reliable, then we do not expect that almost all your memories were corroborated by sense perception later. Of course, you may not recall failed corroborations if either your sense perception or memory is not reliable. However, there is no reason, either, to expect that you obtain the specific (false) memory that almost all your memories were corroborated by sense perception later. So, the memorial evidence e is not coherent with the negation of the hypothesis $\neg h$, and certainly the memorial evidence e is much less coherent with $\neg h$ than it is with the hypothesis h. We can therefore conclude by the principle of probabilistic support (comparative form) that the memorial evidence confirms the hypothesis that both your sense perception and memory are reliable—without the presupposition that either sense perception or memory is reliable. It is a perfectly legitimate case of confirmation with no epistemic circularity

References

Alston, W. (1989). *Epistemic justification.* Ithaca: Cornell University Press.
Alston, W. (1993). *The reliability of sense perception.* Ithaca: Cornell University Press.
Bovens, L., & Hartmann, S. (2003). *Bayesian epistemology.* Oxford: Oxford University Press.
Crupi, V., Tentori, K., & Gonzalez, M. (2007). On Bayesian measures of evidential support: Theoretical and empirical issues. *Philosophy of Science, 74,* 229–252.
Douven, I., & Meijs, W. (2007). Measuring coherence. *Synthese, 156,* 405–425.
Fitelson, B. (1999). The plurality of Bayesian measures of confirmation and the problem of measure sensitivity. *Philosophy of Science, 66,* S362–S378.

Fitelson, B. (2001). *Studies in Bayesian confirmation theory*. Doctoral dissertation, University of Wisconsin-Madison, Madison.

Fitelson, B. (2003). A probabilistic theory of coherence. *Analysis, 63*, 194–199.

Glass, D. (2002). Coherence, explanation and Bayesian networks. *Lecture Notes in Artificial Intelligence, 2464*, 177–182.

Meijs, W. (2005). *Probabilistic measures of coherence*. Doctoral dissertation, Erasmus University, Rotterdam.

Meijs, W. (2006). Coherence as generalized equivalence. *Erkenntnis, 64*, 231–252.

Olsson, E. (2002). What is the problem of coherence and truth? *Journal of Philosophy, 94*, 246–272.

Schupbach, J. (2011). New hope for Shogenji's coherence measure. *British Journal for the Philosophy of Science, 62*, 125–142.

Shogenji, T. (1999). Is coherence truth conducive? *Analysis, 59*, 338–345.

Shogenji, T. (2000). Self-dependent justification without circularity. *British Journal for the Philosophy of Science, 51*, 287–298.

Shogenji, T. (2006). A defense of reductionism about testimonial justification of beliefs. *Noûs, 40*, 331–346.

On Argument Strength

Niki Pfeifer

Abstract Everyday life reasoning and argumentation is defeasible and uncertain. I present a probability logic framework to rationally reconstruct everyday life reasoning and argumentation. Coherence in the sense of de Finetti is used as the basic rationality norm. I discuss two basic classes of approaches to construct measures of argument strength. The first class imposes a probabilistic relation between the premises and the conclusion. The second class imposes a deductive relation. I argue for the second class, as the first class is problematic if the arguments involve conditionals. I present a measure of argument strength that allows for dealing explicitly with uncertain conditionals in the premise set.

Probabilistic approaches to argumentation have become popular in various fields including argumentation theory (e.g., Hahn and Oaksford 2006), formal epistemology (e.g., Pfeifer 2007, 2008), the psychology of reasoning (e.g., Hahn and Oaksford 2007), and computer science (e.g., Haenni 2009). Probabilistic approaches allow for dealing with the uncertainty and defeasibility of everyday life arguments. This chapter presents a procedure to formalize everyday life arguments in probability logical terms and to measure their strength.

"Argument" denotes an ordered triple consisting of (i) a (possibly empty) premise set, (ii) a conclusion indicator (usually denoted by "therefore" or "hence"), and (iii) a conclusion. As an example, consider the following argument $\mathcal{A}$:

(1) If Tweety is a bird, then Tweety can fly.
(2) Tweety is a bird.
(3) Therefore, Tweety can fly.

N. Pfeifer (✉)
Munich Center for Mathematical Philosophy, Ludwig-Maximilians-Universität München, Geschwister-Scholl-Platz 1, 80539 Munich, Germany
e-mail: niki.pfeifer@lrz.uni-muenchen.de

F. Zenker (ed.), *Bayesian Argumentation: The practical side of probability*,
Synthese Library 362, DOI 10.1007/978-94-007-5357-0_10,
© Springer Science+Business Media Dordrecht 2013

In terms of the propositional calculus, $\mathcal{A}$ can be represented by $\mathcal{A}_1$:

(1) $B \supset F$
(2) B
(3) $\therefore F$

where "B" denotes "Tweety is a bird," "F" denotes "Tweety can fly," "$\therefore$" denotes the conclusion indicator, and "$\supset$" denotes the material conditional. The material conditional ($A \supset B$) is false if the antecedent (A) is true and the consequent (B) is false, but true otherwise.[1]

Argument $\mathcal{A}_1$ is an instance of the logically valid *modus ponens*. An argument is logically valid if, and only if, it is impossible that all premises are true and the conclusion is false. In everyday life, however, premises are often uncertain, and conditionals allow for exceptions. Not all birds fly: penguins, for example, are birds that do not fly. Also, the second premise may be uncertain: Tweety could be a nonflying bird or not even a bird. This uncertainty and defeasibility cannot be properly expressed in the language of the propositional calculus. Nevertheless, as long as there is no evidence that Tweety is a bird that cannot fly (e.g., that Tweety is a penguin), the conclusion of $\mathcal{A}$ is rational.

Probability logic allows for dealing with exceptions and uncertainty (e.g., Adams 1975; Hailperin 1996; Coletti and Scozzafava 2002). It provides tools to reconstruct the rationality of reasoning and argumentation in the context of arguments like $\mathcal{A}_1$. Among the various approaches to probability logic, I advocate *coherence-based probability logic* for formalizing everyday life arguments (Pfeifer and Kleiter 2006a, 2009). Coherence-based probability logic combines coherence-based probability theory with propositional logic. It received strong empirical support in a series of experiments on the following: the basic nonmonotonic reasoning System P (Pfeifer and Kleiter 2003, 2005, 2006b), the paradoxes of the material conditional (Pfeifer and Kleiter 2011), the conditional syllogisms (Pfeifer and Kleiter 2007), and on how people interpret (Fugard et al. 2011) and negate conditionals (Pfeifer 2012).

Coherence-based probability theory was originated by de Finetti (1970/1974, 1980). It has been further developed by, among others, by Walley (1991), Lad (1996), Biazzo and Gilio (2000), and Coletti and Scozzafava (2002). In the framework of coherence, probabilities are (subjective) *degrees of belief* and not objective quantities. It seems natural that different people may assign different degrees of belief to the premises of one and the same argument. This does not mean, however, that everything is subjective and therefore no general rationality norms are available. *Coherence* requires that bets which lead to sure loss must be avoided which in turn guarantees that the axioms of probability theory are satisfied.[2]

---

[1] Note that the propositional-logically atomic formulae B and F in argument $\mathcal{A}_1$ can be represented in predicate logic by *bird(Tweety)* and *can_fly(Tweety)*, respectively. Moreover, F may be represented even more fine-grained in modal logical terms by $\Diamond F$, where "$\Diamond$" denotes a possibility operator. However, for the sake of sketching a theory of argument strength, it is sufficient to formalize atomic propositions by propositional variables.

[2] I argued elsewhere (Pfeifer 2008) that violation of coherence is a necessary condition for an argument to be fallacious.

Another characteristic feature of coherence is that conditional probability, $P(B/A)$, is a *primitive* notion. Consequently, the probability value is assigned *directly* to the conditional event, B/A, as a whole. This contrasts with the standard approaches to probability, where conditional probability ($P(B/A)$) is defined by the fraction of the joint and the marginal probability ($P(A \wedge B)/\Pr(A)$). The probability axioms are formulated for conditional probabilities and not for absolute probabilities (the latter is done in the standard approach to probability and is problematic if $P(A) = 0$). Coherence-based probability logic tells us how to propagate the uncertainty of the premises to the conclusion. As an example, consider a probability logical version of the above argument, $\mathcal{A}_2$:

(1) $P(F/B) = x$
(2) $P(B) = y$
(3) $\therefore xy \leq P(F) \leq xy + 1 - y$

where xy and $xy + 1 - y$ are the tightest coherent lower and upper probability bounds, respectively, of the conclusion. $\mathcal{A}_2$ is an instance of the probabilistic modus ponens (see, e.g., Pfeifer and Kleiter 2006a). If premise (1) had been replaced by the probability of the material conditional, then the tightest coherent lower and upper probability bounds of the conclusion would have been different ones. However, paradoxes and experimental results suggest that uncertain conditionals should not be represented by the probability of the material conditional ($P(A \supset B)$) but rather by the conditional probability ($P(B/A)$; Pfeifer and Kleiter 2010, 2011).

The consequence relation between the premises and the conclusion is deductive in the framework of coherence-based probability logic. The probabilities of the premises are transmitted deductively to the conclusion. Depending on the logical and probabilistic structure of the argument, the best possible coherent probability bounds of the conclusion can be a *precise* (point) probability value or an imprecise (interval) probability. Interval probabilities are constrained by a lower and an upper probability bound (see the conclusion of $\mathcal{A}_2$). In the worst case, the unit interval is a coherent assessment of the probability of the conclusion. In this case, the argument form is probabilistically non-informative: zero and one are the tightest coherent probability bounds (Pfeifer and Kleiter 2006a, 2009).

The tightest coherent probability bounds of the conclusion provide useful building blocks for a measure of argument strength. Averages of the tightest coherent lower and upper probabilities of the conclusion given some threshold probabilities of the premises allow for measuring the strength of *argument forms* (like the modus ponens; see Pfeifer and Kleiter 2006a). In the following, I focus on measuring the strength of *concrete arguments* (like argument $\mathcal{A}$).

There are at least two alternative ways to construct measures of argument strength: one presupposes a *deductive* consequence relation, whereas the other one presupposes an *uncertain* consequence relation. As explained above, coherence-based probability logic involves a deductive consequence relation. Theories of confirmation assume that there is an uncertain relation between the evidence and the hypothesis. "Theories of confirmation may be cast in the terminology of argument strength, because $P_1 \ldots P_n$ confirm C only to the extent that $P_1 \ldots P_n / C$ is

Table 1 Measures of confirmation presented in the literature (adapted from Crupi et al. 2007)

$S_d(\mathcal{P},\mathcal{C}) = P(\mathcal{C}/\mathcal{P}) - P(\mathcal{C})$	Carnap (1962)
$S_s(\mathcal{P},\mathcal{C}) = P(\mathcal{C}/\mathcal{P}) - P(\mathcal{C}/\neg\mathcal{P})$	Christensen (1999)
$S_m(\mathcal{P},\mathcal{C}) = P(\mathcal{P}/\mathcal{C}) - P(\mathcal{P})$	Mortimer (1988)
$S_n(\mathcal{P},\mathcal{C}) = P(\mathcal{P}/\mathcal{C}) - P(\mathcal{P}/\neg\mathcal{C})$	Nozick (1981)
$S_c(\mathcal{P},\mathcal{C}) = P(\mathcal{P} \wedge \mathcal{C}) - P(\mathcal{P}) \times P(\mathcal{C})$	Carnap (1962)
$S_r(\mathcal{P},\mathcal{C}) = \frac{P(\mathcal{C}/\mathcal{P})}{P(\mathcal{C})} - 1$	Finch (1960)
$S_g(\mathcal{P},\mathcal{C}) = 1 - \frac{P(\neg\mathcal{C}/\mathcal{P})}{P(\neg\mathcal{C})}$	Rips (2001)
$S_l(\mathcal{P},\mathcal{C}) = \frac{P(\mathcal{P}/\mathcal{C}) - P(\mathcal{P}/\neg\mathcal{C})}{P(\mathcal{P}/\mathcal{C}) + P(\mathcal{P}/\neg\mathcal{C})}$	Kemeny and Oppenheim (1952)

a strong argument" (Osherson et al. 1990, p. 185). Table 1 casts a number of prominent measures of confirmation in terms of argument strength.

The underlying intuition of measures of confirmation is that premise set *P confirms* conclusion *C*, if the conditional probability of the conclusion given the premises is higher than the absolute probability of the conclusion, $P(\mathcal{C}/\mathcal{P}) > P(\mathcal{C})$. $\mathcal{P}$ disconfirms $\mathcal{C}$, if $P(\mathcal{C}/\mathcal{P}) < P(\mathcal{C})$. If $\mathcal{C}$ is stochastically independent of $\mathcal{P}$, that is, $P(\mathcal{C}/\mathcal{P}) = P(\mathcal{C})$, then the premises are *neutral* w.r.t. the confirmation of the conclusion. As pointed out by Fitelson (1999), these three conditions do not impose restrictions on the choice of the measures in Table 1, that is, they are satisfied in the context of the listed measures.

Measures of confirmation may be appropriate for measuring the strength of arguments if we do not want to formalize explicitly the structure of the premise set. However, if the premise set includes conditionals (like argument $\mathcal{A}$), then these measures require a theory of how to combine conditionals and how to conditionalize on conditionals. Consider, for example, argument $\mathcal{A}$ and the general requirement that a strong argument should satisfy the inequality $P(\mathcal{C}/\mathcal{P}) > P(\mathcal{C})$. It is easy to instantiate the conclusion of $\mathcal{A} : P(B/\mathcal{P}) > P(B)$. There are at least two options to instantiate the premise set $\mathcal{P}$. Both options depend on how the conditional in premise 1 is interpreted.

The first option consists in the interpretation of the conditional in terms of a conditional event, B/A. In this case, at least two problems need to be solved. The first one is the combination of the conditional premise(s) with the other premise(s): "(B/A) and A" is not defined.[3] The second problem concerns the conditionalization on conditionals: the meaning of "$P(B/(B/A)\ldots)$" needs to be explicated. This is a deep problem, and an uncontroversial general theory is still missing (for a proposal of how to conditionalize on conditionals, see, e.g., Douven 2012).

The second option consists in the interpretation of the conditional in terms of the material conditional, $A \supset B$. Here, it is straightforward to combine the material

---

[3] Since the conditional event is nonpropositional, it cannot be combined by classical logical conjunction. Conditional events *can* be combined by so-called quasi-conjunctions (Adams 1975, p. 46f). As Adams notes, however, quasi-conjunctions lack some important logical features of conjunctions.

conditionals and to conditionalize on the material conditional. Argument $\mathcal{A}$ is instantiated in the general requirement of strong arguments as follows: $P(B/A \wedge (A \supset B)) > P(B)$. However, coherence requires that $P(B/A \wedge (A \supset B)) = 1$. Thus, the inequality is trivially satisfied (if $P(C) < 1$). It is counterintuitive that every instance—including those with low premise probabilities—of $\mathcal{A}$ is a strong argument. Therefore, measures of confirmation are not appropriate measures of argument strength if we want to explicitly formalize arguments that include conditionals.

I will now turn to a measure of argument strength and show how it allows for formalizing arguments that involve conditionals. The crucial idea is that (i) the precision of a strong argument is high and that (ii) the location of the coherent probability (interval) is close to 1 (Pfeifer 2007). The imprecision is measured by the size of the tightest coherent probability bounds of the conclusion. Let z' and z'' denote the tightest coherent lower and upper bounds, respectively, of an argument $\mathcal{A}_x$. The imprecision of $\mathcal{A}_x$ is measured by $z'' - z'$. Consequently, the *precision* of $\mathcal{A}_x$ is measured by $1 - (z'' - z')$. The location of the coherent conclusion probability is measured by the arithmetic mean of the tightest coherent probability bounds, $\frac{z'+z''}{2}$. The argument strength s of $\mathcal{A}_x$ is equal to the product of the precision and the location of the tightest coherent probability bounds of the conclusion

$$s(\mathcal{A}_x) = [1 - (z'' - z')] \times \frac{z' + z''}{2},$$

where $0 \le s(\mathcal{A}_x) \le 1$, since $0 \le z' \le z'' \le 1$. The values 0 and 1 denote the weakest and the strongest value, respectively.

As an example of the evaluation procedure of the strength of an argument, consider the following instance of argument $\mathcal{A}_2$:

(1) $P(F/B) = .8$
(2) $P(B) = .9$
(3) $\therefore .72 \le P(F) \le .82$

The strength of this argument is .69. In the special case where the premises are certain (i.e., probabilities equal to 1), the strength of the argument obtains its maximum value 1.

Figure 1 presents the behavior of the measure in general. According to the measure, the argument strength increases if the location of the tightest coherent bounds of the conclusion approaches 1. The argument strength decreases if the imprecision increases. Moreover, an argument is weak if the conclusion probability is low. Maximum imprecision implies minimum argument strength. It follows that all probabilistically non-informative arguments are also weak arguments (with $s = 0$). Figure 2 shows the behavior of the measure for coherent lower conclusion probabilities of at least .5. If the conclusion probability is at least .5, then the argument strength varies between .375 and .500. The higher the precision, the higher the strength of the argument.

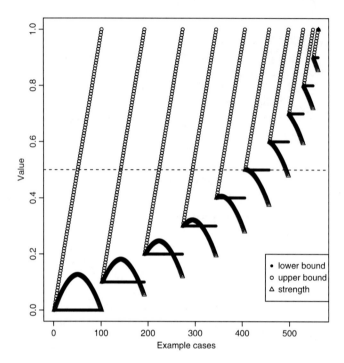

Fig. 1 Let z' denote the tightest coherent lower and z'' denote the tightest coherent upper bound of an argument $\mathcal{A}$. The argument strength of $\mathcal{A}$ is equal to $\left[1 - \left(z'' - z'\right)\right] \times \frac{z'+z''}{2}$. The strength of $\mathcal{A}$ increases if the precision of the conclusion is high and the location of the tightest coherent probability interval is close to 1

The proposed measure contrasts with the traditional measures of confirmation presented in Table 1. The consequence relation remains deductive, while measures of confirmation assume an uncertain relation between the premises and the conclusion. Using probability logic to formalize arguments is advantageous as it does justice to the logical structure: premise sets that include conditionals can be represented explicitly. If a measure of argument strength requires to calculate the conditional probability of the conclusion given some combination of the premises, P(conclusion|premise set), then severe problems arise of how to connect premises containing conditionals with each other and how to conditionalize on conditionals. In the proposed measure, this problem is avoided, as probability logic tells us how to infer the tightest coherent probability bounds of the conclusion from the premises, which are in turn exploited for calculating the argument strength.

The proposed measure s has not only attractive theoretical consequences (as explained above), it also implies at least two psychologically plausible hypotheses. People judge arguments as strong, if the premises imply high conclusion probabilities (i) and if the conclusion probability is—at the same time—precise (ii). The empirical test of these hypotheses is a challenge for future research.

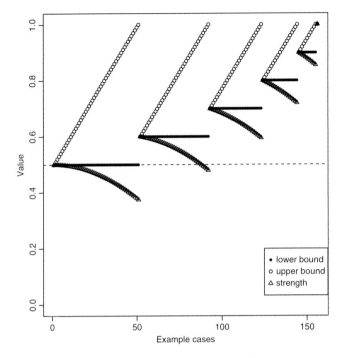

Fig. 2 Detail of Fig. 1, showing the behavior of measure *s* for coherent lower conclusion probabilities of at least .5

Acknowledgments This work is financially supported by the *Alexander von Humboldt Foundation*, the *German Research Foundation* project PF 740/2-1 "Rational reasoning with conditionals and probabilities. Logical foundations and empirical evaluation" (Project leader: Niki Pfeifer; Project within the DFG Priority Program SPP 1516 "New Frameworks of Rationality") and the *Austrian Science Fund* project P20209 "Mental probability logic" (Project leader: Niki Pfeifer).

References

Adams, E. W. (1975). *The logic of conditionals*. Dordrecht: Reidel.
Biazzo, V., & Gilio, A. (2000). A generalization of the fundamental theorem of de Finetti for imprecise conditional probability assessments. *International Journal of Approximate Reasoning, 24*(2–3), 251–272.
Carnap, R. (1962). *Logical foundations of probability* (2nd ed.). Chicago: University of Chicago Press.
Christensen, D. (1999). Measuring confirmation. *Journal of Philosophy, 96*, 437–461.
Coletti, G., & Scozzafava, R. (2002). *Probabilistic logic in a coherent setting*. Dordrecht: Kluwer.
Crupi, V., Tentori, K., & Gonzales, M. (2007). On Bayesian measures of confirmation. *Philosophy of Science, 74*, 229–252.

De Finetti, B. (1974). *Theory of probability* (Vols. 1, 2). Chichester: Wiley. (Original work published 1970)

De Finetti, B. (1980). Foresight: Its logical laws, its subjective sources (1937). In H. J. Kyburg & H. E. Smokler (Eds.), *Studies in subjective probability* (pp. 55–118). Huntington: Robert E. Krieger.

Douven, I. (2012). Learning conditional information. *Mind & Language, 27*(3), 239–263.

Finch, H. A. (1960). Confirming power of observations metricized for decisions among hypotheses. *Philosophy of Science, 27*, 293–207 (part I), 391–404 (part II).

Fitelson, B. (1999). The plurality of Bayesian measures of confirmation and the problem of measure sensitivity. *Philosophy of Science, 66*, 362–378.

Fugard, A. J. B., Pfeifer, N., Mayerhofer, B., & Kleiter, G. D. (2011). How people interpret conditionals: Shifts towards the conditional event. *Journal of Experimental Psychology: Learning, Memory, and Cognition, 37*(3), 635–648.

Haenni, R. (2009). Probabilistic argumentation. *Journal of Applied Logic, 7*(2), 155–176.

Hahn, U., & Oaksford, M. (2006). A normative theory of argument strength. *Informal Logic, 26*, 1–22.

Hahn, U., & Oaksford, M. (2007). The rationality of informal argumentation: A Bayesian approach to reasoning fallacies. *Psychological Review, 114*(3), 704–732.

Hailperin, T. (1996). *Sentential probability logic: Origins, development, current status, and technical applications*. Bethlehem: Lehigh University Press.

Kemeny, J., & Oppenheim, P. (1952). Degrees of factual support. *Philosophy of Science, 19*, 307–324.

Lad, F. (1996). *Operational subjective statistical methods: A mathematical, philosophical, and historical introduction*. New York: Wiley.

Mortimer, H. (1988). *The logic of induction*. Paramus: Prentice Hall.

Nozick, R. (1981). *Philosophical explanations*. Oxford: Clarendon.

Osherson, D. N., Smith, E. E., Wilkie, O., López, A., & Shafir, E. (1990). Category-based induction. *Psychological Review, 97*(2), 185–200.

Pfeifer, N. (2007). Rational argumentation under uncertainty. In G. Kreuzbauer, N. Gratzl, & E. Hiebl (Eds.), *Persuasion und Wissenschaft: Aktuelle Fragestellungen von Rhetorik und Argumentationstheorie* (pp. 181–191). Wien: LIT.

Pfeifer, N. (2008). A probability logical interpretation of fallacies. In G. Kreuzbauer, N. Gratzl, & E. Hiebl (Eds.), *Rhetorische Wissenschaft: Rede und Argumentation in Theorie und Praxis* (pp. 225–244). Wien: LIT.

Pfeifer, N. (2012). Experiments on Aristotle's thesis: Towards an experimental philosophy of conditionals. *The Monist, 95*(2), 223–240.

Pfeifer, N., & Kleiter, G. D. (2003). Nonmonotonicity and human probabilistic reasoning. In *Proceedings of the 6th workshop on uncertainty processing, Hejnice, September 24–27, 2003* (pp. 221–234). Prague: Oeconomica.

Pfeifer, N., & Kleiter, G. D. (2005). Coherence and nonmonotonicity in human reasoning. *Synthese, 146*(1–2), 93–109.

Pfeifer, N., & Kleiter, G. D. (2006a). Inference in conditional probability logic. *Kybernetika, 42*, 391–404.

Pfeifer, N., & Kleiter, G. D. (2006b). Is human reasoning about nonmonotonic conditionals probabilistically coherent? In *Proceedings of the 7th workshop on uncertainty processing, Mikulov, September 16–20, 2006* (pp. 138–150).

Pfeifer, N., & Kleiter, G. D. (2007). Human reasoning with imprecise probabilities: Modus ponens and denying the antecedent. In G. de Cooman, J. Vejnarová, & M. Zaffalon (Eds.), *5th International symposium on imprecise probability: Theories and applications* (pp. 347–356). Prague: SIPTA.

Pfeifer, N., & Kleiter, G. D. (2009). Framing human inference by coherence based probability logic. *Journal of Applied Logic, 7*(2), 206–217.

Pfeifer, N., & Kleiter, G. D. (2010). The conditional in mental probability logic. In M. Oaksford & N. Chater (Eds.), *Cognition and conditionals: Probability and logic in human thought* (pp. 153–173). Oxford: Oxford University Press.

Pfeifer, N., & Kleiter, G. D. (2011). Uncertain deductive reasoning. In K. Manktelow, D. E. Over, & S. Elqayam (Eds.), *The science of reason: A Festschrift for Jonathan St B.T. Evans* (pp. 145–166). Hove: Psychology Press.

Rips, L. J. (2001). Two kinds of reasoning. *Psychological Science, 12*(2), 129–134.

Walley, P. (1991). *Statistical reasoning with imprecise probabilities*. London: Chapman and Hall.

Upping the Stakes and the Preface Paradox

Jonny Blamey

Abstract The preface paradox, first introduced by David Makinson (Analysis 25:205–207, 1961), presents a plausible scenario where an agent is evidentially certain of each of a set of propositions without being evidentially certain of the conjunction of the set of propositions. Given reasonable assumptions about the nature of evidential certainty, this appears to be a straightforward contradiction. We solve the paradox by appeal to stake size sensitivity, which is the claim that evidential probability is sensitive to stake size. The argument is that because the informational content in the conjunction is greater than the sum of the informational content of the conjuncts, the stake size in the conjunction is higher than the sum of the stake sizes in the conjuncts. We present a theory of evidential probability that identifies knowledge with value and allows for coherent stake-sensitive beliefs. An agent's beliefs are represented two-dimensionally as a bid-ask spread, which gives a bid price and an ask price for bets at each stake size. The bid-ask spread gets wider when there is less valuable evidence relative to the stake size and narrower when there is more valuable evidence according to a simple formula. The bid-ask spread can represent the uncertainty in the first-order probabilistic judgement. According to the theory, it can be coherent to be evidentially certain at low stakes, but less than certain at high stakes, and therefore there is no contradiction in the preface. The theory not only solves the paradox but also gives a good model of decisions under risk that overcomes many of the problems associated with classic expected utility theory.

J. Blamey (✉)
Kings College, London, UK
e-mail: jonnyblamey@yahoo.com

F. Zenker (ed.), *Bayesian Argumentation: The practical side of probability*,
Synthese Library 362, DOI 10.1007/978-94-007-5357-0_11,

1   Introduction

A historian writes a history book containing many facts, each of which, as a diligent researcher, she is fully justified in believing are true. The historian, being epistemically modest, acknowledges in the preface to the book that, in spite of her most careful and diligent research, she believes that there is at least one false statement in her book. Given the fallibility of human knowledge and the large number of facts in the book, the statement in the preface might also be considered justified. So here lies the paradox: it seems that she is fully justified in each of a set of propositions taken individually, yet at the same time she is justified in believing the conjunction of the set of propositions to be false.

The preface paradox dramatises a problem at the very heart of evidential justification. Generally speaking, we have many beliefs that we are fully justified in believing given our evidence. These beliefs are settled for us, and our evidence gives us the authority of testimony. Full justification is the greatest degree of justification and can be equated with evidential certainty. When a belief is fully justified, it requires no further justification and any further evidence for the belief is redundant. In this chapter, we will assume that fully justified belief is a necessary condition for knowledge and also for evidence for further conjectures and generalisations. In terms of evidential probability, when a belief is fully justified by the evidence, then the belief has an evidential probability of 1.

But many of our fully justified beliefs are justified on nondeductive grounds. We believe things on the basis of past experience, inductive generalisation, testimony and other more or less reliable grounds. There is always a possibility that our fully justified beliefs could be mistaken. In other words, even our fully justified beliefs are fallible. If we take all of our fully justified beliefs as a whole, we can recognise that there is some probability that some of them are mistaken, yet if we take any of our fully justified beliefs individually, we again find that it is fully justified and evidentially certain. The uncertainty seems to be an emergent feature of the whole, which vanishes in the detail. The preface paradox dramatises this more general problem for evidential justification.

For example, for most practical and scientific purposes, a visual observation is sufficient for evidential certainty. If a lab technician takes a thermometer reading at noon and reads that the temperature is 30°, then he is thereby fully justified in believing that the thermometer read 30° at noon (within an interval that takes into account the relevant level of precision). For the purposes of statistical inference, this reading can be used as a data point and will be accorded an evidential probability of 1. But it is not the case that such observations are infallible. If we were to ask the question whether it is possible that a person could take the wrong reading from a thermometer, then we must surely answer yes and furthermore admit that there is likely to be a non-zero frequency of such misreadings. So when inquiring into the temperature, the observation counts as evidence and is accorded a probability 1, but when inquiring into the reliability of the entire class of observations of this kind, the accuracy of the observation is accorded a probability of less than 1. A change in inquiry, it would appear, can lead to a change in the evidential probability.

The preface paradox could also shed some light on the problem of whether and to what degree a generalisation is confirmed by its instances. We could see the conjunction of all the propositions in the book as the generalisation that all statements in the book are true. Each statement in the book can then be seen as an instance of this generalisation that confirms the generalisation to some degree. We could then use Bayes' theorem to attach a posterior probability to the generalisation on the evidence that all the statements in the book are true. Using this methodology, the paradoxical nature of the preface is clearly revealed. Call the generalisation that all the facts in the book are true "book", and call the evidence formed from the fully justified individual propositions in the book "facts". The posterior probability of the generalisation is then

$$P(\text{Book} \mid \text{Facts}) = \{P(\text{ Facts} \mid \text{Book}) \times P(\text{Book})\}/P(\text{Facts})$$

The problem is that the prior probability that "book" is true surely ought to be the same as the prior probability that all the facts are true. This is because the content of "book" is the same as the content of all the facts since "book" is simply defined as the generalisation that all the facts are true. And the conditional probability that all the facts are true given that "book" is true must surely be 1 for the same reason. Given all this, then the posterior probability of the book given the facts comes out as 1 in all cases where the prior probability of the book is greater than zero. The paradox then is why the preface statement "There is at least one false statement in the book" can seem reasonable to us, when its negation "Every statement in the book is true" has a posterior probability of 1.

We can argue that the preface statement is reasonable in betting terms. Suppose that the book was published and endorsed as a reference book by many great institutions. Supposed it contained the statement that the Battle of Hastings was fought in 1066. It would be then possible to settle bets on the date of the Battle of Hastings by looking it up in the book. But it would not be possible to settle bets on the accuracy of the book itself by checking each fact in the book by looking it up in the book. So while the book does not contain any extra facts that are not in the book, it does appear to fully confirm each claim in the book, without fully confirming a statement to the effect that every statement in the book is true. However, if the reliability of the book is in question, then it is no longer obvious that looking up the Battle of Hastings in the book is sufficient evidence to settle bets on the date of Battle of Hastings.

2   Contextualism

We might frame this in terms of a shift in the context of enquiry. When enquiring into the date of the Battle of Hastings, the evidence that went into the book provides a full justification, but when enquiring into the epistemic standards of the book itself, then the same evidence no longer provides a full justification for ostensibly the same fact.

This may remind us of contextualist ways of meeting the "sceptical challenge" (Cohen 1988; DeRose 1995; Lewis 1996). The sceptical challenge can be illustrated through G.E. Moore's famous proof of the external world. In an ordinary context of enquiry, it seems that Moore is fully justified in believing that he has two hands on the evidence produced by waving his hands in front of his face. But he cannot produce such fully justifying evidence that he is not a brain in a vat. In fact, he can produce no evidence whatsoever that he is not a brain in a vat. But a fully justified belief that he has two hands seems to provide a deductive proof that he is not a brain in a vat. The sceptical challenge, then, is to explain why it is that he knows he has two hands but that he does not know that he is not a brain in a vat, given that if he *is* a brain in a vat, then he does not have two hands. It seems to follow logically that he does not know that he has two hands after all.

Lewis's response to the sceptical challenge can be put like this: in order to know that p your evidence has to eliminate every possibility that $\sim p$. But "every" has a contextually variable scope. In a philosophical sceptical context, "every" can include the brain in the vat hypothesis; whereas in another, more ordinary context, "every" does not include the brain in a vat hypothesis. So G. E. Moore is right in that, ordinarily, he is fully justified in believing he has two hands, but he cannot use this as proof that he is not a brain in a vat, because as soon as the sceptical hypothesis is raised, he no longer knows that he has two hands.

We can see how this might work in the preface paradox. The enquiry as to whether there are any false statements in the book creates a shift in context that makes it necessary to attend to the possibility that at least one statement is false. But in the case of the preface paradox, this does not seem so much a solution, as a restatement of the problem. The problem is *why* are we fully justified at the particular level, but not fully justified at the general level?

3   Threshold Theory

One obvious solution to the preface paradox already in the literature (Hawthorne and Bovens 1999; Sturgeon 2008) is to have a threshold theory of justified belief. The idea is that in order to be fully justified, it is not necessary to be certain, where certainty is a justified degree of belief 1. Instead, the threshold for fully justified belief is some degree of belief below 1. In this case, the probability of the conjunction can be very low, while the probability of the conjuncts is very high. This solution is very appealing because our intuition tells us that the greater the number of facts in the book, the greater the probability that the preface is true. For example, let us suppose all the facts in the book were probabilistically independent and have a probability of 0.9 which is, suppose further, the threshold for justified belief. If there were any more than 21 propositions in the book, then the probability that the preface was true would exceed the threshold of 0.9. (Remember, the preface is true if one or more of the propositions is false, so with 21 propositions the probability that the preface is true is $1-0.9^{21}$, which is greater than 0.9.)

This solution is neat and valid. However, there are two problems with the threshold theory that I will mention; firstly, any threshold will run into the lottery paradox. A consequence of the threshold theory is that there is a lottery such that one is fully justified in believing that each ticket in the lottery will lose before the draw. But it is certain that one ticket will win. Another way of putting this problem is that any threshold will lead to a failure of modus ponens. Any threshold will allow that one is fully justified in all the premises of a valid argument without being fully justified in the conclusion or worse, fully justified in believing the conclusion is false. Without going into too much detail, this seems like a bad result.

Secondly, there seems little motivation to set the threshold at any particular level. Any threshold seems arbitrary. Furthermore, once you take away full justification as a measure of certainty, then it becomes unclear how any probability judgement is to be interpreted. If fully justified statements are not certain, then it is hard to see how anything can be certain beyond logical tautologies. Once certainty is abandoned, then lesser degrees of belief lose their meaning.

However, rather than relying on these general arguments against threshold theories, we will simply allow that a threshold theory could account for many versions of the preface paradox, but no threshold theory can solve a version of the preface where each fact in the book is evidentially certain or, in other words, where each fact has an evidential probability 1. In betting terms, the preface paradox can be stated thus as follows: how can the historian's evidence justify settling bets on each statement in the book, but not justify settling bets on the statement that every proposition in the book is true? The threshold theory fails to solve this version of the paradox because the threshold theory works by denying that the evidence is sufficient to settle bets on the individual propositions.

4   Stake Size Sensitivity: A Sketch of a Solution

The solution we present relies upon the claim that the degree to which a proposition is justified by a body of evidence is sensitive to what is at stake in believing the proposition. Importantly, whether or not a proposition is *fully* justified by a body of evidence can depend on what is at stake, so it is possible that the same evidence can fully justify a belief at low stakes but not fully justify the same belief at high stakes. We assume that fully justified belief is a necessary condition for knowledge, so it follows that it is possible that whether one knows that p on the basis of a fixed set of evidence can also depend on what is at stake.

Given stake size sensitivity, then the paradox is solved by showing that the book is much higher stakes than the sum of the stake sizes on the individual propositions, while the evidence remains constant. So it can be reasonable to be certain of the low-stakes propositions, but less than certain of the high-stakes conjunction.

The stake size sensitivity claim has many proponents, both contemporary and historical. However, the expression of stake size sensitivity depends on the general theory of mind and evidence in which it is imbedded.

4.1   Economic Theory

In economic theory, the stake size sensitivity claim can be expressed in terms of discounting the expected utility of a prospect in proportion to the risk. A high-risk prospect will have an expected value that is lower than its mean return derived from past performance. The magnitude of the discount is based on the variance in the past performance, and risk is defined in terms of variance, which is a measure of how far the outcome deviates from the mean. Variance and its relatives, standard deviation and absolute deviation, are arguably the best measures of second-order uncertainty (Hansson 2009). Higher stakes gambles have a higher variance given equivalent exposure. It is the common practice in the markets to discount due to risk in this way, and risk itself has become a tradable commodity. All the stake size sensitivity claim amounts to in this context is that discounting due to risk as measured by variance is rational.

Understood in this way, stake size sensitivity has a long history going back to Daniel Bernoulli (1738). Sadly, the phenomenon of the lower expected utility of risky prospects has been associated with the diminishing marginal utility of money, which is not obviously related to stake sensitivity in the epistemological sense and therefore could be mistaken for a competing explanation. The idea is that differences in utility are not linearly related to differences in money, specifically differences between large sums of money have less impact on utility than the equivalent differences between small amounts of money, which has the effect that people tend to undervalue large gambles because the utility odds are worse than the money odds.

However, there are several decisions under risk that cannot be explained by either a straightforward diminishing marginal utility curve nor a more complex nonlinear expected utility curve like those introduced by Friedman and Savage (1948). These are principally the Ellsberg problem (1961), the Allais problem (1953) and the reflection effect and framing effects discovered by Kahneman and Tversky (1979). The latter posited "decision weights", which function as degrees of belief in terms of calculating expected utility, but, according to Kahneman and Tversky, do not conform to the axioms of probability (1979, p .280). However, if the theory allows for subjects to have a bid-ask spread, so that their degree of belief varies depending on whether they are buying a prospect or selling it, then all these phenomena can be explained by the theory that bid-ask spreads vary with epistemic factors like variance and weight of evidence. In other words, the less evidence you have for a prospect, the greater the difference between your bid price and your ask price. Bid-ask spreads can easily be measured in the markets and are the subject of a number of studies (Mian 1995; Frank and Garcia 2009). They have been shown to covary with variance, transaction volume and market volume in a way that is consistent with stake size sensitivity.

4.2 Analytic Epistemology

In the setting of analytic epistemology, stake size sensitivity is the claim that whether a subject knows that p, or alternatively, is rational to fully believe that p depends in part on the practical interests of the subject. As a consequence, it is possible that two subjects could have the same evidence for p yet differ in that the one in a low-stakes situation knows that p, while the other in a high-stakes situation does not know that p, or alternatively the one in low stakes could be justified in believing that p, whereas the other in high stakes is not justified in believing that p (Fantl and McGrath 2002; Hawthorne 2004; Stanley 2006; Weatherson 2005).

4.3 Naturalised Epistemology

Another context in which stake size sensitivity finds expression is in naturalised epistemology. If epistemology is viewed as a natural science akin to psychology, then it becomes a significant question as to whether people's and other animals' beliefs actually are sensitive to stake size. If the answer to this question turns out to be yes, then this is enough to posit the hypothesis that beliefs ought to be stake size sensitive if they are to fulfil their proper biological function. The latter normative claim is a little harder to establish from the data alone, but Ruth Millikan at least explicitly states that knowledge is sensitive to stake size from a naturalist perspective.

'Unless the stakes *are* high, we do not require of the person who "knows that p" because he has been told by so-and-so that he be ready to place extremely high stakes on the truth of p' (Millikan 1993, p. 253).

4.4 Stake Size Sensitivity by Whatever Name Solves the Paradox

Given stake size sensitivity, we can solve the preface paradox by showing that the proposition that every statement in the book is true is at higher stakes than the sum of the propositions taken individually given the same interests. Therefore, it is possible that the statements in the book are fully justified taken individually, but not fully justified taken as a whole. The reason for the change in stake size is clear enough. The doubtful conjunction has a great deal more informational content than the fully justified conjuncts. There are more ways the conjunction could be wrong, and so there is a greater investment in believing the conjunction.

5   A Betting Model of Beliefs

In order to be able to argue for this solution to the preface, we must sketch a sufficiently precise model of beliefs. We will use a straightforward betting model of action in which it is assumed that we act on the basis of our beliefs, and these actions resemble bets insofar as their success depends on our beliefs being true. The betting model therefore defines degree of belief as an expected value calculator, such that you calculate the expected value of an action by multiplying the stakes on the action by the degree of belief in success (Ramsey 1926, p.16).

In order to have a betting model of belief, we need to have a measure of value. The sense of value we intend is that which allows a subject to fulfil an essential function and thereby flourish. This is quite different from Ramsey's scale of goods and bads, which is derived from the subject's preferences. Our measure of value assigns to a subject a state of wealth and can measure the differences in states of wealth on a scale that preserves intervals. States of wealth are objective in that being in a certain state of wealth does not entail that you believe that you are in that state of wealth. States of wealth must always be positive, since we assume that whenever a subject reaches a zero state of wealth, then the essential function ceases. So if the subject is a business, then it folds, if it is a person then he dies, and if it is a species then it becomes extinct. We equate value with knowledge, so that it is deliberate increases of value through labour which typifies the appropriation of property and the accumulation of wealth. The most important states of wealth in terms of a bet on p are "B", the state of wealth if p, and the bet is won; "C", the state of wealth if $\sim p$ and the bet is lost; and "A", which is the state of wealth of the subject given by the addition of the bet to his holdings. A is therefore the expected value of his holdings given by the degree of belief in p and will be no lower than C and no higher than B.

A subject's degree of belief can be expressed as a function of the *price* (A–C) of a chance to win the *stakes* (B–C) if p is true. The subject's degree of belief that p in these conditions is equal to the ratio *price/stakes,* or (A–C)/(B–C). As has long been established, price/stakes ratios conform to the laws of probability, which should not be surprising considering that probability theory was developed in the context of pricing bets. We can see straight away that the price should never exceed the stakes, so that the price/stakes should be less than or equal to 1. Furthermore, assuming the stakes are positive, there is little sense in having a negative price. This means that price/stakes is always between 1 and 0 inclusive.

Stakes can be negative as well as positive. A bet with negative stakes is one where the value B is lower than the value C, so that "winning" the bet is in fact a loss. In this case, the price will also be negative, since the value A will now be lower or equal to value C and higher or equal to B. Negative stakes bet prices can be thought of as selling prices, or *ask* prices. For example, a bet at negative stakes £10 on $\sim p$ at price/stakes £1/£10 would be one where you sold a promise to pay £10 if $\sim p$ for the ask price of £1. This would have identical consequences to a positive stakes bet where you *buy* a promise of £10 if p for a bid price of £9. Either way, you gain £1 if ~p and lose £9 if p. Every positive stakes bet can likewise be viewed as a negative stakes bet on the negation.

A feature of stake sensitivity is that it can be coherent to have a different ask price at negative stakes from your bid prices at positive stakes. Coherence demands that the ask prices are higher than the bid prices, and the difference in ask-bid is called the *bid-ask spread*. The width of the bid-ask spread can then be used to measure uncertainty in the first-order probability judgement. It follows from this characterisation of negative stakes that a positive bet on p at price/stakes x/U is identical to a negative bet on ~p at price/stakes $(x-U)/-U$. From this follows a basic law of probability, in its stake-sensitive form:

$$P(p)_U = 1 - P(\sim p)_{-U}$$

The subscripts indicate the stake size. The unique stake size sensitive feature here is that this law only holds when the stakes have the same absolute value, one negative and the other positive.

Ramsey assumed that degrees of belief are stake size invariant when proving the laws of probability, and this assumption allowed him to apply these laws across stake sizes, but we are allowing that degrees of belief are stake sensitive. This is a foundational difference so we have to go back to basics. Using bets as a measure of belief, we can do various mathematical operations on bets on different propositions and thereby establish logical relations between degrees of belief.

We can add bets together. A bet on p at a/U added to a bet on q at b/U where a and b are the prices and U is the stake size, results in a bet with a price $a + b$ which pays U if p, U if q and 2U if both p and q. This composite bet has three possible end states rather than two and so is not reducible to a price/stakes bet on any proposition. Consequently, the sum of these two bets does not represent or measure a degree of belief in any proposition.

We can also subtract bets by subtracting the values of the price and the stakes. So, using the example above, we could subtract a bet of c/U on $(p \& q)$ and derive the first law of probability, the law of disjunction. The resulting bet would have a price of $a + b - c$ and result in U if p OR q. This bet would be identical in consequence to a bet of $(a + b - c)/U$ on the disjunction p OR q. Thus, the law of disjunction

$$P(p\,\text{OR}\,q)_U = P(p)_U + P(q)_U - P(p\&q)_U.$$

It should be noted with great attention that *the law of disjunction does not hold unless the stakes are the same*. If the stakes on p and the stakes on q were different sizes, then the identity would not hold at all, and the bet on the left would have different consequences from the bet on the right, whatever the prices. The bet on the right does not necessarily represent a bet on a single proposition at all unless the stakes are kept constant.

Of course, there are constraints on degrees of belief across stake sizes. The one important constraint I shall call "the minimum constraint".

Minimum. If S has $P(p)_U = x$, then S has $P(p)_V \geq Ux/V$ whenever $V > U$.

This is the rule that you cannot prefer a bet at smaller stakes to a bet at larger stakes for the same price.

Proof: Suppose S had $P(p)_U = $ x and $P(p)_V = $ y such that $y < Ux/V$. The Dutch bookie would simply give S a bet on p at stakes U in exchange for a bet on p at stakes V for a small fee of $xU - yV$, and, if p was true, pay the subject U out of his winnings V, leaving the bookie with a profit of $xU - yV$ if ~p and $V - U$ if p.

The beauty of allowing stake size variation is that is it much more realistic and does not assume that paying a small price for a small bet somehow commits you to paying a much larger price for a much larger bet at the same odds. If this counterintuitive commitment to stake size invariance is dropped, then it is impossible to be Dutch booked on bets at different stake sizes provided that one conforms to the minimum constraint. This allows for considerable variation of degrees of belief across stake sizes without incoherence. The important freedom it allows is to be able to have greater degrees of belief at lower stake sizes and to therefore be able to have a lower bid price from one's ask price, which allows for probabilistically coherent bid-ask spreads.

The second law of probability is the law of conjunction. For the law of conjunction, we need to introduce a new operation on bets, which is a multiplication of bets. To multiply two bets together, you bet the entire stake of the first bet as the price on the second bet. For example, if you were to multiply a bet on 6 on the first role of the die by a bet on 6 on the second role of the die, both at price/stakes £1/£6, then you would place £6 price on the second bet for stakes £36 on condition that the first bet won, otherwise nothing. Multiplying these two bets together would result in winning £36 iff two consecutive sixes were thrown, for a price of £1. We can see that this is identical to a bet at price/stakes £1/£36 on a double six. Notice that the second bet is a conditional bet, which is a measure of conditional beliefs. A conditional bet p given q is a bet on p that is only valid if q. If not q, then the stakes are returned and there is no bet. So as we can see, a bet on p at price/stakes a/U multiplied by a bet on $q \mid p$ at price/stakes U/X is identical in consequence to a bet on p & q at price/stakes a/X where $X = U/P(q \mid p)_X$.

So the stake-sensitive law of conjunction is that

$$P(p\&q)_X = P(p)_U P(q \mid p)_X, \text{where } X = U/P(q \mid p)_X$$

The important feature, unique to stake size-sensitive probability, which allows us to solve the preface paradox, is *stake size escalation*. The stakes on the conjunction are greater than the stakes on the unconditional conjunct by a factor of 1 over the conditional probability. On our theory of evidential probability, the stakes are equivalent to the value of the informational content of the proposition. Stake size escalation reflects the increased informational content in the conjunction over the conjuncts. The degree of stake size escalation is therefore dependent not on the probabilities of the propositions in the conjunction, but on the conditional probabilities between them. If knowledge that p makes it highly probable that q, then knowledge that p & q is not going to be a great deal more useful than knowledge that p on its own. Whereas, if p makes it highly unlikely that q, then knowledge of the conjunction p & q is going to be a lot more informative and valuable than the knowledge that p by itself. For example, knowing that someone is both pregnant and a woman is hardly more valuable than simply knowing that they are pregnant, whereas knowing that someone is pregnant and a man is much more valuable than simply knowing that they are a man.

The stake-sensitive law of conjunction can be iterated many times with the stakes on the conjunction escalating exponentially with each additional conjunct. Since each conditional bet in the chain is at a higher stake size, the conditional probabilities will not remain constant, so that the ordering is important when deriving the conditional probabilities. Conditional probabilities are taken to be primitive and stake size sensitive in this theory, so the conditional probability on a proposition is derived directly from the stakes, and the evidence according to the formula we will give below.

The stake-sensitive law of conjunction allows that you can have a lot lower degrees of belief in the conjunction than in the product of the degrees of belief in the conjuncts without being probabilistically incoherent. Because the stake size is necessarily higher on the conditionals when the conjuncts are multiplied together, it is within the minimum constraint to accept odds on the individual conjuncts, but refuse the same odds when they are chained together conditionally in a multiplier bet. For example, it is perfectly invulnerable to a Dutch book to buy two disjoint bets on consecutive die rolls at price stakes £1/£6 but to decline a bet on double six at £1/£36. This follows because in order to multiply the bets together, you have to accept the second bet at stakes £36 rather than stakes £6, and there is nothing in nature that requires you to accept the same odds at this higher stake size.

The epistemological consequence of this is that the same evidence can rationally lead to a higher degree of belief in the conjuncts than their product in the conjunction, which is the result required to make the preface coherent, because it allows the special case where one may coherently have a degree of belief 1 in the conjuncts, but less than 1 in the conjunction.

In order to show how this works in the epistemological context, we now need a measure of the value of evidence. The value of evidence relative to a particular bet is a measure of how much the evidence changes the expectation on a bet. Because the value of evidence is measured in this way, the value of evidence can be both negative and positive, depending on whether it is evidence for or evidence against. This concept, the value of evidence, is closely related to Turing's "score" (see Gillies 1990), I. J. Good's (1950) "weight of evidence" and Popper's (1974) "severity of test". My chief inspiration for this measure, however, is Ramsey in his obscure note "The value, or weight, of knowledge" (Ramsey 1991) in which he presents a means for calculating how much it is worthwhile to find out a piece of knowledge. The problem with both Popper and Good's measures is that they both ignore stake size completely and frame their measures purely in terms of change in probability. This means that their measures cannot allow for stake size sensitivity.

Our measure of the value of evidence can be understood as a measure of the weighting of evidence for and against a proposition. We can use the metaphor of the scales of justice. Once we have a measure of the value of evidence, we can form odds by taking the ratio of the value of evidence for to the value of evidence against. So for example, if the value of evidence for p was 9 units and the value of evidence against p was 1 unit, then the odds would be 9:1. In this picture, stake size sensitivity would amount to increasing the relative weighting of evidence against as the stakes get higher. So in this example, the degree of belief on this evidence at zero stakes would be 0.9, but at higher stakes the value of evidence for would carry less weight relative to the evidence against and so the stake-sensitive probability would be less than 0.9.

We propose to formalise this stake sensitivity by equating the value of knowledge to the value of the stake size. This is metaphysically profound and amounts to identifying knowledge with value. We can get a sense of the meaning of this identity if we consider that knowledge is a necessary condition for successful deliberate action, and deliberate action is a necessary condition for the creation of value. These are not empirical statements, but a priori statements that follow from the concepts of knowledge, success, action and value.

Another way to put this identity is to say that the value of a bet you know you will win is equal to the entire stake. If C is the state of your wealth if not p, and B the state of wealth if p, then evidence in favour of p is counted up from C, since the value of the bet can be no less than C. Knowledge that p is therefore when the value of the evidence increases the value of the bet from C all the way up to B and therefore is equal to B $-$ C, which is the stake size. This assumes that the value of the bet if one had *no* evidence at all that p would be equal to C, and therefore the degree of belief that one has in a proposition at positive stakes for which one has absolutely no evidence is 0. In case there is no evidence either way, then the degree of belief at positive stakes is 0 in both p and $\sim p$, which in betting terms means your bid price is zero and your ask price is 1 times the stake, making your bid-ask spread the maximum of 1.

Let us call the value of evidence in favour of p "kp". On our theory, the expectation of a bet is equal to C $+$ kp, and the degree of belief justified by the evidence is equal to kp/U, unless $kp > U$, in which case the degree of belief is 1. The value of knowledge and evidence works both ways, so that when a bet is settled by, for example, a direct observation, the value of the evidence given by that observation is equal to U. This observation will then add U to the value of evidence in favour of propositions of type p in similar circumstances. In the case where the evidence in favour of p exceeds U, then $kp/U > 1$ and we have a surplus of evidence. In this case, the belief in p is justifiably certain and has a degree of belief 1, since degrees of belief can by necessity be no higher than 1. But the surplus remains significant, both as an indication of the strength of certainty at stakes U and as measure of the *level of certainty* (Blamey 2008) which is the value kp and can be defined as *the maximum stake size at which* p *is justifiably certain given the evidence.*

Of course, this is only half the story. There is also negative evidence, evidence in favour of ~p. Negative evidence works its way down from B towards C. So, given no evidence whatsoever in favour of ~p, the value of a bet on p is B, and the degree of belief in p is 1, whereas if we know that ~p, then the value of the bet on p is C and the degree of belief in p is 0. The expectation on a bet on p is therefore equal to B + k ~p where k ~p is negative, and the degree of belief in p will equal $1 - k$ ~p/ U.

So far we have only talked about cases where the evidence is one-sided. In the case where there is evidence both for and against p, we will take the total value of evidence K to equal the sum of the absolute values $kp + k - p$, which is the total value of evidence relevant to p. Bigger values for K will mean that the probability judgement has a lot of evidence behind it and will not be so sensitive to stake size.

The mixed evidence probability is given by the odds ratio $C + kp : B + k - p$. In this odds ratio, all values represent states of wealth or information and are therefore positive. The resulting mixed probability is then given as

$$P_K(p)_{B-C} = (C + kp)/(C + B + K) \text{ given that } k \sim p > 0, kp > 0$$

$$P_K(\sim p)_{C-B} = (B + k \sim p)/(C + B + K) \text{ given that } k \sim p > 0, \ kp > 0$$

And to recap, one-sided probabilities are given as

$$\text{If } k \sim p = 0, \ kp > 0, \text{ then } P_K(p)_U = K/U, \text{ or 1 if } K > U$$

$$\text{If } kp = 0, \ k \sim p > 0, \text{ then } P_K(p)_U = (U - K)/(-U), \text{ or 0 if } K > U$$

A careful consideration of this formula will show that it preserves the stake size-sensitive laws of probability and therefore always ensures that those with the same state of evidence cannot be Dutch booked while allowing stake size sensitivity (Blamey 2011). It also allows that one can be certain with relatively little evidence at low stakes provided that there is no evidence against the proposition. Furthermore, the formula gives a bid-ask spread that gets tighter as the value of evidence gets greater relative to the stake size and gets wider the greater the stake size relative to the value of evidence. This last property shows that the formula gives a good representation of how uncertainty devalues prospects and therefore gives a good account of the Ellsberg paradox and the Allais problem, as well as fairly accurately modelling bid-ask price structuring in markets.

On this model of belief and evidence, the updating rule of evidence is very simple. A new piece of evidence in favour of p is simply added to the existing knowledge in favour of p. If there is no negative evidence in relation to a specific bet, this is simply to add the value of evidence directly to the price. So if we already had kp and discovered ke, then, relative to a bet on p at stakes U, the new degree of belief would simply be $(kp + ke)/U$, or 1 if $kp + ke > U$.

6   The Solution

The paradox is solved then by a stake-sensitive theory of evidential probability which measures evidence in terms of increase in expectation. The same increase in expectation at high stakes raises the probability to a lesser degree than the same increase in expectation at lower stakes. We identify knowledge with value by equating the stakes on a proposition with its value in terms of informational content. Given this, we have shown that conjoining propositions escalate the informational content exponentially by 1 over the conditional probability between the conjuncts. Therefore, evidence sufficient for certainty in each of the propositions may only be sufficient to raise the probability of the conjunction by a small amount.

To conclude, we will go through a formal example which contains an element of fantasy. The historian has written a book of two parts, each part containing ten exciting previously undiscovered historical claims. She is satisfied that she has enough evidence to prove beyond reasonable doubt to an educated audience that each claim is true. But before she publishes, she decides to take the ten claims from Part I to the (fictitious) Old Historian's Club and bet on them prior to revealing her evidence. She is fully confident that the OHC will settle in her favour once she shows them her evidence. This kind of bet happens all the time at the OHC, and a committee has been set up to decide on fair odds given the state of knowledge at the club and to assessing the new evidence and deciding whether such bets are settled. The OHC committee assesses that each proposition in Part I has a probability of 1/2 at stakes £100 and offers her £50/£100 per bet. She takes all the bets, lays out £500 and expects to win back a profit of £500. Sure enough, when the committee sees her evidence, they decide that each bet is settled in her favour. This makes her evidence valued at £50 per proposition, totalling £500.

Flushed with success, she returns to the club with a new proposal. Her evidence for the ten propositions in Part II is qualitatively the same, and since she is now confident that the OHC considers that level of evidence sufficient to settle bets, she decides to increase her profits by betting sequentially on a multiplier bet. She bets £50 on the first proposition and bets £100 on the second proposition conditional on winning the first. She then bets on the third proposition conditional on the conjunction of the first and second and so on. Formally, the bet looks like this: $(p1)_{£100} \times (p2 \mid p1)_{£200} \times (p3 \mid p1\&p2)_{£400} \times \ldots \times (p10 \mid p9 \& p8 \& p7 \& p6 \& p5 \& p4 \& p3 \& p2 \& p1)_{£51,200}$.

In effect, she is committing the hubris of betting at huge stakes that everything she has written in Part II is true. We can perhaps see why is it that the informational content of the conjunction is far greater than the sum of its parts. It allows for stake-escalating strategies, which are not possible if the facts are taken on an individual basis.

To her chagrin, the committee decide that her evidence does not support every claim in the book, and she loses her £50 price. In the letter, they tell her that they have a stake size variable theory of probability, and according to this theory, her evidence raised the probability of Part II from 1/1024 to 11/1024, making the expectation on her bet £500. The judgement was broken down as follows:

Value of evidence for Part II already available to the OHC .... KPIIold = £50.
Informational content/stake size ... KPII = £51,200.
Evidential probability at stakes £51,200... $P_{KPIIold}(PII)_{£51,200} = 1/1024$.
Value of new evidence ... KPIInew = £500.
Updated value of evidence ... £550.
Evidential probability at stakes £51,200 ..... $P_{KPIInew}(PII)_{£51,200} = K/U = 11/1024$.

Summary: Although the evidence provided supports the claims in Part II taken on an individual basis at stakes of £100, we do not feel that the evidence supports Part II in its entirety at the much higher stakes of £51,240.

The views expressed in the letter from the OHC are coherent, in that they cannot be Dutch booked even though they assign different probabilities to the same proposition at different stake sizes.

References

Blamey, J. (2008). Probability and certainty. *Praxis, 1*(1), 15–33.
Blamey, J. (2011). *When do I get my money? A probabilistic theory of knowledge*. PhD thesis, King's College, University of London, London.
Cohen, S. (1988). How to be a fallibilist. *Philosophical Perspectives, 2*, 91–123.
DeRose, K. (1995). Solving the skeptical problem. *Philosophical Review, 104*, 1–52.
Fantl, J., & McGrath, M. (2002). Evidence, pragmatics, and justification. *Philosophical Review, 111*, 67–94.
Frank, J., & Garcia, P. (2009, July 26–29). *Bid-ask spreads, volume, and volatility: Evidence from livestock markets*. Selected paper prepared for presentation at the Agricultural & Applied Economics Association 2009 AAEA & ACCI Joint Annual Meeting, Milwaukee, Wisconsin.
Friedman, M., & Savage, L. J. (1948). The utility analysis of choices involving risk. *Journal of Political Economy, 56*, 279–304.
Good, I. J. (1950). *Probability and the Weighing of Evidence*. Charles Griffin Co. London.
Gillies, D. (1990). The Turing-Good Weight of Evidence Function and Popper's Measure of the Severity of a Test. *British Journal for the Philosophy of Science, 41*, 143–146.
Hansson, S. O. (2009). Measuring uncertainty. *Studia Logica, 93*, 21–40.
Hawthorne, J. (2004). *Knowledge and lotteries*. Oxford: Oxford University Press.
Hawthorne, J., & Bovens, L. (1999). The preface, the lottery and the logic of belief. *Mind, 108* (430), 241–264.
Kahneman, D., & Tversky, A. (1979). Prospect theory of decisions under risk. *Econometrica, 47*, 263–291.
Lewis, D. (1996). Elusive knowledge. *Australasian Journal of Philosophy, 74*, 549–567.
Makinson, D. (1965). The paradox of the preface. *Analysis, 25*, 205–207.
Mian, S. (1955). Bid Ask Spread and ownership structure. *Journal of Financial Research*, December.
Millikan, R. (1993). *White queen psychology and other essays for Alice*. Cambridge, MA: MIT Press.
Popper, K. (1974). *The logic of scientific discovery*. London: Hutchinson & Co.
Ramsey, F. P. (1926). Truth and probability. In R. B. Braithwaite (Ed.), *The foundations of mathematics and other logical essays* (pp. 156–198). London: Kegan Paul.

Ramsey, F. P. (1991). Weight or The Value of Knowledge. In M. C. Galavotti (ed.), *Notes on Philosophy Probability and Mathematics Bibliopolis* (pp. 285–287).

Stanley, J. (2006). *Knowledge and practical interests*. Oxford: Oxford University Press.

Sturgeon, S. (2008). Reason and the grain of belief. *Nous, 42*, 139–165.

Weatherson, B. (2005). Can we do without pragmatic encroachment? *Philosophical Perspectives, 19*, 417–443.

Index

F. Zenker (ed.), *Bayesian Argumentation: The practical side of probability*,
Synthese Library 362, DOI 10.1007/978-94-007-5357-0,
© Springer Science+Business Media Dordrecht 2013

Printed by Publishers' Graphics LLC